ACCA
STUDY TEXT

Paper 2.1

Information Systems

BPP's NEW STUDY TEXTS FOR ACCA's NEW SYLLABUS

- Targeted to the syllabus and study guide

- Quizzes and questions to check your understanding

- Clear layout and style designed to save you time

- Plenty of exam-style questions

- Chapter Roundups and summaries to help revision

- Mind Maps to integrate the key points

BPP Publishing
February 2001

First edition 2001

ISBN 0 7517 0728 7

British Library Cataloguing-in-Publication Data
A catalogue record for this book is available from the British Library

Published by

BPP Publishing Limited
Aldine House, Aldine Place
London W12 8AW

www.bpp.com

Published by W M Print
45-47 Frederick Street
Walsall
West Midlands
WS2 9NE

We are grateful to the Association of Chartered Certified Accountants for permission to reproduce past examination questions and questions from the pilot paper. The answers have been prepared by BPP Publishing Limited.

Contents

(iii) *BPP* PUBLISHING

THE BPP STUDY TEXT

Aims of this Study Text

To provide you with the knowledge and understanding, skills and application techniques that you need if you are to be successful in your exams

This Study Text has been written around the **Information Systems** syllabus.

- It is **comprehensive**. It covers the syllabus content. No more, no less.

- It is written at the **right level**. Each chapter is written with the ACCA's **study guide** in mind.

- It is targeted to the **exam**. We have taken account of the **pilot paper**, questions put to the examiners at the recent ACCA conference and the assessment methodology.

To allow you to study in the way that best suits your learning style and the time you have available, by following your personal Study Plan (see page (viii))

You may be studying at home on your own until the date of the exam, or you may be attending a full-time course. You may like to (and have time to) read every word, or you may prefer to (or only have time to) skim-read and devote the remainder of your time to question practice. Wherever you fall in the spectrum, you will find the BPP Study Text meets your needs in designing and following your personal Study Plan.

To tie in with the other components of the BPP Effective Study Package to ensure you have the best possible chance of passing the exam (see page (v))

Recommended period of use	Elements of the BPP Effective Study Package
Three to twelve months before the exam	**Study Text** Use the Study Text to acquire knowledge, understanding, skills and the ability to use application techniques.
One to six months before the exam	**Practice & Revision Kit** Attempt the tutorial questions which are provided for each topic area in the Kit. Then try the numerous examination questions, for which there are realistic suggested solutions prepared by BPP's own authors.
From three months before the exam until the last minute	**Passcards** Work through these short, memorable notes which are focused on what is most likely to come up in the exam you will be sitting.
One to six months before the exam	**Success Tapes** These cover the vital elements of your syllabus in less than 90 minutes per subject with these audio cassettes. Each tape also contains exam hints to help you fine tune your strategy.
Three to twelve months before the exam	**Breakthrough Videos** Use a Breakthrough Video to supplement your Study Text. They give you clear tuition on key exam subjects and allow you the luxury of being able to pause or repeat sections until you have fully grasped the topic.

BPP PUBLISHING

HELP YOURSELF STUDY FOR YOUR ACCA EXAMS

Exams for professional bodies such as ACCA are very different from those you have taken at college or university. You will be under **greater time pressure before** the exam - as you may be combining your study with work. There are many different ways of learning and so the BPP Study Text offers you a number of different tools to help you through. Here are some hints and tips **based on research and experience**.

The right approach

1   The right attitude

Believe in yourself	Yes, there is a lot to learn. Yes, it is a challenge. But thousands have succeeded before and you can too.
Remember why you're doing it	Studying might seem a grind at times, but you are doing it for a reason: to advance your career.

2   The right focus

Read through the Syllabus and Study guide	These tell you what you are expected to know and are supplemented by Exam Guides in the introduction of each chapter.
Study the Exam Paper section	The pilot paper is likely to be a reasonable guide of what you should expect in the exam.

3   The right method

The big picture	You need to grasp the detail - but keeping in mind how everything fits into the big picture will help you understand better. • The **Introduction** of each chapter puts the material in context. • The **Syllabus content, Study guide** and **Exam focus points** show you what you need to **grasp.** • **Mind Maps** show the links and key issues in key topics.
In your own words	To absorb the information (and to practise your written communication skills), it helps **put it into your own words.** • **Take notes.** • Answer the **questions** in each chapter. As well as helping you absorb the information you will practise your written communication skills, which become increasingly important as you progress through your ACCA exams. • Draw **mind maps**. We have some examples. • Try 'teaching' to a colleague or friend.

Give yourself cues to jog your memory	The BPP Study Text uses **bold** to **highlight key points** and **icons** to identify key features, such as **Exam focus points** and **Key terms.**
	• Try **colour coding** with a highlighter pen.
	• Write **key points** on cards.

4   **The right review**

Review, review, review	It is a **fact** that regularly reviewing a topic in summary form can **fix it in your memory**. Because **review** is so important, the BPP Study Text helps you to do so in many ways.
	• **Chapter roundups** summarise the key points in each chapter. Use them to recap each study session.
	• The **Quick quiz** is another review technique to ensure that you have grasped the essentials.
	• Use the **Key term** index as a quiz.
	• Go through the **Examples** in each chapter a second or third time.

Suggested study sequence

Tackle the chapters in the order you find them in the Study Text. Taking into account your individual learning style, you could follow this sequence.

Key study steps	Activity
Step 1 **Topic list**	Each numbered topic is a numbered section in the chapter.
Step 2 **Introduction**	This gives you the **big picture** in terms of the **context** of the chapter. The content is referenced to the **Study Guide**, and **Exam Guidance** shows how the topic is likely to be examined. In other words, it sets your **objectives for study.**
Step 3 **Knowledge brought forward boxes**	In these we highlight information and techniques that it is assumed you have 'brought forward' with you from your earlier studies. If there are topics which have changed recently due to legislation for example, these topics are explained in more detail.
Step 4 **Explanations**	Proceed methodically through the chapter, reading each section thoroughly and making sure you understand.
Step 5 **Key terms and Exam focus points**	• **Key terms** can often earn you *easy marks* if you state them clearly and correctly in an appropriate exam answer (and they are indexed at the back of the text). • **Exam focus points** give you a good idea of how we think the examiner intends to examine certain topics.
Step 6 **Note taking**	Take brief notes if you wish, avoiding the temptation to copy out too much.
Step 7 **Examples**	Follow each through to its solution very carefully.
Step 8 **Case examples**	Study each one, and try to add flesh to them from your own experience - they are designed to show how the topics you are studying come alive (and often come unstuck) in the real world.
Step 9 **Questions**	Make a very good attempt at each one.
Step 10 **Answers**	Check yours against ours, and make sure you understand any discrepancies.
Step 11 **Chapter roundup**	Work through it very carefully, to make sure you have grasped the major points it is highlighting.
Step 12 **Quick quiz**	When you are happy that you have covered the chapter, use the **Quick quiz** to check how much you have remembered of the topics covered.

Key study steps	Activity
Step 13 **Question(s) in the Question bank**	Either at this point, or later when you are thinking about revising, make a full attempt at the **Question(s)** suggested at the very end of the chapter. You can find these at the end of the Study Text, along with the **Answers** so you can see how you did. We highlight those that are introductory, and those which are of the standard you would expect to find in an exam.

Developing your personal Study Plan

Preparing a Study Plan (and sticking closely to it) is one of the key elements in learning success.

Step 1. How do you learn?

First you need to be aware of your style of learning. There are four typical learning styles. Consider yourself in the light of the following descriptions and work out which you fit most closely. You can then plan to follow the key study steps in the sequence suggested.

Learning styles	Characteristics	Sequence of key study steps in the BPP Study Text
Theorist	Seeks to understand principles before applying them in practice	1, 2, 3, 4, 7, 8, 5, 9/10, 11, 12, 13 (6 continuous)
Reflector	Seeks to observe phenomena, thinks about them and then chooses to act	
Activist	Prefers to deal with practical, active problems; does not have much patience with theory	1, 2, 9/10 (read through), 7, 8, 5, 11, 3, 4, 9/10 (full attempt), 12, 13 (6 continuous)
Pragmatist	Prefers to study only if a direct link to practical problems can be seen; not interested in theory for its own sake	9/10 (read through), 2, 5, 7, 8, 11, 1, 3, 4, 9/10 (full attempt), 12, 13 (6 continuous)

Step 2. How much time do you have?

Work out the time you have available per week, given the following.

- The standard you have set yourself
- The time you need to set aside later for work on the Practice & Revision Kit and Passcards
- The other exam(s) you are sitting
- Very importantly, practical matters such as work, travel, exercise, sleep and social life

BPP PUBLISHING

Note your time available in box A.

A ☐

Step 3. Allocate your time

- Take the time you have available per week for this Study Text shown in box A, multiply it by the number of weeks available and insert the result in box B.

B ☐

- Divide the figure in Box B by the number of chapters in this text and insert the result in box C.

C ☐

Step 4. Implement

Set about studying each chapter in the time shown in box C, following the key study steps in the order suggested by your particular learning style.

This is your personal **Study Plan**.

Short of time: *Skim study technique?*

You may find you simply do not have the time available to follow all the key study steps for each chapter, however you adapt them for your particular learning style. If this is the case, follow the **skim study** technique below (the icons in the Study Text will help you to do this).

- Study the chapters in the order you find them in the Study Text.

- For each chapter, follow the key study steps 1-3, and then skim-read through step 4. Jump to step 11, and then go back to step 5. Follow through steps 7 and 8, and prepare outline answers to questions (steps 9/10). Try the Quick quiz (step 12), following up any items you can't answer, then do a plan for the Question (step 13), comparing it against our answers. You should probably still follow step 6 (note-taking), although you may decide simply to rely on the BPP Passcards for this.

Moving on...

However you study, when you are ready to embark on the practice and revision phase of the BPP Effective Study Package, you should still refer back to this Study Text, both as a source of **reference** (you should find the list of key terms and the index particularly helpful for this) and as a **refresher** (the Chapter roundups and Quick quizzes help you here).

And remember to keep careful hold of this Study Text - you will find it invaluable in your work.

SYLLABUS

Aim

To develop the knowledge and understanding of information systems development and delivery required to take an informed and active role in information systems solutions.

Objectives

On completion of this paper candidates should be able to:

- Explain how to effectively use information systems and information systems resources in an organisation

- Identify and apply methods of organising and accounting for information systems delivery and information systems projects

- Explain the principles of initiating, planning and controlling information systems projects

- Participate in the definition and specification of user and system requirements

- Describe how an appropriate solution might be defined to fulfil the specified user requirements

- Participate in the implementation, monitoring and maintenance of an information systems solution

- Participate in the quality assurance of an information systems project

- Identify how computer software can assist effective information systems management, development and quality assurance

Position of the paper in the overall syllabus

The paper assumes a familiarity with the basic applications of information technology.

The paper provides the knowledge and understanding of information systems required to enable the candidate to progress to the more strategic perspectives considered in Paper 3.4 Business Information Management.

The ideas introduced in this paper are also drawn upon in Paper 2.6 Audit and Internal Review, Paper 3.1 Audit and Assurance Services and Paper 3.5 Strategic Planning and Development.

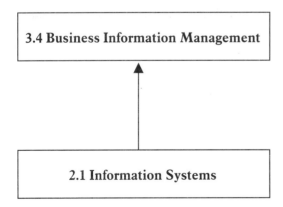

BPP PUBLISHING

SYLLABUS

1 Managing information systems (IS)

(a)   Business strategy and IS/IT alignment.

(b)   Delivering information systems - organisational arrangements.

(c)   Delivering information systems - accounting issues.

(d)   Organising information systems - structural issues.

(e)   Feasibility study.

(f)   Project initiation.

(g)   Project planning.

(h)   Project monitoring and control.

(i)   Software support for project management.

2 Designing information systems

(a)   The information systems development process.

(b)   Investigating and recording user requirements.

(c)   Documenting and modelling user requirements - processes.

(d)   Documenting and modelling user requirements - static structures.

(e)   Documenting and modelling user requirements – events.

(f)   External design.

(g)   Developing a solution to fulfil requirements.

(h)   Software package selection.

(i)   Software support for the systems development process.

3 Evaluating information systems

(a)   Technical information systems requirements.

(b)   Legal compliance in information systems.

(c)   Implementing security and legal requirements.

(d)   Quality assurance in the management and development process.

(e)   Systems and user acceptance testing.

(f)   Implementation issues and implementation methods.

(g)   Post-implementation issues.

(h)   Change control in systems development and maintenance.

(i)   Relationship of management, development process and quality.

Excluded topics

Detailed systems design – file/database design, program design is an excluded topic. Computer hardware will not be explicitly examined.

Key areas of the syllabus

The syllabus has three key areas:

- Managing information systems
- Designing information systems
- Evaluating information systems

BPP PUBLISHING

Paper 2.1

Information Systems

Study Guide

1 BUSINESS STRATEGY AND IS/IT ALIGNMENT

- Explain an approach that an organisation may follow to formulate its strategic business objectives.

- Discuss how information systems may be used to assist in achieving these objectives.

- Identify current trends in information technology (IT) and the opportunities they offer to organisations.

- Distinguish between a business strategy and an information systems strategy.

- Identify responsibility for the ownership of the IS strategy.

2 DELIVERING INFORMATION SYSTEMS – ORGANISATIONAL ARRANGEMENTS

- Describe the traditional structure of a centralised Information Systems department and the roles and responsibilities of each function.

- Explain the principles of a decentralised Information Systems function.

- Discuss the advantages and disadvantages of centralising or decentralising the Information Systems function.

- Explain the principles of outsourcing the Information Systems function.

- Describe the advantages and disadvantages of outsourcing the Information Systems function.

3 DELIVERING INFORMATION SYSTEMS - ACCOUNTING ISSUES

- Briefly describe the types of cost incurred in delivering information systems.

- Describe how the costs of the Information Systems function may be distributed between customer departments.

- Explain the principles, benefits and drawbacks of cross-charging costs.

- Discuss the issues raised by establishing the Information Systems function as a cost or profit centre.

- Describe the advantages and disadvantages of establishing the Information Systems function as separate company.

- Explain the problems of accounting for shared infrastructure costs.

4 ORGANISING INFORMATION SYSTEMS - STRUCTURAL ISSUES

- Describe the typical hardware, software, data and communications infrastructures found within Information Systems functions.

- Discuss the meaning and need for a disaster recovery plan.

- Discuss the meaning and need for a risk management process.

- Describe the meaning and implications of legacy systems.

- Discuss the relationship of Information Systems with end-users and the implications of the expectations and skills of end-users.

5 FEASIBILITY STUDY

- Explain the purpose and objectives of a feasibility study.

- Evaluate the technical, operational, social and economic feasibility of the proposed project.

- Describe and categorise the benefits and costs of the proposed project.

- Apply appropriate investment appraisal techniques to determine the economic feasibility of a project.

- Define the typical content and structure of a feasibility study report.

6 PROJECT INITIATION

- Define the content and structure of terms of reference.

- Describe the typical contents of a Project Quality Plan and explain the need for such a plan.

- Identify the roles and responsibilities of staff who will manage and participate in the project.

- Define in detail the role and responsibilities of the project manager.

- Explain the concept of a flat management structure and its application to project-based systems development.

7 PROJECT PLANNING

- Assist in splitting the project into its main phases.

- Participate in the breakdown of work into lower-level tasks.

- Assist in the estimation of the time taken to complete these lower-level tasks.

- Define dependencies between lower-level tasks.

- Construct and interpret a project network.

- Construct and interpret a Gantt Chart.

8 PROJECT MONITORING AND CONTROL

- Describe methods of monitoring and reporting progress.

- Define the reasons for slippage and how to deal with slippage when it occurs.

- Discuss the reasons for changes during the project and the need for a project change procedure.

- Reflect the effects of progress, slippage and change requests on the project plan.

- Discuss the particular problems of planning and controlling Information Systems projects.

9 SOFTWARE SUPPORT FOR PROJECT MANAGEMENT

- Define the meaning of a project management software package and give a brief list of representative products.

- Describe a range of features and functions that a project management software package may provide.

- Explain the advantages of using a project management software package in the project management process.

10 THE INFORMATION SYSTEMS DEVELOPMENT PROCESS

- Define the participants in the systems development process - managers, analysts, designers, programmers and testers.

- Describe the waterfall approach to systems development and identify its application in a representative systems development methodology.

- Describe the spiral approach to systems development and identify its application in a representative systems development methodology.

- Discuss the relative merits of the waterfall and spiral approaches, including an understanding of hybrid methodologies that include elements of both.

11 INVESTING AND RECORDING USER REQUIREMENTS

- Define the tasks of planning, undertaking and documenting a user interview.

- Identify the potential role of background research, questionnaires and special purpose surveys in the definition of requirements.

- Describe the purpose, conduct and recording of a facilitated user workshop.

- Explain the potential use of prototyping in requirement's definition.

- Explain how requirements can be collected from current computerised information systems.

- Discuss the problems users have in defining, agreeing and prioritising requirements.

12 DOCUMENTING AND MODELLING USER REQUIREMENTS - PROCESSES

- Describe the need for building a business process model of user requirements.

- Briefly describe difference approaches to modelling the business process.

- Describe in detail the notation of one of these business process models.

- Construct a business process model of narrative user requirements using this notation.

- Explain the role of process models in the systems development process.

13 DOCUMENTING AND MODELLING USER REQUIREMENTS - STATIC STRUCTURES

- Describe the need for building a business structure model of user requirements.

- Briefly describe different approaches to modelling the business structure.

- Describe in detail the notation of one of these business structure models.

- Construct a business structure model of narrative user requirements using this notation.

- Explain the role of structure models in the systems development process.

14 DOCUMENTING AND MODELLING USER REQUIREMENTS - EVENTS

- Describe the need for building a business event model of user requirements.

- Briefly describe different approaches to modelling business events.

- Describe in detail the notation of one of these business event models.

- Construct a business even model of narrative user requirements using the notation.

- Explain the role of event models in the systems development process.

15 EXTERNAL DESIGN

- Define the characteristics of a 'user-friendly' system.
- Describe the task of external design and distinguish it from internal design.

- Design effective output documents and reports.

- Select appropriate technology to support the output design.

- Design effective inputs.

- Select appropriate technology to support input design.

- Describe how the user interface may be structured for ease of use.

- Explain how prototyping may be used in defining an external design.

16 DEVELOPING A SOLUTION TO FULFIL REQUIREMENTS

- Define the bespoke software approach to fulfilling the user's information systems requirements.

- Briefly describe the tasks of design, programming and testing required in developing a bespoke systems solution.

- Define the application software package approach to fulfilling the user's information systems requirements.

- Briefly describe the tasks of package selection, evaluation and testing required in selecting an appropriate application software package.

- Describe the relative merits of the bespoke systems development and application software package approaches to fulfilling an information systems requirement.

17 SOFTWARE PACKAGE SELECTION

- Describe the structure and contents of an Invitation to Tender (ITT).

- Describe how to identify software packages and how their suppliers may potentially fulfil the information systems requirements.

- Develop suitable procedures for distributing an ITT and dealing with subsequent enquiries and bids.

- Describe a process for evaluating the application software package, the supplier of that package and the bid received from the supplier.

- Describe risks of the application software package and how these might be reduced or removed.

18 SOFTWARE SUPPORT FOR THE SYSTEMS DEVELOPMENT PROCESS

- Define a Computer Aided Software Engineering (CASE) tool and give a brief list of representative products.

- Describe a range of features and functions that a CASE tool may provide. Explain the advantages of using a CASE tool in the systems development process.

- Define a Fourth General Language and give a brief list of representative products.

- Explain the advantages of using a CASE tool in the systems development process.

- Describe a range of features and functions that a Fourth Generation Language may provide.

- Explain how a Fourth Generation Language contributes to the prototyping process.

19 TECHNICAL INFORMATION SYSTEMS REQUIREMENTS

- Define and record performance and volume requirements of information systems.

- Discuss the need for archiving, backup and restore, and other 'house-keeping' functions.

- Explain the need for a software audit trail and define the content of such a trail.

- Examine the need to provide interfaces with other systems and discuss the implications of developing these interfaces.

- Establish requirements for data conversion and data creation.

20 LEGAL COMPLIANCE IN INFORMATION SYSTEMS

- Describe the principles, terms and coverage typified by the UK Data Protection Act.

- Describe the principles, terms and coverage typified by the UK Computer Misuse Act.

- Explain the implications of software licences and copyright law in computer systems development.

- Discuss the legal implications of software supply with particular reference to ownership, liability and damages.

21 IMPLEMENTING SECURITY & LEGAL REQUIREMENTS

- Describe methods to ensure the physical security of IT systems.

- Discuss the role, implementation and maintenance of a password system.

- Explain representative clerical and software controls that should assist in maintaining the integrity of a system.

- Describe the principles and application of encryption techniques.

- Discuss the implications of software viruses and malpractice.

- Discuss how the requirements of the UK Data Protection and UK Computer Misuse legislation may be implemented.

22 QUALITY ASSURANCE IN THE MANAGEMENT AND DEVELOPMENT PROCESS

- Define the characteristics of a quality software product.

- Define the terms, quality management, quality assurance and quality control.

- Describe the V model and its application to quality assurance and testing.

- Explain the limitations of software testing.

- Participate in the quality assurance of deliverables in requirement specification using formal static testing methods.

- Explain the role of standards and, in particular, their application in quality assurance.

- Briefly describe the task of unit testing in bespoke systems development.

23 SYSTEMS AND USER ACCEPTANCE TESTING

- Define the scope of systems testing.

- Distinguish between dynamic and static testing.

- Use a cause-effect chart (decision table) to develop an appropriate test script for a representative systems test.

- Explain the scope and importance of performance testing and usability testing

- Define the scope and procedures of user acceptance testing

- Describe the potential use of automated tools to support systems and user acceptance testing.

24 IMPLEMENTATION ISSUES AND IMPLEMENTATION METHODS

- Plan for data conversion and creation.

- Discuss the need for training and suggest different methods of delivering such training.

- Describe the type of documentation needed to support implementation and comment on ways of effectively organising and presenting this documentation.

- Distinguish between parallel running and direct changeover and comment on the advantages and disadvantages of each.

25 POST-IMPLEMENTATION ISSUES

- Describe the metrics required to measure the success of the system.

- Discuss the procedures that have to be implemented to effectively collect the agreed metrics.

- Identify what procedures and personnel should be put in place to support the users of the system.

- Explain the possible role of software monitors in measuring the success of the system.

- Describe the purpose and conduct of an end-project review and a post-implementation review.

- Describe the structure and content of a report from an end-project review and a post-implementation review.

26 CHANGE CONTROL IN SYSTEMS DEVELOPMENT AND MAINTENANCE

- Describe the different types of maintenance that a system may require.

- Explain the need for a change control process for dealing with these changes.

- Describe a maintenance lifecycle.

- Explain the meaning and problems of regression testing.

- Discuss the role of user groups and their influence on system requirements.

27 RELATIONSHIP OF MANAGEMENT, DEVELOPMENT PROCESS AND QUALITY

- Describe the relationship between project management and the systems development process

- Describe the relationship between the systems development process and quality assurance

- Explain the time/cost/quality triangle and its implications for information systems projects.

- Discuss the need for automation to improve the efficiency and effectiveness of information systems management, delivery and quality assurance.

- Explain the role of the accountant in information systems management, delivery and quality assurance.

OXFORD BROOKES BSc (Hons) IN APPLIED ACCOUNTING

The standard required of candidates completing Part 2 is that required in the final year of a UK degree. Students completing Parts 1 and 2 will have satisfied the examination requirement for an honours degree in Applied Accounting, awarded by Oxford Brookes University.

To achieve the degree, you must also submit two pieces of work.

- A 5,000 word **Research and Analysis Project** on a chosen topic, which demonstrates that you have acquired the necessary research and IT skills.

- A 1,500 word **Key Skills Statement,** indicating how you have developed your analytical and communication skills.

BPP has been selected by the ACCA to produce the official text *Success in your Research and Analysis Project* to support students in this task. The book pays particular attention to key skills not covered in the professional examinations.

> AN ORDER FORM FOR THE NEW SYLLABUS MATERIAL, INCLUDING THE OXFORD BROOKES PROJECT TEXT, CAN BE FOUND AT THE END OF THIS STUDY TEXT.

BPP PUBLISHING

THE EXAM PAPER

The examination is a **three hour paper** divided into **two sections**.

		Number of Marks
Section A:	3 compulsory questions (20 marks each)	60
Section B:	Choice of 2 from 3 questions (20 marks each)	40
		100

Section A is based on a short narrative scenario. This section will have three compulsory questions from across the syllabus linked to the narrative scenario. Each question will be worth 20 marks giving a total of 60 marks for this section.

Section B contains three independent questions, one question from each main area of the syllabus. Each question is worth 20 marks. The candidate must answer two questions giving a total of 40 marks for this section.

Additional information

The examination does not assume any use of any systems development methodology. Practical questions will be set in such a way that they that they can be answered by any methodology. However the following examples of models may be useful:

Syllabus heading	*Example models*
Documenting and modelling user requirements – processes	Data Flow Diagram Flowchart
Documenting and modelling user requirements – static structures	Entity-relationship model Object Class model
Documenting and modelling user requirements – events	Entity Life History State Transition Diagram

Analysis of pilot paper

Section A scenario – Insurance company has developed an unsatisfactory information system

1 Project risk assessment
2 Solving and preventing system problems
3 Quality assurance and testing in systems development

Section B

4 Outsourcing; Legacy systems; Project management software
5 Systems analysis interviews; Event model construction
6 Post-implementation review; Measuring software effectiveness; Controlling change

Part A
Managing information systems

Chapter 1

INFORMATION SYSTEMS AND BUSINESS STRATEGY

Topic list	Syllabus reference
1 Strategic planning	1(a)
2 Developing a strategy for information systems and information technology	1(a)

Introduction

Welcome to Paper 2.1 Information Systems. This Study Text follows the structure of the official ACCA syllabus and study guide wherever possible. The front page of each chapter provides syllabus and study guide references showing the areas covered within the chapter.

We start with a look at the concept of **business strategy** and **strategic planning**. Later in this chapter we examine the relationships between **business strategy**, **information systems** (IS) and **information technology** (IT).

Study guide

Part 1.1 – Business strategy and IS/IT alignment

- Explain an approach that an organisation may follow to formulate its strategic business objectives

- Discuss how information systems may be used to assist in achieving these objectives (this issue is relevant throughout this text)

- Distinguish between a business strategy and an information systems strategy

- Identify responsibility for the ownership of the IS strategy (also see Chapter 10)

Exam guide

The scenario that will appear in Section A of the examination provides the examiner with an ideal opportunity to test your understanding of the importance of an organisation's IS/IT strategy complimenting the overall business strategy.

1 STRATEGIC PLANNING

1.1 **Strategic planning** is a complex process which involves taking a view of the **organisation** and the **future** that it is likely to encounter, and then attempting to organise the structure and resources of the organisation accordingly.

> **KEY TERM**
>
> **Strategy** can be defined as 'a course of action, including the specification of resources required, to achieve a specific outcome'.

BPP PUBLISHING

> **KEY TERM**
>
> **Strategic planning** is the formulation, evaluation and selection of strategies for the purpose of preparing a long-term plan of action to attain objectives.

1.2 Three general levels of strategy can be identified: corporate, business and functional/operational.

Corporate strategy

1.3 **Corporate strategy** is concerned with what types of business the organisation is in. It denotes the most general level of strategy in an organisation.

Business strategy

> **KEY TERM**
>
> **Business strategy** is concerned with how an organisation approaches a particular product or market.

1.4 This can involve decisions as to whether, in principle, a company should:

(a) Segment the market and specialise in particularly profitable areas.
(b) Compete by offering a wider range of products.

1.5 Some large, diversified firms have separate **strategic business units** dealing with particular areas.

1.6 **Characteristics of decisions relating to corporate and\or business strategy**

Characteristic	Comment
Scope of activities	Products and markets – decisions might involve diversifying into a new line of business or into a new market. It might mean global expansion or contraction.
Environment	The organisation counters threats and exploits opportunities in the environment (customers, clients, competitors).
Capability	The organisation matches its activities to its resources: ie it does what it is able to do.
Resources	Strategy involves choices about allocating or obtaining resources now and in future.
Operations	Strategic decisions always affect operations.
Values	The value systems of people in power influence them to understand the world in a certain way.
Direction	Strategic decisions have a medium or long-term impact.
Complex	Strategic decisions involve uncertainty about the future, integrating the operations of the organisation and change.

1.7 The relationship between corporate, business and operational strategies is shown in the following diagram.

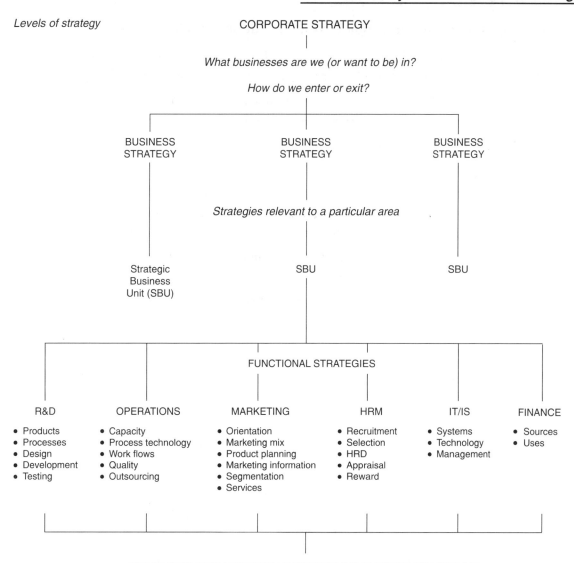

Levels of strategy

CORPORATE STRATEGY

What businesses are we (or want to be) in?

How do we enter or exit?

BUSINESS STRATEGY   BUSINESS STRATEGY   BUSINESS STRATEGY

Strategies relevant to a particular area

Strategic Business Unit (SBU)   SBU   SBU

FUNCTIONAL STRATEGIES

R&D	OPERATIONS	MARKETING	HRM	IT/IS	FINANCE
• Products	• Capacity	• Orientation	• Recruitment	• Systems	• Sources
• Processes	• Process technology	• Marketing mix	• Selection	• Technology	• Uses
• Design	• Work flows	• Product planning	• HRD	• Management	
• Development	• Quality	• Marketing information	• Appraisal		
• Testing	• Outsourcing	• Segmentation	• Reward		
		• Services			

STRATEGIES INVOLVING MANY FUNCTIONS (EG CHANGE MANAGEMENT, TOTAL QUALITY, RE-ENGINEERING)

Functional/operational strategies; information systems strategy

1.8 Information systems strategy is an example of a **functional/operational strategy** (although in some cases it may have strategic implications). Functional/operational strategies deal with specialised areas of activity.

Functional area	Comment
Information systems	A firm's information systems are becoming increasingly important, as an item of expenditure, as administrative support and as a tool for competitive strength.
Marketing	Devising products and services, pricing, promoting and distributing them, in order to satisfy customer needs at a profit.
Production	Factory location, manufacturing techniques, outsourcing etc.
Finance	Ensuring that the firm has enough financial resources to fund its other strategies.
Human resources	Secure personnel of the right skills in the right quantity at the right time.
R&D	New products and techniques.

Formulating strategic business objectives: The rational model

1.9 Strategic planning divides into a number of different stages: strategic **analysis**, strategic **choice** and **implementation**. This is represented on the diagram on page 7.

(a) **Strategic analysis** (Relevant models referred to are covered throughout this Text.)

	Stage	Comment	Key tools, models, techniques
Step 1.	Mission and/or vision	Mission denotes values, the business's rationale for existing; vision refers to where the organisation intends to be in a few years time	• Mission statement
Step 2.	Goals	Interpret the mission to different stakeholders	• Stakeholder analysis
Step 3.	Objectives	Quantified embodiments of mission	• Measures such as profitability, time scale, deadlines
Step 4.	Environmental analysis	Identify opportunities and threats	• PEST analysis • Porter's 5 forces • Scenario building
Step 5.	Position audit or situation analysis	Identify strengths and weaknesses Firm's **current** resources, products, customers, systems, structure, results, efficiency, effectiveness	• Resource audit • Distinctive competence • Value chain • Product life cycle • Boston (BCG) matrix • Marketing audit
Step 6.	Corporate appraisal	Combines Steps 4 and 5	• SWOT analysis charts
Step 7.	Gap analysis	Compares outcomes of Step 6 with Step 3	• Gap analysis

Question 1

List five ways in which corporate and business strategy are relevant to the types of information system required in an organisation?

Answer

Five ways are shown below. You may have come up with others.

(a) Information is needed to shape corporate and business strategy.

(b) Information systems provide information that monitors progress towards strategic objectives.

(c) Business objectives are becoming increasingly customer focused. Good customer service requires good quality information available on demand.

(d) A strategy of growth will require a corresponding increase in the information system.

(e) A change of strategy may mean a new information system is required.

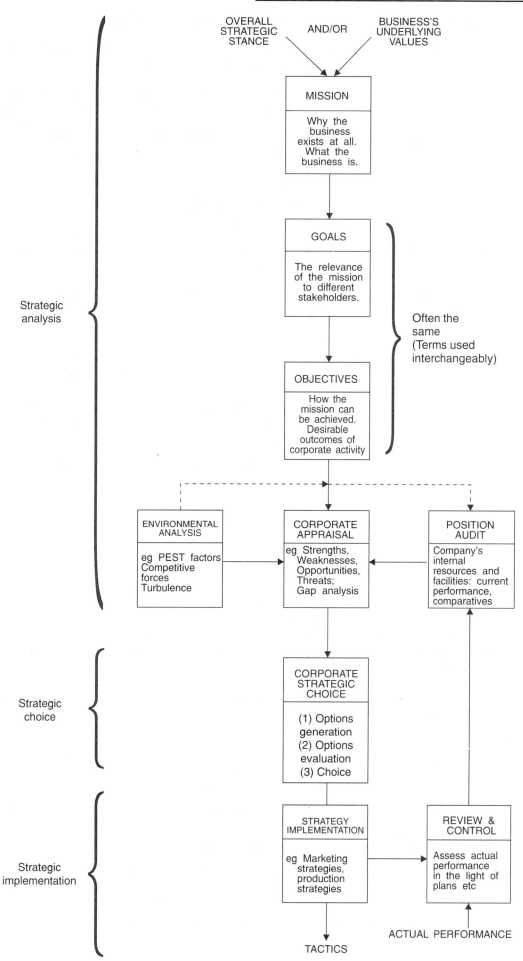

BPP
PUBLISHING

(b) **Strategic choice**

Stage	Comment	Key tools, models, techniques
Strategic options generation	Come up with new ideas: • How to compete (competitive advantage) • Where to compete • Method of growth	• Value chain analysis • Scenario building • Porter's generic strategic choices • Ansoff's growth vector • Acquisition vs organic growth
Strategic options evaluation	Normally, each strategy has to be evaluated on the basis of • Acceptability • Suitability • Feasibility • Environmental fit	• Stakeholder analysis • Risk analysis • Decision-making tools such as decision trees, matrices, ranking and scoring methods • Financial measures (eg ROCE, DCF)

(c) **Strategy selection** involves choosing between the alternative strategies.

   (i)   The **competitive strategies** are the generic strategies for competitive advantage an organisation will pursue. They determine **how you compete**.

   (ii) **Product-market strategies** (which markets you should enter or leave) determine **where you compete** and the direction of growth.

   (iii) **Institutional strategies** (ie relationships with other organisations) determine the **method of growth**.

Strategy implementation

1.10   Strategy implementation is the **conversion** of the strategy into detailed plans or objectives for operating units. This involves:

   • **Resource** planning (ie finance, personnel) involves assessing the key tasks
   • **Operations** planning
   • **Organisation** structure and control systems

Case example

Goold and Quinn (in *Strategic Control*) cite Ciba-Geigy, a Swiss-based global firm with chemicals and pharmaceuticals businesses, as an example of formal strategic control and planning processes.

(a) Strategic planning starts with the identification of strategic business sectors, in other words, areas of activity where there are identifiable markets and where profit, management and resources are largely independent of the other sectors.

(b) Strategic plans containing:

   (i)   Long term objectives
   (ii) Key strategies
   (iii) Funds requirements

   are drawn up, based on a 'comprehensive analysis of market attractiveness', competitors etc.

(c) At corporate level, these plans are reviewed. Head office examines all the different plans and, with a 7-10 year planning horizon, the total risk, profitability, cash flow and resource requirements are assessed. Business sectors are allocated specific targets and funds.

Information systems and corporate / business strategy

1.11 It is widely accepted that an organisation's information system should **support** corporate and business strategy. In some circumstances an information system may have a greater influence and actually help **determine** corporate / business strategy. For example:

(a) IS/IT may provide a possible source of competitive advantage. This could involve new technology not yet available to others or simply using existing technology in a different way.

(b) The information system may help in formulating business strategy by **providing information** from internal and external sources.

(c) Developments in IT may provide **new channels** for distributing and collecting information, and /or for conducting transactions eg the Internet.

1.12 An important role of both the finance and information technology functions is to help ensure the agreed strategy is proceeding according to plan. The table below (devised by the US Institute of Management Accountants) outlines the rationale behind this view.

	Traditional view	**Strategic implications**
Cost	The finance and information technology functions can be relatively expensive	Shared services and outsourcing could be used to capture cost savings
IT	IT has traditionally been transaction based	IT/IS should be integrated with business strategy
Value	The finance and IT functions do not add value	Redesign the functions
Strategy	Accountants and IT managers are seen as scorekeepers and administrators rather than as a business partner during the strategic planning process	Change from cost-orientated to market-orientated ie development of more effective strategic planning systems

2 DEVELOPING A STRATEGY FOR INFORMATION SYSTEMS AND INFORMATION TECHNOLOGY

Vision and reality

2.1 A company that has a **vision** of its own future, and some idea of how information technology can be used to turn that vision into **reality,** may be able to use new technologies for strategic advantage.

2.2 **One approach to creating a vision** is to adopt a familiar three step approach, involving answering three questions about the organisation.

- Where are we now?
- Where do we want to be?
- How will we get there?

2.3 The first question can be answered using standard techniques such as a strengths, weaknesses, opportunities, threats **(SWOT) analysis**. This approach ensures that both internal and external factors are considered. We cover SWOT analysis in the context of a feasibility study in Chapter 5.

2.4 Answering the second question requires vision. This does not have to be a continuation in the organisation's current direction. It must be challenging, attainable and communicated to those who will implement it.

2.5 Once this has been done, the strategy (in answer to the third question) can be defined.

2.6 **A second approach** takes the view that insiders are too tied to 'the way we do things now', and recommends the involvement of **outsiders**. An outsider may be able to more readily anticipate dramatic shifts which might occur in the future. Additionally, an outsider does not have the insider's investment in **maintaining the status quo**.

Information and competitive advantage

2.7 It is now recognised that information can be used as a source of competitive advantage. This has led to formal management strategies and plans for information.

2.8 A strategy is needed for areas in which decisions have the potential to have a major impact on an organisation. Many organisations have recognised the importance of information and developed an **information strategy**, covering both IS and IT.

2.9 Information systems should be **tied in some way to business objectives**.

(a) The **corporate strategy** is used to plan functional **business plans** which provide guidelines for information-based activities.

(b) On a year by year basis, the **annual plan** would try to tie in business plans with information systems projects for particular applications, perhaps through the functioning of a **steering committee**.

Information systems strategy

> **KEY TERM**
>
> The **information systems (IS) strategy** refers to the long-term plan concerned with exploiting IS and IT either to support business strategies or create new strategic options.

2.10 An IS strategy therefore deals with the integration of an organisation's information requirements and information systems planning with its **long-term overall goals** (customer service etc). IS strategy is formulated at the level of business where specific customer needs etc can be delineated. It deals with what applications should be developed, and where resources should be deployed.

2.11 The **information technology (IT) strategy** leads on from the IS strategy above. It deals with the **technologies** of:

- Computing
- Communications

- Data
- Application systems

2.12 This provides a framework for the analysis and design of the **technological infrastructure** of an organisation. This strategy indicates how the information systems strategies that rely on technology will be **implemented**.

Why have an IS/IT strategy?

2.13 A strategy for information systems and information technology is **justified** on the grounds that IS/IT.

- Involves **high costs**
- Is **critical to the success** of many organisations
- Is now used as part of the commercial strategy in the battle for **competitive advantage**
- Impacts on **customer service**
- Affects **all levels of management**
- Affects the way **management information** is created and presented
- **Requires effective management** to obtain the maximum benefit
- Involves many **stakeholders** inside and outside the organisation

IS/IT is a high cost activity

2.14 Many organisations invest large amounts of money in IS, but not always wisely.

2.15 The unmanaged proliferation of IT is likely to lead to expensive mistakes. Two key benefits of IT - the ability to **share** information and the avoidance of duplication – are likely to be lost.

2.16 All IT expenditure should therefore require approval to ensure that it enhances rather than detracts from the overall information management strategy.

IS/IT is critical to the success of many organisations

2.17 When developing an IS/IT strategy a firm should assess **how important IT is** in the provision of products and services. The role that IT fills in an organisation will vary depending on the type of organisations. IS/IT could be:

- A **support** activity
- A **key** operational activity
- **Potentially** very important
- A **strategic** activity (without IT the firm could not function at all)
- A source of **competitive advantage**

IT as required by the economic context

2.18 IT is an **enabling** technology, and can produce dramatic changes in individual businesses and whole industries. For example, the deregulation of US airline system encouraged the growth of computerised seat-reservation systems (eg SABRE, as used by American Airlines

BPP
PUBLISHING

which always displayed American Airlines flights preferentially). IT can be both a **cause** of major changes in doing business and a **response** to them.

IT affects all levels of management

2.19 IT has become a routine a feature of office life, **a facility for everyone to use**. IT is no longer used solely by specialist staff.

IT and its effect on management information

2.20 The use of IT has permitted the design of a range of **Management Information Systems (MIS)**. Executive Information Systems (EIS), Decision Support Systems (DSS), and expert systems can be used to enhance the flexibility and depth of MIS. (We look at different types of information system in Chapter 2.)

2.21 IT has also had an effect on **production processes**. For example, Computer Integrated Manufacturing (CIM) changed the methods and cost profiles of many manufacturing processes. The techniques used to **measure and record costs** have also adapted to the use of IT.

IT and stakeholders

2.23 Parties interested in an organisation's use of IT are as follows.

(a) **Other business users** - for example to facilitate Electronic Data Interchange (EDI).

(b) **Governments** – eg telecommunications regulation, regulation of electronic commerce.

(c) **IT manufacturers** looking for new markets and product development. User-groups may be able to influence software producers.

(d) **Consumers** - for example as reassurance that product quality is high, consumers may also be interested if information is provided via the Internet.

(e) **Employees** - as IT affects work practices.

Developing an IS/IT strategy

2.24 An IS/IT strategy must deal with three issues.

- The organisation's overall **business needs**
- The organisation's **current use** of IT
- The potential **opportunities** and **threats** that IT can bring

2.25 Each of these three issues involves different personnel, and requires a slightly different approach. A diagrammatic representation of IT strategy development follows.

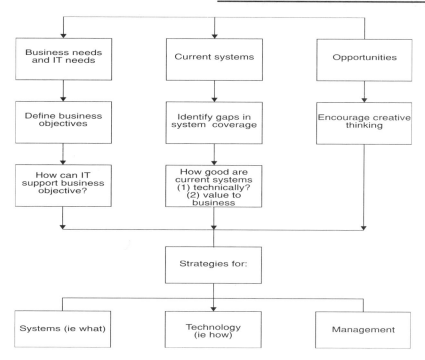

2.26 The inputs and outputs of the IS/IT strategic planning process are summarised on the following diagram.

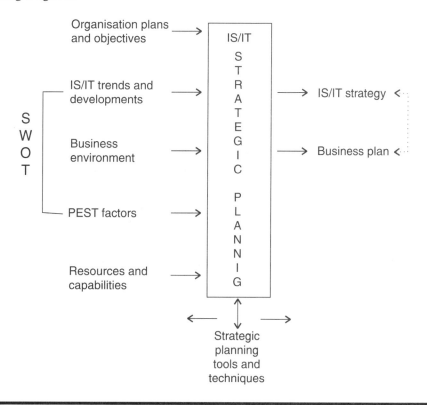

Question 2

Think about the role of Information Systems (IS) and Information Technology (IT) in achieving business objectives and securing an advantage over competitors. Try to think of an example of each of the following.

(a)   The use of IT to 'lock out' competitors.

(b)   The use of IS/IT to reduce the likelihood of customers changing suppliers.

(c)   The use of IS/IT to secure a performance advantage.

BPP PUBLISHING

(d)   How IT may generate a new product or service.

Answer

(a)   An example is an organisation that invests so heavily in technology that potential competitors lack both the expertise and the funds to compete successfully. Microsoft has not completely locked competitors out of the office software market but its domination is increasing.

(b)   Once a bank customer has gone to the effort of installing a home banking system, he or she is unlikely to make a decision to change banks.

(c)   Accurate stock systems that facilitate Just-In-Time stock management, and organisations participating in Electronic Data Interchange (EDI) are two examples of how IT can increase efficiency and facilitate better service - providing an advantage over competitors. (They may also make an organisation more dependent on existing suppliers therefore discouraging the changing of suppliers.)

(d)   Internet Service Providers (ISPs) did not exist before the advent of the Internet.

Chapter roundup

- A **strategy** is a general statement of long-term objectives and goals and the ways by which these will be achieved. **Strategic planning** is the formulation, evaluation and selection of strategies for the purpose of preparing a long-term plan of action to attain objectives.

- There are three levels of strategy: **corporate, business and functional**/operational.

- Corporate strategy is concerned with what types of business the organisation is in.

- Business strategy is concerned with how an organisation approaches a particular product market area.

- Information systems and Information Technology (IS/IT) strategy refers to the long-term plan concerned with exploiting IS and IT either to support business strategies or create new strategic options.

- IS/IT strategy is an example of a functional/operational strategy, but may have strategic implications.

- A strategy is needed for IS/IT because these areas involve **high costs**, are **critical to the success** of many organisations, can be used as a **strategic weapon** and affects internal and external **stakeholders**.

- IS/IT are sufficiently important and widespread to require proper **planning** and management attention.

- A **vision** can be defined as a statement of how someone wants the future to be or believes it will be. A vision may form the basis of the strategic direction taken by a firm and the **reality** it tries to create.

- Developing strategy involves taking a number of steps, from setting strategic objectives right through to evaluating actual performance. Three basic issues are the organisation's **overall business objectives** and in consequence its **IS/IT needs**, the organisation's **current IT usage** and the potential **opportunities** that IT can bring.

Quick quiz

1   List three levels of strategy.

2   Corporate strategy and business strategy are the same thing. TRUE or FALSE?

3   Distinguish between an organisation's mission and a business objective.

4   List five reasons why an organisation should have a strategy for IS/IT.

5   What three issues must an IS/IT strategy deal with?

Answers to quick quiz

1   Corporate, business and functional/operational.

2   FALSE. Corporate strategy is concerned with what types of business the organisation is in. Business strategy is concerned with how an organisation approaches a particular product or market.

3   A mission is the rationale behind the company's existence: what it is for. An objective is more precise. It is a particular desired outcome.

4   [Five of]

   IT involves high costs.

   IT is critical to the success of many organisations.

   IT is now used as part of the commercial strategy in the battle for competitive advantage.

   IT is required by customers.

   IT affects all levels of management.

   IT affects the way management information is created and presented.

   IT requires effective management to obtain the maximum benefit.

   IT involves many stakeholders inside and outside the organisation.

5   The organisation's overall business needs.

   The organisation's current use of IT.

   The potential opportunities and threats that IT can bring.

The material covered in this Chapter, together with the material in Chapter 2, is tested in Question 15 in the Exam Question Bank. Study Chapter 2 before attempting Question 15.

Chapter 2

THE IMPACT OF INFORMATION TECHNOLOGY

Topic list	Syllabus reference
1 Manual systems	1(a)
2 The computer	1(a)
3 Input devices	1(a)
4 Output devices	1(a)
5 Storage devices	1(a)
6 Software	1(a)
7 Data processing in a computerised environment	1(a)
8 Developments in communications	1(a)
9 The effect of office automation on business	1(a)
10 The Internet	1(a)
11 The quality of information	1(a)

Introduction

We will now look at some of the ways that businesses are utilising information technology. We include newer technologies (such as the Internet) and established tools of office automation (eg PCs).

Study guide

Part 1.1 – Business strategy and IS/IT alignment

- Identify current trends in information technology (IT) and the opportunities they offer to organisations

Part 1.4 – Organising information systems; structural issues

- Describe the typical hardware, software, data and communications infrastructures found within information systems functions (also see Chapter 3)

Exam guide

Much of the information provided in this chapter would not be examined directly – but is required to gain an understanding of current trends in information technology and the opportunities they offer to organisations. Exam questions are likely to focus on how organisations could use technology, rather than directly testing your knowledge of a particular technology.

1 MANUAL SYSTEMS

1.1 Many **people like manual methods** of working and find it more convenient to jot down notes with pen and paper or tap out a few figures with a calculator than to use a computer. This is especially true of people who have not been brought up with computers.

1.2 People also enjoy **communicating face to face,** not just to fulfil their social needs but also because it is the most effective means of communication for many everyday tasks.

1.3 Computers can waste time, especially if the user is not properly trained or if the system has deficiencies.

Manual systems v computerised systems

1.4 However, there are a number of reasons why **manual** office systems are **less beneficial** than computerised systems.
   (a) Labour **productivity** is usually lower, particularly for routine tasks.
   (b) Processing is **slower.**
   (c) Complex processing may not be practicable using manual methods.
   (d) The **risk of errors** is greater.
   (e) Information is generally **less accessible.**
   (f) It is difficult to make **corrections or alterations.**
   (g) Output appears less professional.
   (h) Paper based systems are generally very **bulky** both to handle and to store.

2 THE COMPUTER

2.1 The definition of a 'computer' given in CIMA's *Computing Terminology* is as follows.

> A device which will accept input data, process it according to programmed logical and arithmetic rules, store and output data and/or calculate results.

Types of computer

2.2 Computers can be classified as follows.

- Supercomputers
- Mainframe computers
- Minicomputers
- Microcomputers, now commonly called PCs

2.3 A **supercomputer** is used to process **very large amounts of data very quickly**. They are particularly useful for occasions where high volumes of calculations need to be performed, for example in meteorological or astronomical applications.

2.4 A **mainframe** computer system uses a powerful central computer, linked by cable or telecommunications to terminals. A mainframe has many times more **processing power** than a PC and offers **extensive data storage** facilities.

2.5 Mainframes are used by organisations such as banks that have very large volumes of processing to perform and have special security needs. Many organisations have now replaced their old mainframes with networked 'client-server' systems of mid-range computers and PCs because this approach is thought to be cheaper and offer more flexibility.

2.6 A **minicomputer** is a computer whose size, speed and capabilities lie somewhere between those of a mainframe and a PC. The term was originally used before PCs were developed, to describe computers which were cheaper but less well-equipped than mainframe computers.

2.7 With the advent of PCs and of mainframes that are much smaller than in the past, the definition of a minicomputer has become rather vague. There is really no definition which distinguishes adequately between a PC and a minicomputer.

2.8 PCs are now the norm for small to medium-sized business computing and for home computing, and most larger businesses now use them for day-to-day needs such as word-processing. Often they are linked together in a **network** to enable sharing of information between users.

Portables

2.9 The original portable computers were heavy, weighing around five kilograms, and could only be run from the mains electricity supply. Subsequent developments allow true portability.

(a) The **laptop** or **notebook** is powered either from the electricity supply or using a rechargeable battery and can include all the features and functionality of desktop PCs.

(b) The **palmtop** or handheld is increasingly compatible with true PCs. Devices range from basic models which are little more than electronic organisers to relatively powerful processors running 'cut-down' versions of Windows and Microsoft Office, and including communications features.

2.10 It is estimated that portable computers now represent over 50% in volume of all types of personal computer sold.

A typical PC specification

2.11 Here is the specification for a **fairly powerful PC,** from an advertisement that appeared in early 2001. This PC cost around £800.

PC SPECIFICATION	
Intel 650 MHz Pentium III Processor	3.5" (1.44MB) Floppy Disk Drive
10GB hard disk drive	15" SVGA Monitor
56 kpbs internal fax modem	105 Key Windows Keyboard
512K CPU Cache	Logitech 2 button mouse
128MB RAM High speed 64-bit data path to memory	Midi Tower Case 3 × 5.25"& 3 × 3.5" drive bays, 2 serial ports, 1 parallel port
32 Speed CD ROM	Windows ME pre-loaded

The processor

2.12 The processor is the **'brain'** of the computer. The processor may be defined as follows. The processor (sometimes referred to as the central processing unit or CPU) is divided into three areas:

- Arithmetic and logic unit
- Control unit
- Main store or memory

2.13 The processing unit may have all its elements - arithmetic and logic unit, control unit, and the input/output interface on a single '**chip**'. A chip is a small piece of silicon upon which is etched an integrated circuit, on an extremely small scale.

2.14 The chip is mounted on a carrier unit which in turn is 'plugged' on to a circuit board - called the motherboard - with other chips, each with their own functions.

2.15 The most common chips are those made by the Intel company. Each generation of Intel CPU chip has been able to perform operations in fewer clock cycles than the previous generation, and therefore works more quickly.

MHz and clock speed

2.16 The processor receives program instructions and sends signals to peripheral devices. The number of cycles produced per second is usually measured in **MegaHertz** (MHz). 1 MHz = one **million** cycles per **second**. A typical modern business PC might have a specification of 450 MHz, but models with higher clock speeds (eg 700 MHz) are now common.

Memory

2.17 The computer's memory is also known as main store or internal store. The memory will hold the following.

- **Program instructions**
- The **input data** that will be processed next
- The **data** that is **ready for output** to an output device

Bits and bytes

2.18 Each individual storage element in the computer's memory consists of a simple circuit which can be switched **on** or **off**. These two states can be conveniently expressed by the numbers 1 and 0 respectively.

2.19 Each 1 or 0 is a **bit**. Bits are grouped together in groups of eight to form **bytes**. A byte may be used to represent a **character**, for example a letter, a number or another symbol.

2.20 Business PCs now make use of **32 bit** processors. Put simply, this means that data travels around from one place to another in groups of 16 or 32 bits, and so modern PCs operate considerably faster than the original 8 bit models.

2.21 The processing capacity of a computer is in part dictated by the capacity of its memory. Capacity is calculated in kilobytes (1 kilobyte = 2^{10} (1,024) bytes) and megabytes (1 megabyte = 2^{20} bytes) and gigabytes (2^{30}). These are abbreviated to Kb, Mb and Gb.

RAM

2.22 RAM (Random Access Memory) is memory that is directly available to the processing unit. It holds the data and programs in current use. RAM in microcomputers is 'volatile' which means that the contents of the memory are erased when the computer's power is switched off.

2.23 The RAM on a typical business PC is likely to have a capacity of 32 to 128 megabytes. The size of the RAM is **extremely** important. A computer with a 500 MHz clock speed but only 32 Mb of RAM will not be as efficient as a 300 MHz PC with 128 Mb of RAM.

BPP
PUBLISHING

Cache

2.24 The **cache** is a small capacity but **extremely fast** part of the memory which saves a second copy of the pieces of data most recently read from or written to main memory. When the cache is full, older entries are 'flushed out' to make room for new ones.

ROM

2.25 ROM (**Read-Only Memory**) is **a memory chip into which fixed data is written permanently** at the time of its manufacture.

2.26 When you turn on a PC you may see a reference to **BIOS** (basic input/output system). This is part of the ROM chip containing all the programs needed to control the keyboard, screen, disk drives and so on.

3 INPUT DEVICES

3.1 Input is a labour-intensive process. The process of inputting data can also be achieved through a variety of **data capture** techniques.

The keyboard

3.2 Computer keyboards are derived from the basic 'QWERTY' typewriter keyboard.

The VDU

3.3 A VDU (visual display unit) or '**monitor**' displays text and graphics. The screen's **resolution** is the number of pixels that are lit up. More and smaller pixels enable detailed high-resolution display. Super VGA, or **SVGA**, is the standard for newer monitors and offers resolutions up to 1,280 × 1,024.

3.4 **Touch-sensitive** screens have been developed but they are expensive.

Mouse

3.5 A **mouse** is generally used in conjunction with a keyboard. A mouse is a handheld device with a rubber or metal ball protruding from a small hole in its base used to instruct the cursor on screen.

Document reading methods

3.6 **Document reading methods** save time and money and also **reduce errors.** Some common document reading methods are described below.

Magnetic ink character recognition (MICR)

3.7 **MICR** is the recognition by a machine of special formatted characters printed in magnetic ink (such as those as on a cheque). The characters are read using a specialised reading device. The main advantage of MICR is its accuracy, but MICR documents are expensive to produce, and so MICR has only limited application in practice.

Optical mark reading (OMR)

3.8 **Optical Mark Reading** involves the marking of a pre-printed form with a ballpoint pen or typed line or cross in an appropriate box. The card is then read by an OMR device which senses the mark in each box using an electric current and translates it into machine code. Applications in which OMR is used include National Lottery entry forms, and answer sheets for multiple choice questions.

Scanners and OCR

3.9 A scanner is device that can **read text or illustrations** printed on paper and translate the information into a **form the computer can use**. A scanner works by digitising an image, the resulting matrix of bits is called a **bit map.**

3.10 To edit text read by an optical scanner, you need **Optical Character Recognition (OCR)** software to translate the picture into text format. Most scanners sold today come with OCR software.

3.11 Scanners may be used to set up a **Document Image Processing (DIP)** system. Document Image Processing converts paper documents into electronic form.

3.12 The **advantages** of DIP are:

- Reduced office **space** needed for paper files
- The same file can be viewed by **different users** simultaneously
- **Safer** as a digital file is on disk
- **Faster retrieval** of files than with a manual system

3.13 Applications of DIP include the management of accounting transactions - the documentation relating to an accounting transaction can be referenced to the ledger record: an entry in the sales ledger for example could be accompanied by images of all the related paperwork.

Bar coding and EPOS

3.14 **Bar codes** are groups of marks which, by their spacing and thickness, indicate specific codes or values. Look at the back cover of this book for an example of a bar code.

3.15 Large retail stores are introducing **Electronic Point of Sale (EPOS)** devices, which include bar code readers. This enables the provision of immediate sales and stock level information.

Question 1

The next time you are at the supermarket check-out, think of the consequences of the operator simply scanning one bar code. What effect does this quick and simple action have?

Answer

(a) The price of the item is added to your bill.

(b) The supermarket stock 'number on shelf' is reduced by one, and if the predetermined minimum has been reached the 'shelf restock required' indicator will be activated.

(c) The overall stock on hand figure will be reduced, and if the minimum stock holding has been reached the 'reorder from supplier' indicator will be activated.

(d) The relevant accounting entries will be made, or be sent to a pending file awaiting the running of the month-end routine.

(e) Marketing information will be obtained – what time the purchase was made, what else was purchased and if your loyalty card was swiped – who purchased it.

BPP PUBLISHING

You may have thought of others. The key point to grasp from this exercise is that **efficient information collection** can be achieved using appropriate technology.

Magnetic stripe cards

3.16 The **standard magnetic stripe card** contains machine-sensible data on a **thin strip of magnetic recording tape** stuck to the back of the card. The magnetic card reader converts this information into directly computer-sensible form. The widest application of magnetic stripe cards is as **bank credit or service cards**.

EFTPOS

3.17 Many retailers have now introduced **EFTPOS systems (Electronic Funds Transfer at the Point of Sale)**. Customers in shops and at petrol stations can use a plastic card (usually a credit card or debit card) to purchase goods or services, and using an EFTPOS terminal in the shop, the customer's credit card account or bank current account will be debited automatically. EFTPOS systems **combine point of sale systems with electronic funds transfer**.

Smart cards

3.18 A **smart card** is **a plastic card in which is embedded a microprocessor chip**. A smart card would typically contain a **memory** and a **processing capability**. The information held on smart cards can therefore be updated (eg using a PC and a special device).

Voice recognition

3.19 Computer software has been developed that can **convert speech into computer sensible form**: the input device needed in this case is a microphone. Users are required to speak clearly and reasonably slowly.

4 OUTPUT DEVICES

4.1 The commonest methods of computer output are printers and screen display. Other methods include output to a computer file, onto **microfilm** or to microfiche. Many computers also produce sound output through **speakers**.

The choice of output medium

4.2 Choosing a suitable output medium depends on a number of factors.

Factor	Comment
Hard copy	Is a printed version of the output needed?
Volume	For example, a VDU screen can hold a certain amount of data, but it becomes more difficult to read when information goes 'off-screen' and can only be read a 'page' at a time.
Speed	For example if a single enquiry is required it may be quicker to make notes from a VDU display.

Factor	Comment
Suitability for further use	Output to a file would be appropriate if the data will be processed further, maybe in a different system. Large volumes of reference data might be held on microfilm or microfiche.
Cost	The 'best' output device may not be justifiable on the grounds of cost - another output medium should be chosen.

Printers

4.3 A **line printer** prints a complete line in a single operation. They offer the operational speeds necessary for **bulk printing requirements**.

4.4 **Character printers** print a single character at a time. An examples is a dot matrix printers. Dot matrix printers are still reasonably widely used in accounting departments. Their main drawback is their **low-resolution.** They are also relatively **slow** and **noisy.**

4.5 **Bubblejet** and **inkjet** printers are small and reasonably cheap (under £100), making them popular where a 'private' output device is required. They work by sending a jet of ink on to the paper to produce the required characters. They are fairly **quiet and fast**, but they may produce **smudged** output if the paper is not handled carefully.

4.6 **Laser printers** print a whole page at a time, rather than line by line. The quality of output with laser printers is **very high**.

The VDU

4.7 Screens were described earlier, as they are used together with computer keyboards for **input**. They can be used as an **output** medium, primarily where the volume of output is low, for example a single enquiry.

4.8 The input/output process using a VDU is usually conducted via a **Graphical User Interface** (GUI). GUIs were designed to make computers more 'user-friendly'. A GUI involves the use of **W**indows, **I**cons, **M**ouse and **P**ull-down menus or 'WIMP'.

4.9 A GUI allows the screen to be divided into sections or windows. This enables two or more documents to be viewed and edited together, and sections of one to be inserted into another. The Windows operating system utilises WIMP features.

5 STORAGE DEVICES

Hard disks

5.1 Disks offer **direct access** to data. A modern business PC invariably has an **internal hard disk**. At the time of writing the average new **PC** has a hard disk size of around 5 **Gigabytes**, but 15 Gb disks are not uncommon. In larger computer systems **removable disk packs** are commonly used.

Floppy disks

5.2 The floppy disk provides a **cost-effective** means of on-line storage for **small** amounts of information. A $3^1/2$" disk can hold up to **1.44 Mb** of data.

BPP PUBLISHING

5.3   A **Zip disk** is a different type of **removable** disk, with much larger capacity (100 Mb) that requires a special Zip drive. A Zip disk is suitable for back-up, storage or for moving files between computers.

Tape storage

5.4   Tape cartridges have a **much larger capacity** than floppy disks and they are still widely used as a **backing storage** medium. Fast tapes which can be used to create a back-up file very quickly are known as **tape streamers**.

5.5   Like an audio or video cassette, data has to be recorded **along the length** of a computer tape and so it is **more difficult to access** than data on disk (ie direct access is not possible with tape). Reading and writing are separate operations.

CD-ROM(Compact Disc – Read Only Memory)

5.6   A CD-ROM can store 650 megabytes of data.

5.7   The **speed** of a CD-ROM drive is relevant to how fast data can be retrieved: an **eight speed** drive is quicker than a **four speed** drive.

5.8   CD recorders are now available for general business use with blank CDs (CD-R) and **rewritable disks** (CD-RW) are now available.

DVD (Digital Versatile Disc)

5.9   The CD format has started to be superseded by DVD. DVD development was encouraged by the advent of multimedia files with video graphics and sound - requiring greater disk capacity.

5.10 **Digital Versatile Disk (DVD)** technology can store almost 5 gigabytes of data on one disk. Access speeds are improved as is sound and video quality. Many commentators believe DVD will not only replace CD-ROMs, but also VHS cassettes, audio CDs and laser discs.

Question 2

Briefly outline two features and one common use of magnetic disks, magnetic tapes and optical disks (CD-ROMs).

Answer

(a)   *Magnetic disks* offer fast access times, direct access to data and offer suitability for multi-user environments. Magnetic disk storage is therefore the predominant storage medium in most commercial applications currently. Direct access is essential for many commercial applications (eg databases) and in addition speed is necessary for real-time applications.

(b)   *Magnetic tapes* offer cheap data storage, portability and serial or sequential access only. Magnetic tape is most valuable as a backup medium.

(c)   *Optical disks* (eg CD-ROMs) offer capacity to store vast amounts of data but offer slower access speeds than magnetic disks. They are most suitable for backup and archiving, or keeping old copies of files which might need to be retrieved. However, the technology behind optical drives is still in development, and it may not be too long before they are a viable alternative to magnetic disk drives for most applications.

---

6   SOFTWARE

The operating system

6.1   The **operating system** provides the interface between the computer hardware and both the user and the other software.

6.2   Operating software can be defined as a program or suite of programs which provide the 'bridge' between **applications** software (such as word processing packages, spreadsheet or accounting packages) and the hardware.

6.3   An operating system will typically perform the following tasks.

(a)   Initial **set-up** of the computer, when it is switched on.

(b)   Checking that the **hardware** (including peripheral devices such as printers) is functioning properly.

(c)   Calling up of **program files and data files** from external storage into memory.

(d)   **Opening and closing** of files, checking of file labels etc.

(e)   Maintenance of **directories** in external storage.

(f)   Controlling **input and output devices**, including the interaction with the user.

(g)   Controlling system **security** (for example monitoring the use of passwords).

(h)   Handling of **interruptions** (for example program abnormalities or machine failure).

(i)   Managing **multitasking.**

6.4   **Multitasking** means doing more than one task at once, for example printing out a Word document while you work in Excel.

UNIX

6.5   The UNIX operating system was developed as a **non-proprietary** (ie not specific to one manufacturer) operating system that could be portable to different computer architectures. UNIX works equally well in a PC network environment as in a **mainframe** or **minicomputer** system, though it is more common in the latter.

Windows

6.6   Early incarnations of Windows, culminating in **Windows 3.1** were not genuine operating systems in their own right, but were an operating environment for an older Microsoft system called **MS-DOS**. This meant that MS-DOS was always running underneath any applications and users were therefore still constrained by, for example, **eight-character file names** and various problems relating to the conventional memory of a PC.

6.7   In 1993, Microsoft launched **Windows NT**, a complete operating system in its own right, designed for **networks.** Today Windows NT provides strong competition for other network operating systems like Novell Netware. For PCs and smaller networks there is **Windows 95** and **Windows 98**. Windows ME (an upgrade to Windows 98) and Windows 2000 (an upgrade to Windows NT) are not yet in common use (January 2001).

Windows 98/ME/2000

6.8   Features of the Windows operating system include the following.

BPP PUBLISHING

Feature	Comment
Easy to use	User interface enhancements include easier navigation, such as **single-click launching** of applications, icon highlighting, forward/backward buttons, and an easy to customise Start Menu.
	A '**desktop**', from which everything in the system branches out. Disk drives, folders (directories), applications and files can all be placed on the desktop.
	A '**taskbar**' which includes a **Start** button (featured in advertising around the time of the release) and buttons representing every open application.
	Long file names are supported (up to 256 characters).
Faster	**Multitasking**.
	A **Tune-Up Wizard** helps the PC to maintain itself automatically and provide the best possible performance. File storage is more efficient, freeing up hard drive space.
Web integration	The Microsoft Web browser **Microsoft Internet Explorer** is included. There are a variety of features designed to enhance **Internet access** and technologies. For instance it is possible to access a website directly from the 'Explorer' file management system.
Entertaining	Windows has good **graphics** and **video capabilities** and supports **Digital Versatile Disks** (DVD).
Manageable	Tools such as Dr. Watson and System Information Utility make it easier for IT support staff to **diagnose and correct problems**.
	There is a **Recycle Bin** for easy deletion and recovery of files.
	Easy integration with **networking** software

6.9 Although it has bugs and irritations for the experienced user, Microsoft Windows provides a **comprehensive working environment**, enabling a wide range of programs written by many software companies to look and feel similar to other programs.

Apple Macs

6.10 There are some computer users, particularly those working in design and graphics, who prefer the **Apple Macintosh** system.

Other operating systems

6.11 Other competitors to Windows exist, such as **Linux** but, since the majority of PC manufacturers send out their products with Windows pre-loaded, this is the system that is likely to predominate.

Applications software

6.12 Applications software consists of **programs which carry out a task for the user** as opposed to programs which control the workings of a computer.

Application packages and general purpose packages

6.13 A distinction can be made between application packages and more general purpose packages.

    (a) An **application package** is a program or set of programs that will carry out a **specific** processing application - for example, a **payroll** package would be specific to payroll processing.

    (b) A **general purpose** package is an off-the-shelf program that can be used **for processing of a general type:** the user can apply the package to a variety of uses. **Spreadsheet** packages and **word processing** packages are examples.

Integrated software

6.14 Integrated software refers to programs, or packages of programs, that perform a **variety of different processing operations**, using **data which is compatible** with whatever operation is being carried out.

6.15 **Accounts packages** often consist of program 'modules' that can be integrated into a larger accounting system. There will be a module for each of the sales ledger system, the purchase ledger system, the nominal ledger, and so on. Output from one 'module' in an integrated system can be used as input to another, without the need for re-entry of data.

6.16 **'Office'** software allows the user to carry out a variety of processing operations, such as word processing, using spreadsheets and creating and using a database. The best known example is Microsoft Office, the basic version of which includes word processing (Word), spreadsheet (Excel), and a presentation package (PowerPoint).

The spreadsheet

> **KEY TERM**
>
> A **spreadsheet** is a general purpose software package for **modelling**, 'spreadsheet' being a term loosely derived from the application's likeness to a 'spreadsheet of paper' divided into **rows** and **columns**.

6.17 The spreadsheet was originally used mainly as an aid to accountants or financial specialists, but it is now widely used in most offices. The most widely used packages are **Microsoft Excel** and **Lotus 1-2-3**.

6.18 The spreadsheet user generally **constructs a model** by doing the following.

    (a) Identifying what data goes into each row and column, by **inserting text**, for example column headings and row identifications.

    (b) Specifying how the **numerical data** in the model should be **derived**.

6.19 Spreadsheets are **versatile** tools that can be used for a wide variety of tasks and calculations. The absence of imposed formats or contents gives the spreadsheet great flexibility and it is this that users find so valuable in **decision making**.

6.20 Spreadsheets are particularly useful at **tactical** level.

    (a) At **operational** level, decisions are more structured and routine and therefore more suited to specific application packages.

(b) At **strategic** level, decisions are less structured and relevant factors are less likely to be able to be incorporated into a computer package.

(c) Much tactical management, however, involves the **analysis and interpretation** of operational information. The '**what if?**' manipulation of data, for example, is an important facility of a spreadsheet package.

As a simple illustration, a manager planning activities for the next six months might want to know how the department's cash flow would be affected if interest rates changed. It is a simple matter to set up a spreadsheet so that the interest rate is entered in a separate cell and treated as a variable in the cash flow calculations. The value in this cell can then be changed at will to see **what** happens to cash flow **if** the rate is 5%, 6%, 7% and so on.

Potential drawbacks

6.21 Spreadsheets are immensely popular and can be used for a very wide range of modelling tasks. However, because each model is **designed from scratch**, there are risks in their use.

(a) Spreadsheets may be **badly designed**, increasing the risk of errors or inefficiency.

(b) Users are unlikely to **document** the workings of their spreadsheet, as they consider it 'obvious'. This makes it difficult for other staff (temporary replacement or permanent successor) to understand, use or modify the model.

(c) The '**macro**' is an important feature of many spreadsheets. Macros can be **difficult to write and to understand** and are not as conducive to tight control as the use of a programming language.

(d) The **lack of a proper audit trail** can be a disadvantage. Because spreadsheets are usually saved by overwriting the current file, it is unlikely that a record of the intermediate stages of the model will be maintained.

Word processing

> **KEY TERM**
>
> **Word processing** is the **processing of text information**. Typically, word processing software may be used for the production of standard letters and for the drafting and redrafting of documents.

6.22 Word processing enables the person preparing the text to check the input visually on the VDU as it is being keyed in, and to **correct errors immediately**.

6.23 Changes can be made quickly and simply. For example, a company might hold its rules and procedures books, or its price lists, on a WP file and update them just before they are to be reprinted.

6.24 The WYSIWYG (What You See Is What You Get) facility is another helpful feature for users who wish to see on screen exactly the **format and typeface** (italics, bold etc) they will get on paper.

Question 3

What are the advantages of word processing over a manual system.

Answer

The advantages of word processing include the following.

(a) The ability to produce personalised letters of a standard type.
(b) The ability to amend, correct or update text on screen easily.
(c) A low error rate in the text.
(d) Speed of keying text and corrections.
(e) Easy formatting of text.
(f) Quality is improved.
(g) Security may be enhanced.

Presentation packages

6.25 Presentation programs allow the user to build up a series of images (or slides) which can be used for presentation eg Microsoft PowerPoint.

Graphics

6.26 Another use of computers is the production of information in the form of **pictures, diagrams or graphs**. Widely used packages include CorelDraw and Paint Shop Pro.

6.27 **Spreadsheets** and **word processing packages** also commonly incorporate some graphics facilities eg excellent graphs can be produced using Microsoft Excel.

7 DATA PROCESSING IN A COMPUTERISED ENVIRONMENT

7.1 In data processing a data **file** is a collection of **records** with similar characteristics. Examples of data files include the sales ledger, the purchase ledger and the nominal ledger.

7.2 A **record** in a file consists of data relating to one logically definable unit of business information. A collection of similar records makes up a file. For example, the records for a sales ledger file consist of customer records (or 'customer accounts').

7.3 Records in files consist of **fields** of information. For example, a customer record on the sales ledger file will include name, address, customer reference number, balance owing, and credit limit.

7.4 Records on a file should contain one **key field**. This is an item of data within the record by which it can be uniquely identified.

7.5 Files are conventionally classified into **transaction** files, and **master** files. These distinctions are particularly relevant in batch processing applications.

7.6 A transaction file is a file containing records that relate to individual transactions. The sales day book entries are examples of transaction records in a transaction file.

7.7 A **master file** contains reference data and also cumulative transaction data. For example, in a purchase ledger system, the master file is the purchase ledger itself. This is a file consisting of:

(a) **Reference data** for each supplier (supplier name and address, reference number, amount currently owed etc) and

(b) **Cumulative transaction data** for each supplier – periodic totals for purchases, purchase returns and payments.

7.8 Both manual and computer data processing can be divided into two broad types: batch processing and real-time processing. Batch processing systems are becoming less common, particularly if the process concerned impacts on customer service.

Batch processing

7.9 **Batch processing** is the processing **as a group** of a number of transactions of a similar kind. For example a payroll office may divide transaction records into a **batch per department**. Transactions will be collected over a period of time. Some **delay** in processing the transactions must therefore be acceptable - for example in a payroll system daily timesheets may be stored and processed weekly.

7.10 Batch input allows for **control** over the input data, because data can be grouped and totalled in numbered **batches**. Output listings of the processed transactions are usually organised in batch order.

Real-time processing

7.11 **Real-time processing** is the continual receiving and processing of data. Real-time processing uses an **'on-line'** computer system (see below) to interrogate or update files as requested, rather than batching for subsequent processing.

7.12 Real time systems are the norm in modern business. Examples include the following.

(a) As a sale is made in a department store or a supermarket and details are input via the bar code reader on the point of sale terminal, the stock records are updated in real-time.

(b) In (some) banking systems where account details are updated immediately a transaction is processed.

(c) Travel agents and theatre ticket agencies use real-time systems. Once a hotel room, plane seat or theatre seat is booked it must not show as still being available.

On-line

7.13 On-line refers to a machine which is under the **direct control** of the **central processor**. A terminal is said to be on-line when it communicates interactively with the central processor. Modern computers such as PCs are on-line by definition (they have their own processor), but mainframe-based systems may not be. (The term is increasingly being used to describe an active connection to the Internet.)

7.14 Response times are a significant feature of on-line processing. This is the time that elapses between initiating an on-line enquiry or transaction and receiving the result.

8 DEVELOPMENTS IN COMMUNICATIONS

8.1 The 1990s saw significant developments in communications.

KEY TERMS

Digital means 'of digits or numbers'. Digital information is information in a coded (binary) form.

Information in **analogue** form uses continuously variable signals.

Modems and digital transmission

8.2 New technologies require **transmission systems** capable of delivering substantial quantities of data at great speed.

8.3 For data transmission through the existing 'analogue' telephone network to be possible, there has to be a device at each end of the telephone line that can convert (MOdulate) the data from digital form to analogue form, and (DEModulate) from analogue form to digital form, depending on whether the data is being sent out or received along the telephone line. This conversion of data is done by devices called **modems**. There must be a modem at each end of the telephone line.

Integrated Systems Digital Networks (ISDN)

8.4 An ISDN line enables the sending of voice, data, video and fax communications from a single desktop computer system over the telecommunication link, without using a modem.

Asymmetric Digital Subscriber Line (ADSL)

8.5 ADSL offers data transfer rates of up to 8 Mbps (Megabytes per second), considerably faster than ISDN. ADSL allows information to be sent out over ordinary copper wires and simultaneous use of the normal telephone service. A special ADSL modem is required.

Mobile communications

8.6 **Networks** for portable telephone communications, also known as 'cellular phones', have boomed in developed countries since the early 1990s.

8.7 **Digital networks** have been developed which are better able to support data transmission than the older analogue networks, with **higher transmission speeds** and **less likelihood of data corruption**.

8.8 This means that a salesperson out on the road, say, can send or receive a fax or e-mail simply by plugging a lap-top PC into a mobile handset. A combined palmtop computer and cellular phone is already on the market.

8.9 In theory it is now possible to do any kind of 'office' activity outside on the move, although **limitations in battery power** (a technology lagging far behind others described here) impose restrictions.

8.10 The mobile services available are increasing all the time. Here are some examples.

   (a) **Messaging services** such as: voice mail; short message service (SMS) which allows messages of up to 160 characters to be transmitted over a standard digital phone; and paging services

BPP
PUBLISHING

(b) **Call handling services** such as: call barring, conference calls and call divert

(c) **Corporate services** such as: integrated numbering, so that people have a single contact number for both the phone on their desk and for their mobile; and virtual private networks that incorporate mobile phones as well as conventional desktop phones, so that users can dial internal extension numbers directly.

(d) **Internet access.** The speed of transmission when downloading information is relatively slow at present, but improving.

(e) **Dual mode handsets** are due to be released shortly which allow users to use both cheap cordless technology when in the office and cellular technology when outside.

(f) There are several **satellite projects** in progress which by about 2002 will mean that business people can contact each other at a modest cost using a mobile phone from virtually any point on Earth.

Which communication tool?

8.11   Technological advances have increased the number of communication tools available. The features and limitations of ten common tools are outlined in the following table.

Tool	Features / Advantages	Limitations
Conversation	Usually unstructured so can discuss a wide range of topics Requires little or no planning Gives a real impression of feelings	Temptation to lose focus May be easily forgotten
Meeting	Allows multiple opinions to be expressed Can discuss and resolve a wide range of issues	Can highlight differences if not managed efficiently – have been known to turn into time-wasting confrontations 'Louder' personalities may dominate Costly in terms of personnel time A focused agenda and an effective Chair should minimise the impact of these limitations
Presentation	Complex ideas can be communicated Visual aids such as slides can help the communication process The best presentations will leave a lasting impression	Requires planning and skill Poorly researched or presented material can lead to audience resentment

Tool	Features / Advantages	Limitations
Telephone	Good for communications that do not require (or you would prefer not to have) a permanent written record Can provide some of the 'personal touch' to people in geographically remote locations Conference calls allow multiple participants	Receiver may not be available; 'phone-tag' is a frustrating pass-time! (Voice-mail may help) Can be disruptive to receiver if in the middle of another task No written record gives greater opportunity for misunderstandings
Facsimile	Enables reports and messages to reach remote locations quickly	Easily seen by others Fax machine may not be checked for messages Complex images do not transmit well
Memorandum	Provides a permanent record Adds formality to internal communications	If used too often or the message is too general people may ignore it Can come across as impersonal
Letter	Provides a permanent record of an external message Adds formality to external communications Use a clear, simple structure, eg…<ul><li>Letterhead</li><li>Reference or heading</li><li>Date</li><li>Recipient name and address</li><li>Greeting/salutation</li><li>Subject</li><li>Substance</li><li>Close</li><li>Signature</li><li>Author name and position</li><li>Enclosure/copy reference</li></ul>	If inaccurate or poorly presented provides a permanent record of incompetence May be slow to arrive depending on distance and the postal service

BPP PUBLISHING

Tool	Features / Advantages	Limitations
Report	Provides a permanent, often comprehensive written record Use a clear, simple structure. There is no one correct format. An example that could be adapted to suit the report requirements is… • Meaningful Title • Author name and position • Purpose/Terms of Reference • Procedure followed • Findings • Conclusion / Recommendations Where necessary use a hierarchy of headings to aid clarity, eg… • 1 Section heading • (a) sub heading • (i) sub point	Complex messages may be misunderstood in the absence of immediate feedback Reports that reach (necessarily) negative conclusions can lead to negative impressions of the author
Electronic mail	Provides a written record Attachments (eg Reports or other documents) can be included Quick – regardless of location Automated 'Read receipts' or a simple request to acknowledge receipt by return message mean you know if the message has been received Can be sent to multiple recipients easily, can be forwarded on to others	Requires some computer literacy to use effectively People may not check their e-mail regularly Lack of privacy – can be forwarded on without your knowledge Long messages (more than one 'screen') may best be dealt with via other means, or as attached documents
Video-conference	This is in effect a meeting conducted using a computer and video system Provides more of a personal touch than the telephone, but less than a 'physical' meeting Some non-verbal messages (eg gestures) will be received	The hardware is expensive compared to telephone May be dominated by the most confident participant(s) Cross-border cultural differences may be unintentionally ignored as participants feel 'at home' Image quality is often poor – resulting in not much more than an expensive telephone conference call!

Voice messaging systems

8.12 Voice messaging systems answer and route telephone calls. Typically, when a call is answered a **recorded message** tells the caller to dial the extension required, or to hold if they want to speak to the operator. Sometimes other options are offered, such as 'press 2 if you want to know about X service and 3 if you want to know about Y'.

8.13 Such systems **work well** if callers often have **similar needs** and these can be accurately anticipated. They can be **frustrating** for callers with **non-standard enquiries**.

Case example: Interactive voice response (IVR)

Several pharmaceutical companies have installed sophisticated interactive voice response systems to deal with enquiries from doctors, chemists or patients. For example some allow the caller to press a number on their handset and have details of possible side effects sent back to them by fax.

Computer Telephony Integration (CTI)

8.14 Computer Telephony Integration (CTI) systems **gather information about callers** such as their telephone number and customer account number or demographic information (age, income, interests etc). This is stored on a customer database and can be **called up and sent to the screen** of the person dealing with the call, perhaps before the call has even been put through.

Computer bulletin boards

8.15 A computer bulletin board consists of a central mailbox or area on a computer server where people can **deposit messages** for everyone to see, and, in turn, **read what other people have left** in the system.

8.16 Bulletin boards can be appropriate for a team of individuals at different locations to compare notes. It becomes a way of keeping track of progress on a **project** between routine team meetings.

Videoconferencing

8.17 Videoconferencing is the use of computer and communications technology to **conduct meetings**.

8.18 Videoconferencing has become increasingly common as the Internet and webcams have brought the service to desktop PCs at reasonable cost. More expensive systems feature a **separate room with several video screens**, which show the images of those participating in a meeting.

Electronic Data Interchange (EDI)

8.19 EDI is a form of computer-to-computer **data** interchange. Instead of sending each other reams of paper in the form of invoices, statements and so on, details of inter-company transactions are sent via telecoms links, **avoiding the need for output** and paper at the sending end, and **for re-keying of data** at the receiving end.

Electronic Funds Transfer (EFT)

8.20 EFT describes a system whereby organisations are able to use their computer system to **transfer funds** - for example make payments to a **supplier,** or pay salaries into **employees'** bank accounts.

9 THE EFFECT OF OFFICE AUTOMATION ON BUSINESS

9.1 Office automation has an enormous effect on business.

Routine processing

9.2 The processing of routine data can be done in **bigger volumes,** at **greater speed** and with **greater accuracy** than with non-automated, manual systems.

The paperless office

9.3 There might be **less paper** in the office (but not necessarily so) with more data-processing done by keyboard. Data handling is likely to shift from moving and storing paper to moving and storing data electronically.

Management information

9.4 The nature and **quality of management information** will change.

(a) Managers are likely to have **access to more information** - for example from a database. Information is also likely to be **more accurate, reliable and up to date**. The range of **management reports** is likely to be wider and their content more comprehensive.

(b) **Planning activities** should be more thorough, with the use of **models** (eg spreadsheets for budgeting) and **sensitivity analysis**.

(c) Information for **control** should be more readily available. For example, a computerised sales ledger system should provide prompt reminder letters for late payers, and might incorporate other credit control routines. Stock systems, especially for companies with stocks distributed around several different warehouses, should provide better stock control.

(d) **Decision making** by managers can be helped by **decision support systems.**

Organisation structure

9.5 The **organisation structure** might change. PC networks give local office managers a means of setting up a good **local management information system,** and **localised data processing** while retaining access to **centrally-held databases** and programs. Office automation can therefore encourage a tendency towards **decentralisation** of authority within an organisation.

9.6 On the other hand, such systems help **head office** to **keep in touch** with what is going on in local offices. Head office can therefore readily monitor and control the activities of individual departments, and retain a co-ordinating influence.

Customer service

9.7 Office automation, in some organisations, results in **better customer service**. When an organisation receives large numbers of telephone enquiries from customers, the staff who take the calls should be able to provide a prompt and helpful service if they have **on-line access** to the organisation's data files.

Homeworking or remote working

9.8 Advances in communications technology have, for some tasks, **reduced the need for the actual presence of an individual in the office**.

9.9 The **advantages to the organisation** of homeworking are as follows.

(a) **Cost savings on space**. Office rental costs and other charges can be very expensive. If firms can move some of their employees on to a homeworking basis, money can be saved.

(b) A **larger pool of labour**. The possibility of working at home might attract more applicants for clerical positions, especially from people who have other demands on their time (eg going to and from school) which cannot be fitted round standard office hours.

(c) If the homeworkers are **freelance**, then the organisation **avoids the need to pay them** when there is insufficient work, when they are sick, on holiday etc.

9.10 The **advantages to the individual** of homeworking are as follows.

(a) No time is wasted commuting.

(b) Work can be organised around domestic commitments.

9.11 **Problems** for the organisation might be as follows.

(a) **Co-ordination** of the work of different homeworkers. The job design should ensure that homeworkers perform to the required standard.

(b) **Training**. If a homeworker needs a lot of help on a task, this implies that the task has not been properly explained.

(c) **Culture**. A homeworker is relatively isolated from the office and therefore, it might be assumed, from the firm. However, questions of loyalty and commitment do not apply for an organisation's sales force, whose members are rarely in the office.

(d) A loss of direct **control**.

9.12 **Problems for homeworkers** may include:
- Isolation
- Interruptions
- Adequate space
- Possibly fewer employment rights (if employed on a 'casual' basis)

Technological change

9.13 Technological change can affect the activities of organisations as follows.

(a) **The type of products or services that are made and sold**. For example, consumer markets have seen the emergence of home computers, compact discs and satellite dishes for receiving satellite TV; industrial markets have seen the emergence of custom-built microchips, robots and local area networks for office information systems.

(b) **The way in which products are made**. There is a continuing trend towards the use of modern labour-saving production equipment, such as robots. The manufacturing environment is undergoing rapid changes with the growth of advanced manufacturing technology. These are changes in both apparatus and technique.

(c) **The way in which services are provided**. High-street banks encourage customers to use 'hole-in-the-wall' cash dispensers, or telephone or PC banking. Most larger shops now use computerised **Point of Sale terminals** at cash desks. Many organisations are starting to use **e-commerce**: selling products and services over the Internet.

(d) **The way in which markets are identified**. Database systems make it much easier to analyse the market place.

(e) **The way in which employees are mobilised**. Computerisation encourages delayering of organisational hierarchies, and greater workforce empowerment and skills. Using technology frequently requires changes in working methods. This is a change in organisation.

9.14 The benefits of technological change might therefore be as follows.

- To **cut production costs**
- To develop **better quality** products and services
- To develop **new** products and services
- To **provide** products or services to customers **more quickly or effectively**
- To **free staff** from repetitive work and to tap their creativity

9.15 Organisations that operate in an environment where the pace of technological change is very fast **must be flexible enough to adapt to change quickly** and must **plan** for change and innovation. Technological change can be planned for by **developing strategies** for improved productivity and for innovation.

The importance of management

9.16 It is argued that **success or failure** in implementing IT is a result not so much of the systems themselves but the **management effort** behind them. For example, information systems will fail for any of the following reasons.

(a) They are used to tackle the **wrong problem** (ie the use of IT has not been thought through in the context of the wider organisational context).

(b) **Senior management are not interested**.

(c) **Users are ignored** in design and development.

(d) No attention is given to **behavioural factors** in design and operation.

9.17 If an organisation develops and follows a realistic **strategy** for information systems and technology then there is less chance that these problems will arise.

Types of information system

Management information system (MIS)

KEY TERM

A **management information system (MIS) converts data** from internal and external sources into **information,** and communicates that information in an appropriate form to **managers** at all levels.

9.18 An MIS provides **regular formal information** gleaned from normal commercial data. For example, an MIS might provide information on the following.

(a) **Product information.** On-line, categorised information at the fingertips.

(b) **Sales ledger.** Information will be immediately available relating to **customer turnover** and **payment records. Trend analysis** will identify customers whose business is growing or has fallen away.

(c) **Marketing.** As enquiries and sales arise, the MIS can summarise this data to assist in forward planning. **Customer satisfaction** can be measured by post-purchase surveys and questionnaires. This information will be processed by the MIS and summarised for use by the management, both in **report** and **graphical form**.

(d) **Supplier information.** Information such as **amount spent** with each supplier, and **reliability indicators** (cancellations by the supplier, satisfaction of the customers) will prove useful when negotiating and making strategic decisions.

(e) **Accounting.** Because the **transactions** of the company are on the system, information will be available to trial balance stage of the nominal ledger. This will be available to the accounts department with **comparable budget and prior year information**, through drill down enquiry and also available in report formats.

(f) **Modelling.** Key data from the above areas can be combined into reports, possibly via **spreadsheets**, to create **strategic** and 'what if' models.

Transaction processing systems

9.19 Transaction processing systems, or data processing systems, are the **lowest level** in an organisation's use of information systems. They are used for **routine tasks** in which data items or transactions must be processed so that operations can continue. Handling sales orders, purchase orders, payroll items and stock records are typical examples.

9.20 Transaction processing systems provide the **raw material** which is often used more extensively by management information systems, databases or decision support systems. In other words:

(a) Transaction processing systems might be used to produce **management information**, such as reports on cumulative sales figures to date, total amounts owed to suppliers or owed by debtors and so on.

(b) However, the **main purpose** of transaction processing systems is as an integral part of **day-to-day operations**.

Decision support systems (DSS)

9.21 Decision support systems are used by management to assist in making decisions on issues which are **unstructured**, with high levels of uncertainty about the true **nature** of the problem, the various **responses** which management could undertake or the likely **impact** of those actions.

9.22 The term decision support system is usually taken to mean computer systems which are designed to produce information in such a way as to help managers to make better decisions. They are now often associated with information 'at the touch of a button' at a manager's personal computer or workstation. DSS can describe a **range of systems**, from fairly simple information models based on **spreadsheets** to **expert systems**.

9.23 Decision support systems **do not make decisions**. The objective is to allow the manager to consider a number of **alternatives** and evaluate them under a variety of potential conditions.

Executive Information Systems (EIS)

9.24 An executive information system is a type of DSS which gives the senior executive easy access to key internal and external data'. An EIS is likely to have the following features.

(a) Provision of **summary-level** data, captured from the organisation's main systems.

(b) A facility which allows the executive to **drill down** from higher levels of information to lower).

(c) **Data manipulation** facilities (for example comparison with budget or prior year data, trend analysis).

(d) **Graphics**, for user-friendly presentation of data.

(e) A **template** system. This will mean that the same type of data (eg sales figures) is presented in the same format, irrespective of changes in the volume of information required.

Expert systems

9.25 Expert systems are a form of DSS that allow users to benefit from expert knowledge and information. The system will consist of a **database** holding specialised data and **rules** about what to do in, or how to interpret, a given set of circumstances.

9.26 For example, many financial institutions now use expert systems to process straightforward **loan applications**. The user enters certain key facts into the system such as the loan applicant's name and most recent addresses, their income and monthly outgoings, and details of other loans. The system will then process the application and make a decision.

Intranets and Extranets

9.27 Organisations are increasingly using **intranets** and **extranets** to **disseminate information**.

(a) An **intranet** is like a mini version of the Internet (covered in the following section). Organisation members use networked computers to access information held on a server. The user interface is a browser – similar to those used on the Internet. The intranet offers access to information on a wide variety of topics, and often includes access to the Internet.

(b) An **extranet** is an intranet that is accessible to **authorised outsiders**, using a valid username and password. The user name will have access rights attached - determining which parts of the extranet can be viewed. Extranets are becoming a very popular means for business partners to exchange information.

10   THE INTERNET

KEY TERM

The **Internet** is a global network connecting millions of computers.

10.1   The Internet is the name given to the technology that allows any computer with a telecommunications link to **send and receive information** from any other suitably equipped computer.

10.2   The **World Wide Web** is the multimedia element which provides facilities such as full-colour, graphics, sound and video. Web-sites are points within the network created by members who wish to provide an information point for searchers to visit and benefit by the provision of information and/or by entering into a transaction.

10.3   Most companies now have a **Website** on the Internet. A site is a collection of screens providing **information in text and graphic form,** any of which can be viewed simply by clicking the appropriate button, word or image on the screen.

Current uses of the Internet

10.4   The scope and potential of the Internet are still developing. Its uses already embrace the following:

(a) **Dissemination** of information.

(b) **Product/service development** - through almost instantaneous test marketing.

(c) **Transaction processing** (electronic commerce or e-commerce) - both business-to-business and business-to-consumer.

(d) **Relationship enhancement** - between various groups of stakeholders.

(e) **Recruitment** and job search - involving organisations worldwide.

(f) **Entertainment** - including music, humour, art, games and some less wholesome pursuits!

10.5   It is estimated that over 32% of households in the UK will have Internet access by the end of 2001, with the figure rising to 40 per cent by 2002.

10.6   The Internet provides opportunities to organise for and to automate tasks which would previously have required more costly interaction with the organisation. These have often been called low-touch or zero-touch approaches.

BPP
PUBLISHING

10.7 Tasks which a **website may automate** include:

(a) **Frequently-Asked Questions (FAQs)**: carefully-structured sets of answers can deal with many customer interactions.

(b) **Status checking**: major service enquiries (Where is my order? When will the engineer arrive? What is my bank balance?) can also be automated, replacing high-cost human service processes, and also providing the opportunity to proactively offer better service and new services.

(c) **Keyword search**: the ability to search provides web users with opportunities to find information in large and complex websites.

(d) **Wizards (interview style interface) and intelligent algorithms**: these can help diagnosis, which is one of the major elements of service support.

(e) **E-mail and systems to route and track inbound e-mail**: the ability to route and/or to provide automatic responses will enable organisations to deal with high volumes of e-mail from actual and potential customers.

(f) **Bulletin boards**: these enable customers to interact with each other, thus facilitating self-activated customer service and also the opportunity for product/service referral. Cisco in particular has created communities of Cisco users who help each other - thus reducing the service costs for Cisco itself.

(g) **Call-back buttons**: these enable customers to speak to someone in order to deal with and resolve a problem; the more sophisticated systems allow the call-centre operator to know which web pages the users were consulting at the time.

Problems with the Internet

10.8 To a large extent the Internet has grown organically **without any formal organisation**. There are specific communication rules, but it is not **owned** by any one body and there are no clear guidelines on how it should develop.

10.9 The **quality** of much of the information on the Internet leaves much to be desired.

10.10 Speed is a major issue. Data only downloads onto the user's PC at the speed of the slowest telecommunications link - downloading data can be a painfully **slow** procedure.

10.11 So much information and entertainment is available that employers worry that their **staff will spend too much time** browsing through non-work-related sites.

10.12 Connecting an information system to the Internet exposes the system to numerous security issues. We will explore these issues in Chapter 10.

11 THE QUALITY OF INFORMATION

11.1 Advances in IS and IT should provide organisations with **better quality information**. 'Good' information is information that **adds to the understanding of a situation**. The qualities of good information are outlined in the following table.

Quality	Example
A ccurate	Figures should **add up**, the degree of **rounding** should be appropriate, there should be **no typos**, items should be allocated to the **correct category, assumptions should be stated** for uncertain information.
C omplete	Information should includes everything that it **needs** to include, for example external data if relevant, or comparative information.
C ost-beneficial	It should not **cost more** to obtain the information than the **benefit** derived from having it. Providers or information should be given efficient means of collecting and analysing it. Presentation should be such that users do not waste time working out what it means.
U ser-targeted	The **needs of the user** should be borne in mind, for instance senior managers need summaries, junior ones need detail.
R elevant	Information that is **not needed** for a decision should be omitted, no matter how 'interesting' it may be.
A uthoritative	The **source** of the information should be a reliable one (**not**, for instance, 'Joe Bloggs Predictions Page' on the Internet unless Joe Bloggs is known to be a reliable source for that type of information).
T imely	The information should be available **when it is needed**.
E asy to use	Information should be **clearly presented, not excessively long**, and sent using the **right medium** and **communication channel** (e-mail, telephone, hard-copy report etc)

> **Exam focus point**
> You will **not be asked simply to produce a list** of the qualities of good information in the exam. Exam questions may require you to be able to **recognise information deficiencies and suggest improvements**.

Improvements to information

11.2 The table on the following page contains suggestions as to how the quality of information can be **improved**.

BPP PUBLISHING

Feature	Example of possible improvements
Accurate	Use **computerised** systems with automatic input checks rather than manual systems.
	Allow **sufficient time** for collation and analysis of data if pinpoint accuracy is crucial.
	Incorporate elements of **probability** within projections so that the required response to **different future scenarios** can be assessed.
Complete	Include **past data** as a reference point for future projections.
	Include any **planned developments,** such as new products.
	Information about **future demand** would be more useful than information about past demand.
	Include **external** data.
Cost-beneficial	Always bear in mind whether the benefit of having the information is greater than the cost of obtaining it.
User-targeted	Information should be **summarised** and presented together with relevant **ratios or** percentages.
Relevant	The **purpose** of the report should be defined. It may be trying to fulfil too many purposes at once. Perhaps **several shorter reports** would be more effective.
	Information should include **exception reporting**, where only those items that are worthy of note - and the **control actions taken** by more junior managers to deal with them - are reported.
Authoritative	Use **reliable sources** and **experienced personnel**.
	If some figures are derived from other figures the **method of derivation** should be explained.
Timely	Information **collection and analysis** by production managers needs to be **speeded up** considerably, probably by the introduction of better information systems
Easy-to-use	**Graphical** presentation, allowing **trends** to be quickly assimilated and relevant action decided upon.
	Alternative methods of presentation should be considered, such as **graphs or charts**, to make it easier to review the information **at a glance**. **Numerical** information is sometimes best summarised in **narrative** form or vice versa.
	A '**house style**' for reports should be devised and adhered to by all. This would cover such matters as number of decimal places to use, table headings and labels, paragraph numbering and so on.

Chapter roundup

- In many circumstances, **manual** systems are **less productive** than computerised systems.

- **Computers** can be classified as supercomputers, mainframes, minicomputers and PCs.

- The amount of **RAM** and the **processor speed** are key determinants of computer performance. Hard drive size is another important factor.

- The **operating system** provides the interface between hardware, software and user.

- There are a range of **input** and **output** devices available. The most efficient method will depend on the circumstances of each situation.

- Hard disks are used for internal **storage** - external storage may be on floppy disk, zip disk, CD-ROM or DVD.

- The **operating system** is software which supervises the running of other programs, providing a 'bridge' between applications software and the hardware.

- **General purpose software** allows data to be handled in a particular way, for example in a spreadsheet.

- Data can be collected from within and beyond an organisation. **Information systems** are used to convert this **data** into **information** and to communicate it to management at all levels.

- A system receives **inputs** which it **processes** and generates into **outputs**. Any system can be thought of in terms of inputs, processing and outputs.

- The **channel of communication** will impact on the effectiveness of the communication process. The characteristics of the message will determine what communication tool is best for a given situation.

- Different types of information systems exist with different characteristics - reflecting the different **roles** they perform.

- Technological **change** may be used:

  - To cut production costs

  - To develop better quality products and services

  - To develop new products and services

  - To provide products or services to customers more quickly or effectively

  - To free staff from repetitive work and to tap their creativity

- Many organisations are now utilising **the Internet** as a means of gathering and disseminating information, and conducting transactions.

- Developments in IS/IT should provide organisations with better quality information. ACCURATE is a handy mnemonic for the qualities of good information.

Quick quiz

1   List four reasons why manual office systems maybe less beneficial than computerised systems.

2   What is RAM?

3   List five ways an organisation could input or capture data.

4   What does the term 'what if?' mean in relation to spreadsheets?

5   Distinguish between batch and real-time processing.

6   What is EDI and how could it encourage a closer relationship between organisations?

7   Distinguish between an intranet and an extranet.

8   List four general business uses of the Internet.

9   List five tasks a website may automate.

10 Do you agree with the statement 'information derived from the Internet is unreliable'? Justify your answer.

Answers to quick quiz

1 Manual systems may be slower, more prone to error, require more labour and may be unable to handle large volumes of data. (This assumes the computerised system is operating correctly, is reliable and that staff know how to utilise it fully.)

2 RAM stands for Random Access Memory. It holds the data and programs in current use. RAM and processor speed are important indicators of processing power.

3 [Five of]

Keyboard.

Mouse.

Scanner and OCR.

Bar codes and scanner.

MICR.

OMR.

EPOS.

EFTPOS.

Touch sensitive screen.

Voice recognition software and a microphone.

4 This refers to the ability to set up a financial model to automatically show the effect of a change in a variable (or variables). The user need only change the variable(s) and the model calculates the other figures.

5 Batch processing is the processing as a group of a number of transactions of a similar kind in a batch. Real-time processing is the continual receiving and processing of data. Real-time processing uses an 'on-line' computer system to interrogate or update files as requested, rather than batching for subsequent processing.

6 Electronic Data Interchange (EDI) is a form of computer-to-computer data interchange. Instead of sending reams of paper in the form of invoices, statements and so on, details of transactions are sent via telecoms links. An efficient EDI link encourages a closer relationship between organisations as it encourages organisations to do business with those organisations it has EDI links with. Faster document transmission should reduce order lead times.

7 An intranet is available to those inside an organisation - members use networked computers to access information held on a server. The user interface is a browser – similar to those used on the Internet. An extranet is an intranet that is accessible to authorised outsiders. Extranets are becoming a very popular means for business partners to exchange information.

8 [Four of]

External e-mail.

Dissemination of information.

Product/service development - through almost instantaneous test marketing.

Transaction processing (electronic commerce or e-commerce).

Relationship enhancement - between various groups of stakeholders.

Recruitment and job search - involving organisations worldwide.

9   [Five of]

Frequently-Asked Questions (FAQs).

Status checking service enquiries.

Keyword search.

Bulletin boards that enable customers to interact with each other.

Call-back buttons that enable customers to request a customer services representative contacts them.

10   The Internet provides a means of accessing information from a wide range of organisations. Some of these organisations will provide good quality information (eg ACCA, BBC, FT etc), others may provide information that proves to be unreliable. Who is behind the information is a more significant indicator of reliability than the fact that the information was transmitted over the Internet.

The material covered in this Chapter is tested in Question 15 in the Exam Question Bank.

BPP PUBLISHING

Chapter 3

THE INFORMATION SYSTEMS FUNCTION: ORGANISATIONAL ISSUES

Topic list	Syllabus reference
1 Centralisation and decentralisation	1(b)
2 Multi-user and distributed systems	1(b)
3 LANs, WANs and client-server computing	1(d)
4 Accounting issues	1(c)
5 Other organisational issues	1(d), 3(a)
6 Outsourcing	1(b)

Introduction

We begin this chapter by looking at the different ways of structuring the information systems function. Later, we explore wider organisational issues including accounting for the costs associated with information systems. The chapter concludes with the advantages and disadvantages of outsourcing.

Study guide

Part 1.2 – Delivering information systems; organisational arrangements

- Describe the traditional structure of a centralised information systems department and the roles and responsibilities of each function

- Explain the principles of a decentralised information systems function

- Discuss the advantages and disadvantages of centralising or decentralising the information systems function

- Explain the principles of outsourcing the information systems function

- Describe the advantages and disadvantages of outsourcing the information systems function

Part 1.3 – Delivering information systems; accounting issues

- Briefly describe the types of cost incurred delivering information systems (also see Chapter 7)

- Describe how the costs of the information systems function may be distributed between customer departments

- Explain the principles, benefits and drawbacks of cross-charging costs

- Discuss the issues raised by establishing the information systems function as a cost or profit centre

- Describe the advantages and disadvantages of establishing the information systems function as a separate company

- Explain the problems of accounting for shared infrastructure costs

Study guide (continued)

Part 1.4 – Delivering information systems; structural issues

- Describe the typical hardware, software, data and communications infrastructures found within information systems functions (also see Chapter 2)

- Describe the meaning and implications of legacy systems

Part 3.19 – Technical information system requirements

- Examine the need to provide interfaces with other systems

Exam guide

The material covered in this chapter lends itself to both longer scenario type questions (eg a miss-match between organisation information requirements and the IS structure) and shorter Section B questions (eg accounting for information systems costs).

1 CENTRALISATION AND DECENTRALISATION

1.1 An important issue is whether the IS function is centralised or decentralised.

Centralised systems

1.2 Centralised systems have the data/information processing done in a central place, such as a computer centre at head office. Data will be collected at 'remote' (ie geographically separate) offices and other locations and sent in to the central location, by post, by courier or by telecommunications link. Processing could be in either batch processing mode or on-line.

1.3 At the central location there will be:

- A central computer, probably a large mainframe computer
- Central files, containing all the files needed for the system

1.4 **Advantages** of centralised processing.

(a) There is **one set of files**. Everyone uses the same data and information.

(b) It gives **better security/control** over data and files. It is easier to enforce standards.

(c) **Head office** is in a better position to know what is going on.

(d) An organisation might be able to afford a **very large central computer,** with extensive processing capabilities that smaller 'local' computers could not carry out.

(e) There may be **economies of scale** available in purchasing computer equipment and supplies.

(f) Computer staff are in a single location, and **more expert staff** are likely to be employed. Career paths may be more clearly defined.

1.5 **Disadvantages** of centralised processing.

(a) Local offices might have to **wait** for data to be processed.

(b) **Reliance on head office**. Local offices have to rely on head office to provide information they need.

(c) If the central computer **breaks down,** or the software develops a fault, the entire system goes out of operation.

Decentralised systems

1.6 Decentralised systems have the data/information processing carried out at several different locations, away from the centre or head office. Each region, department or office will have its own processing systems, and so:

    (a) There will be several different and **unconnected computers** in the various offices.

    (b) Each computer will operate with its own **programs** and its own **files.**

1.7 **Advantages** of decentralised processing.

    (a) Each office can introduce an information system specially **tailored** for its individual needs. Local changes in business requirements can be taken into account.

    (b) If data **originates locally** it might make sense to process it locally too.

    (c) Each office has **control over its own** data.

    (d) There is likely to be easy/quick **access to information** when it is needed.

    (e) Any **breakdowns** in the system are **restricted** to just one part of the system.

    (f) It fits in with the organisation **structure**, and **responsibility accounting** systems (profit centres).

    (g) It allows staff to concentrate on **business objectives** rather than being constrained by IT objectives.

1.8 **Disadvantages** of decentralised processing.

    (a) Many different and **uncoordinated information systems** will be introduced.

    (b) Decentralisation encourages **lack of co-ordination between departments**.

    (c) One office might be **unable to obtain information** from the information system of another office.

    (d) There might be a **duplication of data**, with different offices holding the same data on their own separate files.

2 MULTI-USER AND DISTRIBUTED SYSTEMS

Multi-user systems

2.1 With a multi-user system the terminals are **dumb terminals**, which means that they do not include a CPU and so **cannot do independent data processing**. A dumb terminal relies on the central computer for its data processing power.

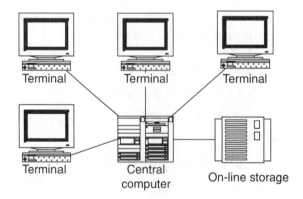

2.2 Many users, each with their own VDU and keyboard, might be connected to the same computer, with the capability for all the users to carry out processing work **simultaneously**. (In practice user requirements are often processed successively, according to defined priorities for that system, though to users it will appear that they have simultaneous access.)

2.3 The terminals in a multi-user system might be sited in the **same room** or building as the central computer, or may be **geographically distant** from the central computer, connected by an external data link. Terminals can be used:

(a) For **interactive computing** with the central computer.

(b) To **input data** ('transactions' data) into the computer from a remote location.

> **KEY TERMS**
>
> **Remote access** describes access to a central computer installation from a terminal which is physically 'distant'.
>
> The term **remote job entry** is used to describe a method of processing in which the user inputs data from a remote terminal.

Advantages

2.4 **Benefits** of multi-user systems are:

(a) More departments or sections can have **access** to the computer, its data files and its programs. This improves the data processing capabilities of 'local' offices.

(b) By giving departments more computing power and access to centralised information files, multi-user systems also make it easier for an organisation to **decentralise authority** from head office to local managers.

(c) The **speed of processing**, for both local offices and head office, is very fast.

(d) Local offices **retain their input documents**, and do not have to send them to a remote computer centre for processing.

Distributed processing

2.5 Distributed processing links several computers together. A typical system might consist of a mainframe computer with PCs as **intelligent terminals**, with a range of peripheral equipment and with files either held centrally or at dispersed sites.

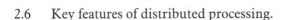

> **KEY TERM**
>
> A **distributed system** is a combination of processing hardware located at a central place, eg a mainframe computer, with other, usually smaller, computers located at various sites within the organisation. The central and dispersed computers are linked by a communications network.
>
> (CIMA, *Computing Terminology*)

2.6 Key features of distributed processing.

(a) Computers distributed or spread over a **wide geographical area**.

(b) A computer can **access** the information files of **other computers** in the system.

(c) The ability for computers within the system to **process data 'jointly'** or **'interactively'**.

(d) **Processing** is **either** carried out centrally, or at dispersed locations.

(e) **Files** are held **either** centrally or at local sites.

(f) **Authority is decentralised** as processing can be performed autonomously by local computers.

(g) **End-users** of computing facilities are given responsibility for, and control over, their own data.

2.7 One form of distributed data processing system is shown in the following illustration.

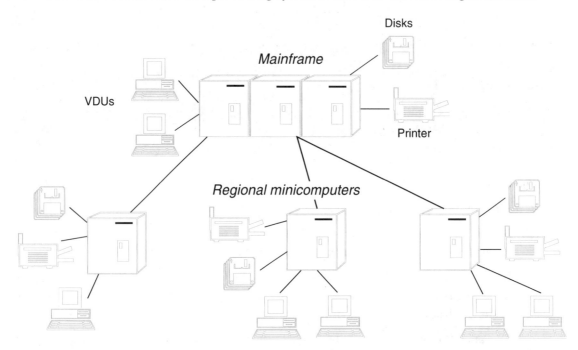

Advantages and disadvantages of distributed processing

2.8 **Advantages**.

(a) There is **greater flexibility** in system design. The system can cater for both the specific needs of each local user of an individual computer and also for the needs of the organisation as a whole, by providing communications between different local computers in the system.

(b) Since data files can be held locally, **data transmission is restricted** because each computer maintains its own data files which provide most of the data it will need. This reduces the costs and security risks in data transmission.

(c) **Speed of processing** for both local branches and also for the central (head office) branch.

(d) There is a possibility of a **distributed database**. Data is held in a number of locations, but any user can access all of it for a global view.

(e) The effect of **breakdowns** is **minimised,** because a fault in one computer will not affect other computers in the system. With a centralised processing system, a fault in the mainframe computer would put the entire system out of service.

(f) The fact that it is possible to acquire powerful PCs at a 'cheap' price enables an organisation to dedicate them to particular applications. This in turn means that the computer system can be more readily **tailored** to the organisation's systems, rather than forcing the organisation to change its systems to satisfy the requirements for a mainframe computer.

(g) Decentralisation allows for **better localised control** over the physical and procedural aspects of the system.

(h) Decentralised processing may facilitate **greater user involvement** and increase familiarity with the use of computer technology. The end user must accept responsibility for the accuracy of locally-held files and local data processing.

2.9 **Disadvantages**.

(a) Minicomputers and PCs have **not had a large storage capacity** in the past, and the high-level language programs needed for distributed processing have used up much of the storage capacity available. This disadvantage is now being eliminated by the development of more powerful small machines.

(b) There may be a **duplication of data** on the files of different computers incurring unnecessary storage costs.

(c) A distributed network can be more **difficult to administer** and to **maintain** with service engineers.

(d) The items of equipment used in the system must be **compatible** with each other.

2.10 In practice, information systems do not have to be entirely centralised or entirely decentralised, and these days a suitable **mixture of centralisation and decentralisation** will normally be used.

(a) Local offices can have their own **local systems**, perhaps on PC, and also input some data to a centralised processing system.

(b) Computer systems can be **networked**, and there might be:

   (i) A **multi-user system**.
   (ii) A **'distributed'** data processing system.

Question 1

When would you expect a **stand-alone** computer to be used?

Answer

Stand-alone computers are used in the following situations.

(a) When the data processing requirements can be handled by one user with one computer, for example for developing a personal spreadsheet model.

(b) When security could be compromised by the use of a multi-user system.

Networks

> **KEY TERM**
>
> A **network** is an interconnected collection of **autonomous** processors.

2.11 A network differs slightly from a distributed system as strictly, in a 'distributed' system, the user should be unaware that the system has more than one processor..

BPP PUBLISHING

2.12   There are two main types of network, a local area network (**LAN**) and a wide area network (**WAN**).

2.13   The key idea of a network is that users need **equal access to some resources** (such as data), but they do not necessarily have to have equal computing power.

3   LANS, WANS AND CLIENT-SERVER COMPUTING

Local area networks (LANs)

3.1   A local area network is a network of computers located in a single building or on a **single site**. The parts of the network are linked by **computer cable** rather than via telecommunications lines. This means that a LAN does not need modems.

Network topologies

3.2   Network topology means the physical arrangement of **nodes** in a network. A node is any device connected to a network: it can be a computer, or a peripheral device such as a printer.

3.3   There are several types of LAN system configuration. For example, in a **bus structure** (shown below), messages are sent out from one point along a single communication channel, and the messages are received by other connected machines.

3.4   Each device can **communicate with every other device** and communication is quick and reliable. Nodes can be **added or unplugged** very easily.

Bus system

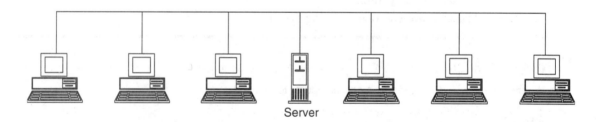

Server

3.5   Local area networks have been **successful** for a number of reasons. First of all, personal computers of sufficient **power** and related software were developed, so that network applications became possible. Some organisations who could not afford a mainframe or minicomputer with terminal links have been able to afford a LAN with personal computers.

Wide area networks (WANs)

3.6   **Wide area networks** are networks on a number of sites, perhaps on a wide geographical scale. WANs often use minicomputers or mainframes as the 'pumps' that keep the data messages circulating, whereas shorter-distance LANs normally use PCs for this task.

3.7   A wide area network is similar to a local area network in concept, but the key differences are:

   (a)   The **geographical area** covered by the network is greater, not being limited to a single building or site.

(b) WANs will send data over **telecommunications links**, and so will need modems unless ISDN links are used. LANs use direct cables only for transmitting data.

(c) WANs will often use a **larger computer** as a file server.

(d) WANs are usually larger than LANs, with **more terminals or computers** linked to the network.

(e) A WAN can link two or more LANs.

Client-server computing

3.8 The term 'client-server' is a way of describing the relationship between the devices in a network. With client-server computing, tasks are distributed among the machines on the network.

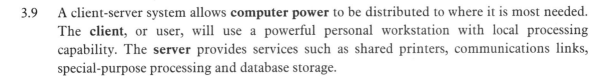

KEY TERMS

A **client** is a machine which requests a service, for example a PC running a spreadsheet application which the user wishes to print out.

A **server** is a machine which is dedicated to providing a particular function or service requested by a client. Servers include file servers (see below), print servers and e-mail servers.

3.9 A client-server system allows **computer power** to be distributed to where it is most needed. The **client**, or user, will use a powerful personal workstation with local processing capability. The **server** provides services such as shared printers, communications links, special-purpose processing and database storage.

3.10 This approach has a number of benefits.

(a) It reduces network **communications** costs.

(b) It allows the central computer to be used for **administrative** tasks such as network management.

(c) The flexibility of this type of system allows the use of **sophisticated applications.**

3.11 A server computer (or file server) may be a powerful PC or a minicomputer. As its name implies, it **serves** the rest of the network offering a large generally-accessible hard disk.

3.12 Clients on a network generally also have their **own hard disk** storage.

File servers

3.13 File servers must be powerful enough to handle **multiple user requests** and provide **adequate storage**. File servers are typically classified as 'low end' or 'high end'.

(a) A **low end file server** might be used in a network of around six users running 'office' type software. A low end server will be usually be a highly specified standard PC.

(b) A **mid range server** might support 10-30 users.

(c) A **high end file server** might be used in a large department network of anything from 30-250 users, handling transaction processing and an accounting system. High end servers have now been joined by **superservers** and 'enterprise servers' (effectively, mainframes). These are either departmental or organisation-wide, running sophisticated mission-critical systems and offering fault tolerance features. They might support upwards of 250 users.

Network operating systems

3.14 To carry out the administrative tasks connected with operating a network a special operating system is required. This establishes the links between the nodes of the network, monitors the operation of the network and controls recovery processes when the system or part of it breaks down. The main examples are **Novell Netware, Microsoft Windows NT,** and the recent upgrade to NT, Windows 2000.

The advantages of client/server computing

3.15

Advantage	Comment
Greater resilience	**Processing is spread** over several computers. If one server breaks down, other locations can carry on processing.
Scalability	They are highly **scalable.** Instead of having to buy computing power in large quantities you can buy just the amount of power you need to do the job.
Shared programs and data	Program and data files held on a file server can be **shared** by all the PCs in the network. With stand-alone PCs, each computer would have its own data files, and there might be unnecessary duplication of data.
	A system where everyone uses the same data will help to improve data processing and decision making.
Shared work-loads	Each PC in a network can do the **same work.**
	If there were separate stand-alone PCs, A might do job 1, B might do job 2, C might do job 3 and so on. In a network, any PC, (A, B or C) could do any job (1, 2 or 3). This provides flexibility in sharing work-loads.
Shared peripherals	**Peripheral** equipment can be **shared.** For example, in a LAN, five PCs might share a single on-line printer, whereas if there were stand-alone PCs, each might be given its own separate printer.
Communication and time management	LANs can be linked up to the office **communications network,** thus adding to the processing capabilities in an office. Electronic mail can be used to send messages, memos and electronic letters from node to node. Electronic calendar and diary facilities can also be used.
Compatibility	Client/server systems are more likely than centralised systems to have Windows **interfaces,** making it easier to move information between applications such as spreadsheets and accounting systems.
Ad hoc enquiries	They enable information to be moved to a separate server, allowing managers to make **ad hoc enquiries** without disrupting the main system.

3.16   The **disadvantages** of client/server computing.

(a)   **Mainframes** are better at dealing with **very large volumes** of transactions.

(b)   It is easier to **control** and **maintain** a system centrally. In particular it is easier to keep data **secure**.

(c)   It may be **cheaper** to 'tweak' an existing mainframe system rather than throwing it away and starting from scratch: for example it may be possible to give it a graphical user interface and to make data exchangeable between Windows and non-Windows based applications.

4   ACCOUNTING ISSUES

4.1   As information systems support a wide variety of functions in an organisation, and information systems incur significant capital and revenue costs, it is not surprising that many organisations should seek to develop costing systems so that **user departments pay for their usage** of information systems.

4.2   There are three broad possibilities. The information systems function can be treated as a central administrative **overhead**, it can be **charged out 'at cost'**, or it can be **charged out at market rates**, generating a profit (or loss) for the information systems (IS) department. (We look at the types of costs associated with information systems in Chapter 7.)

Information technology as a corporate overhead

4.3   Under this system IT/IS costs are treated as a general administrative expense, and are **not allocated** to user departments.

4.4   **Advantages** of this approach are.

(a)   It is **simple** and **cheap to administer,** as there is no chargeout system to operate.

(b)   It encourages **innovation** and **experimentation** by the information systems department which user departments might be unwilling to pay for. (However, the existence of a unit for research and development within the IS department should be sufficient for this purpose.)

(c)   There is **minimal conflict,** over costs at least, between the IS department and user departments.

4.5   **Disadvantages** of this approach.

(a)   The IS department has **no incentive to control costs** or use available resources efficiently.

(b)   It does not encourage **responsible use** of the IS resource by user departments, who do not have the cost information to prioritise their requirements. Also, IS department management are not given the right cost information to choose between competing projects.

Information technology charged out on a cost basis

4.6   A cost-based chargeout means that users are **charged a proportion** of the costs of the IS department according to some measure, preferably reflecting actual use. Cost-based chargeout systems should motivate users to employ computer resources efficiently.

(a) Chargeout rates should be based on a tangible service which the user can **understand**. Examples are: cost per transaction processed; cost per page; cost per hour of programmer's and/or analyst's time; cost per number of terminals/workstations; cost per unit of CPU time.

(b) **Standard costing** systems should be used. This is so that:

    (i) User departments are not penalised for **inefficiencies** in the IS department.

    (ii) The **IS department is not penalised** with variances caused by user departments' increased usage.

    (iii) User departments are not charged with those **long-term fixed costs** of the IS department itself (eg its building), over which they have **no control**.

4.7 The **advantages** of the cost based chargeout system.

(a) It is conceptually **simple**.

(b) It **motivates user departments** to consider the cost of their usage of IT services and to regulate it efficiently.

(c) It ties in with costing systems which use **responsibility accounting** as a means of controlling costs.

4.8 **Disadvantages** exist, too.

(a) Unless precautions are taken, **inefficiencies** in the IS department are merely **passed on** to users. Programmers could actually design programmes to take lots of CPU time so that the IT department made more money.

(b) Although simple in concept, it is **complex** in practice.

(c) It is often difficult to determine an **appropriate cost unit** on which to base the chargeout system (eg how easy is it to assess the cost of a single transaction? How easily can indirect costs be allocated?)

(d) In many circumstances users are faced, effectively, with a **monopoly supplier.** What may be perceived as over-charging could cause resentment.

(e) Overhead costs of the department **have to be met**, even if the IT services are not used.

4.9 Under both the corporate overhead approach and the charge out at cost approach the IS function is treated as a cost centre. This can influence the way in which information systems and technology are viewed within an organisation – it encourages the view that they are a **drain on resources** rather than tools in the quest for **competitive advantage**.

Market-based chargeout methods

4.10 Under market-based methods the IS department acts as a **profit centre.** It sets its own prices and charges for its services to make a profit, perhaps as a separate business unit or subsidiary.

4.11 Advantages of the market-based chargeout method.

(a) **External standards** of service and price are available.
(b) It encourages an **entrepreneurial** attitude.
(c) Prices are **negotiable.**

4.12 **Disadvantages**.

    (a) There may be **no comparable service** outside the organisation where services of the type and intensity that users require can be purchased.

    (b) It is difficult to implement where **common or shared resources** are concerned.

    (c) It may not be in the organisation's strategic interest for user departments to buy from outsiders: the IS function's fixed costs still have to be covered, and there may result an **under-use of resources** available within the organisation.

    (d) There may be a **lack of appropriate management skills** in the department. Running a company is likely to be much more challenging than running a department

5 OTHER ORGANISATIONAL ISSUES

Organisation structure

5.1   The structure of the organisation and the structure of the organisations information systems are related. PCs give local office managers a means of setting up a **good local management information system**, and localised data processing. Multi-user systems and distributed data processing systems also put more processing 'power' into local offices.

Constant change

5.2   Office automation commits an organisation to **continual change**. The pace of technological change is rapid, and computer systems - both hardware and software - are likely to be superseded after a few years.

Power and privacy

5.3   The power of computer systems makes them a threat to the **privacy of the individual**. If every significant action is recorded in a computer system, and programs are available for analysing them, the daily activities of each individual could become open to scrutiny.

5.4   From another point of view information is a **source of power** in an organisation.

    (a) If you know something that your colleagues or managers do not know, you have the power to **exploit** that knowledge for your own advancement, or else **withhold** that knowledge if you wish.

    (b) Somebody working in an accounts department or a personnel office has access to a great deal of **personal information** about his or her colleagues and this raises a variety of **ethical** issues.

Interoperability

5.5   **Interoperability** means that any company, individual or institution can readily share and exchange information and facilities with any other company, individual or institution. Moreover, they can do so without having to use the same service provider as the other party, without having to use the same technology platform, or even know what technology platform is used by the other party. They need have only a minimum of concern about data structures, and there is a minimum need for new skills when using new applications and technologies.

BPP
PUBLISHING

Backward compatibility

5.6 A new version of a **program** is said to be backward compatible if it can use files and data created with an **older version** of the same program. Computer **hardware** is said to be backward compatible if it can run the same software as **previous models.**

5.7 Backward compatibility is important because it **eliminates the need to start afresh** when upgrading to a newer product. A backward-compatible word processor, for instance, allows users to edit documents created with a previous version of the program. In general, manufacturers try to keep their products backward compatible. Sometimes, however, it is necessary to **sacrifice** backward compatibility to take advantage of **new technology**.

Legacy system

5.8 A legacy system is a computer system or application program which **continues to be used** because of the **prohibitive cost of replacing or redesigning it** and often despite its poor competitiveness and compatibility with modern equivalents. The implication is that the system is **large, monolithic and difficult to modify.**

5.9 Legacy **software** may only run on antiquated **hardware,** and the cost of maintaining this may eventually outweigh the cost of replacing both the software and hardware.

Open systems

5.10 Organisations develop computerised systems over a period of time, perhaps focusing on different functions at different times. The ease with which systems interact with each other is important for organisation efficiency. Examples of inefficiencies caused by systems incompatibility include:

(a) Hardware supplied by different **manufacturers** that can not interact.
(b) **Data duplicated** in different areas of the business as separate systems can not use the same source.
(c) Software that is unable to interact with other packages.

5.11 **Open systems** aim to ensure compatibility between different systems. An open systems infrastructure supports **organisation-wide functions** and allows interoperability of networks and systems. Authorised users are able to access applications and data from any part of the system.

6 OUTSOURCING

6.1 **Outsourcing,** also referred to as facilities management, is not a concept which is limited to the arena of computing. Any company which contracts out necessary services to a third party is using facilities management (FM) in one form or another.

6.2 Buying in services is seen as a better way of **managing resources** and of **obtaining access to specialists** in particular fields. The practice has been firmly established for years in such activities as sandwich-making, laundry services and office cleaning.

6.3 As the significance of IT grew, a large proportion of many companies' workforces were engaged in IT activities, and IT expenditure was frequently in excess of budget. This experience clashed with the belief held by many executives that **IT should be a critical but subordinate function of the core business,** whether operating in international financial markets or running a UK county council. Facilities management enabled many organisations simply to pick a supplier, draw up a contract and hand over the entire responsibility for running the organisation's IT function.

6.4 The third party supplier, or FM company, usually takes over the **employment contracts** of the organisation's IT staff. Their terms and conditions of employment are protected by legislation in the form of the **Transfer of Undertakings (Protection of Employment) Regulations,** or **TUPE**. It may also take over the organisation's computer centre.

6.5 The scope of FM contracts can vary considerably.

(a) **Systems integration** is a project-based approach which is designed to get a single system developed and operational.

(b) **FM** usually denotes the outsourcing of computer operations.

(c) **Third party maintenance** can involve qualified third party contractors carrying out certain support services.

Case example: Sears

The retailer Sears recently outsourced the management of its vast information technology and accounting functions to Andersen Consulting (now known as Accenture). Savings are estimated at £14 million per annum. This is clearly considerable, although re-organisation costs relating to redundancies, relocation and asset write-offs are thought to be in the region of £35 million. About 900 staff are involved: under the transfer of undertakings regulations (which protect employees when part or all of a company changes hands) Andersen is obliged to take on the existing Sears staff. This appears to mean new opportunities for the staff who are moving, while those whom Sears are retaining are free to concentrate on strategy, development and management direction.

Advantages of outsourcing arrangements

6.6 The **advantages** of facilities management are as follows.

(a) Facilities management is an effective form of **cost control**, as there is often a long-term contract where services are specified in advance for a **fixed price**. If the computing services are inefficient, the costs will be borne by the FM company. This is also an incentive to the FM company to provide a high quality service, of course.

(b) **Long-term contracts** (maybe up to ten years) allow much greater certainty in **planning for the future**.

(c) A facilities management company has **economies of scale**. Several organisations will employ the same FM company, and so the FM company's research into new products on the market or new technologies will be shared between them.

(d) **Skills and knowledge are retained.** Many organisations do not have a sufficiently well-developed IT department to offer existing staff good opportunities for personal development. They find that talented staff leave to pursue their careers elsewhere, taking their skill and knowledge (much of which may have been acquired at the expense of the original organisation) with them. An FM company that takes over the contracts of existing employees will be able to offer them the advancement they are looking for.

(e) **New skills and knowledge become available.** An FM company can **share** staff with **specific expertise** (such as programming in HTML to produce Web pages) between several clients. This means that the outsourcing company can take advantage of new developments without the need to recruit new people or re-train existing staff, and without the cost.

(f) **Resources employed can be scaled up or down** depending upon demand. For instance, during a major changeover from one system to another the number of IT staff needed may be twice as large as it will be once the new system is working satisfactorily. This is likely to be difficult to manage and to cause morale problems in an in-house IT facility.

An outsourcing organisation, however, is likely to arrange its work on a **project** basis, whereby some staff will expect to be moved periodically from one project to the next.

Disadvantages of outsourcing arrangements

6.7 The **drawbacks**, however, can be quite considerable.

(a) It is arguable that information and its provision is **an inherent part of the business and of management**. Unlike office cleaning, or catering, an organisation's IS services may be too important to be contracted out. Information is at the heart of management.

(b) A company may have highly **confidential information** and to let outsiders handle it could be seen as highly **risky** in commercial and/or legal terms.

(c) Information strategy can be used to gain **competitive advantage**. Opportunities may be missed if a third party is handling IS services, because there is no onus upon internal management to keep up with new developments and have new ideas. If the FM company has a good new idea there is nothing to prevent it from selling it to more than one company.

(d) Once an organisation has handed over its computing to an FM company, it is **locked in** to the contract. The decision may be very difficult to reverse. If the FM company supplies unsatisfactory levels of service for whatever reason (takeover, financial difficulties etc), then the effort and expense an organisation would have to incur to rebuild its own computing function and expertise would be enormous.

(e) The use of FM does not encourage a **proper awareness of the potential costs and benefits** of IT amongst managers. If managers cannot manage in-house IT resources effectively, then it could be argued that they will not be able to manage an arrangement to outsource IT effectively either.

The contract

6.8 As indicated above (under both advantages and disadvantages), a vital aspect of any FM contract is the **service level contract** (SLC) or **service level agreement** (SLA). This should specify clearly minimum levels of service to be provided. It should also contain arrangements for an exit route, addressing what happens if the contract is handed over to another contractor or brought in-house. The responsibilities of the outgoing FM company should be clearly specified.

6.9 Some companies have found that aspects of information systems management that they believed would be included in their FM contract have turned out to be **extras**, for which considerable **extra fees** are payable. It is probably not possible to draw up a contract that covers every eventuality, particularly as some eventualities, such as new technologies, may not even be imaginable at the time when the contract is first drawn up.

Other organisations

Software houses

6.10 Software houses concentrate on the provision of **software services**. These services include feasibility studies, systems analysis and design, development of operating systems software, provision of application program packages, 'tailor-made' application programming, specialist systems advice, and so on. For example, a software house might be employed to write a computerised system for the London Stock Exchange.

6.11 A software house may offer a wide range of services or may **specialise** in a particular area.

Consultancy firms

6.12 Some consultancy firms work at a fairly high level, giving advice to management on the general approach to solving problems and on the types of system to use. Others specialise in giving more particular systems advice, carrying out feasibility studies and recommending computer manufacturers/software houses that will supply the right system. As always, whenever a consultancy firm is used, the terms of the contract should be agreed at the outset.

6.13 The use of consultancy services enables management to learn directly or indirectly from the experience of others. The success of an individual consultancy project will depend largely on the expertise of the firm approached and more particularly on the individual consultant or consultants employed. Many larger consultancies are owned by big international accountancy firms; smaller consultancies may consist of one or two person outfits with a high level of specialist experience in one area.

BPP PUBLISHING

Chapter roundup

- **Centralised processing** means having the data/information processing done in a central place, such as a computer centre at head office.

- **Decentralised processing** means having the data/information processing carried out at several different locations.

- Information systems do not have to be entirely centralised or entirely decentralised, and these days a suitable **mixture of centralisation and decentralisation** will normally be used.

- With a **multi-user system** the terminals are dumb terminals, which means that they do not include a CPU.

- **Distributed processing** links several computers together. A typical system might consist of a mainframe computer with PCs as intelligent terminals.

- A **distributed system** is a combination of processing hardware located at a central place, eg a mainframe computer, with other, usually smaller, computers located at various sites.

- A **network** is an interconnected collection of autonomous processors. A local area network (LAN) is a network of computers located in a single building or on a single site. Wide area networks (WANs) are networks on a number of sites.

- A **client-server** system allows computer power to be distributed to where it is most needed. The client, or user, will use a powerful personal workstation with local processing capability. The server provides services such as shared printers, communications links, special-purpose processing and database storage.

- Many organisations should seek to develop costing systems so that **user departments pay** for their use of information systems.

- Some organisations choose to **outsource** the IS/IT function to a facilities management (or similar) company. Outsourcing has **advantages** (eg use of highly skilled people) and **disadvantages** (eg lack of control).

Quick quiz

1. List four advantages of centralised processing.
2. List four disadvantages of centralised processing.
3. List four advantages of decentralised processing.
4. List four disadvantages of decentralised processing.
5. What is a 'dumb terminal'?
6. Define 'legacy system'.
7. Distinguish between a centralised information systems department and an information centre. *(If you do not know what an information centre is, quickly refer to Chapter 1,1 section 4.)*
8. List four advantages of outsourcing the IS/IT function.
9. List four disadvantages of outsourcing the IS/IT function.
10. What would a SLA contain?

Answers to quick quiz

1 [Four of]

Data inconsistencies should be eliminated as there is only one set of files.

Provides better security/control over data and files.

It is easier to enforce standards.

A large powerful central computer may be purchased with greater capabilities than a series of smaller machines.

The IS/IT team would be in a single location providing enabling them to pool their expertise.

2 Local offices might have to wait for data to be processed centrally.

Local offices have to rely on head office for management information.

If the central computer breaks down, or the software develops a fault, the entire organisation is without computer facilities.

Local staff are unlikely to develop the computer literacy required in the modern business environment.

3 [Four of]

Each office can introduce an information system specially tailored for its individual needs.

If data originates locally it makes sense to process it locally.

Each office has control over its own data.

There is likely to be easy/quick access to information when it is needed.

Any breakdowns in the system are restricted to just one part of the system.

Fits in with the organisation structure, and responsibility accounting systems (profit centres).

Allows staff to concentrate on business objectives.

4 [Four of]

A lack of co-ordination and consistency across information systems.

May encourage a lack of co-ordination between departments in other areas.

One office might be unable to obtain information from the information system of another office.

Data duplication.

Errors and inconsistencies between systems.

5 A dumb terminal is a VDU connected via cable to a central computer. Dumb terminals do not include a CPU – they rely on a central computer for processing power.

6 A legacy system is a system which continues to be used because of the prohibitive cost of replacing or redesigning it.

7 A centralised information systems department is usually associated with centralised processing - having all an organisations data/information processing done in a central place. An information centre (IC) is a unit of staff with a good technical awareness of computer systems, who provide a support function to computer users within the organisation. An information centre could exist in organisations using centralised or decentralised processing.

8 [Four of]

Cost control - services are specified in advance for a fixed price.

Certainty - long-term contracts allow greater certainty in planning for the future.

Economies of scale. Several organisations will employ the same FM company - the cost of FM company's research into new technologies will be shared.

Skills and knowledge are retained within the FM company who can offer staff career development.

New skills and knowledge become available. An FM company can share staff with specific expertise (such as programming in HTML to produce Web pages) between several clients.

Flexibility - resources employed can be scaled up or down depending upon demand.

9   [Four of]

An organisation's IS services may be too important to be contracted out. Information is at the heart of management.

Risky – confidential or commercially sensitive information could be leaked.

Opportunities may be missed to use IS for competitive advantage - there is no onus upon internal management to keep up with new developments and have new ideas.

Locked in - an organisation may be locked into a contract with a poor service provider.

Hard to reverse - the effort and expense an organisation would have to incur to rebuild its own computing function and expertise would be enormous.

The use of FM does not encourage a proper awareness of the potential costs and benefits of IT amongst managers.

10   The Service Level Agreement (SLA) or Service Level Contract (SLC) is a vital aspect of any outsourcing arrangement. It should specify minimum levels of service, arrangements for an exit route, transfer arrangements and dispute procedures.

The material covered in this Chapter is tested in Questions 4(a), 4(b), 4(c) and 12 in the Exam Question Bank.

Chapter 4

THE PROJECT MANAGER AND PROJECT STAKEHOLDERS

Topic list	Syllabus reference
1 What is a project?	1(f)
2 The project manager	1(f)
3 The project team	1(f)
4 Project stakeholders	1(f)

Introduction

This chapter will introduce the subject of project management, explain what project management is and outline what a **project manager** does. Later in the chapter we look at how a **project team** should be put together, and examine the **stakeholders** of a project and the relationships between them.

Project management tools and techniques will be covered in Chapter 5.

Study guide

Part 1.6 – Project initiation

- Identify the roles and responsibilities of staff who will manage and participate in the project
- Define in detail the role and responsibilities of the project manager
- Explain the concept of a flat management structure and its application to project-based systems development

Exam guide

It is highly likely that the exam scenario will be based around an information systems project.

1   WHAT IS A PROJECT?

1.1   To understand project management it is necessary to first define what a project is.

> **KEY TERMS**
>
> A **Project** is 'an undertaking that has a beginning and an end and is carried out to meet established goals within cost, schedule and quality objectives'. (Haynes, *Project Management*)

1.2 In general, the work organisations undertake involves either **operations** or **projects**. Operations and projects are planned, controlled and executed. So how are projects distinguished from 'ordinary work'?

Projects	Operations
Have a defined beginning and end	On-going
Have resources allocated specifically to them, although often on a shared basis	Resources used 'full-time'
Are intended to be done only once (eg organising the Year 2001 London Marathon – the 2002 event is a separate project)	A mixture of many recurring tasks
Follow a plan towards a clear intended end-result	Goals and deadlines are more general
Often cut across organisational and functional lines	Usually follows the organisation or functional structure

1.3 Common examples of projects include:
- Producing a new product, service or object
- Changing the structure of an organisation
- Developing or modifying a new information system
- Implementing a new information system

What is project management?

> ### KEY TERM
>
> **Project management** is the combination of systems, techniques, and people used to control and monitor activities undertaken within the project. Project management co-ordinates the resources necessary to complete the project successfully.

1.4 The objective of project management is a successful project. A project will be deemed successful if it is completed at the **specified level of quality, on time** and **within budget**.

Objective	Comment
Quality	The end result should conform to the project specification. In other words, the result should achieve what the project was supposed to do.
Budget	The project should be completed without exceeding authorised expenditure.
Timescale	The progress of the project must follow the planned process, so that the 'result' is ready for use at the agreed date. As time is money, proper time management can help contain costs.

1.5 Projects present some management challenges.

Challenge	Comment
Teambuilding	The work is carried out by a team of people often from varied work and social backgrounds. The team must 'gel' quickly and be able to communicate effectively with each other.
Expected problems	Expected problems should be avoided by careful design and planning prior to commencement of work.
Unexpected problems	There should be mechanisms within the project to enable these problems to be resolved quickly and efficiently.
Delayed benefit	There is normally no benefit until the work is finished. The 'lead in' time to this can cause a strain on the eventual recipient who is also faced with increasing expenditure for no immediate benefit.
Specialists	Contributions made by specialists are of differing importance at each stage.
Potential for conflict	Projects often involve several parties with different interests. This may lead to conflict.

1.6 Project management ensures responsibilities are clearly defined and that resources are **focussed** on specific objectives. The **project management process** also provides a structure for communicating within and across organisational boundaries.

1.7 All projects share similar features and follow a similar process. This has led to the development of **project management tools and techniques** that can be applied to all projects, no matter how diverse. For example, with some limitations similar processes and techniques can be applied to whether building a major structure or implementing a company-wide computer network.

1.8 All projects require a person who is ultimately responsible for delivering the required outcome. This person is the **project manager**.

2 THE PROJECT MANAGER

2.1 Some project managers have the job title 'Project Manager'. These people usually have one major responsibility: the project. Most people in business will have 'normal work' responsibilities outside their project goals – which may lead to conflicting demands on their time. Anybody responsible for a project (large or small) is a project manager.

> **KEY TERMS**
>
> The person who takes ultimate responsibility for ensuring the desired result is achieved on time and within budget is the **Project Manager**.
>
> The way in which a project manager co-ordinates a project from initiation to completion, using project management and general management techniques, is known as the **Project Management process**.

2.2 The role a project manager performs is in many ways similar to those performed by other managers. There are however some important differences, as shown in the table below.

BPP PUBLISHING

Project manager	Operations manager
Are often 'generalists' with wide-ranging backgrounds and experience levels	Usually specialists in the areas managed
Oversee work in many functional areas	Relate closely to technical tasks in their area
Facilitate, rather than supervise team members	Have direct technical supervision responsibilities

2.3   The duties of a project manager are summarised below.

Duty	Comment
Outline planning	Project planning (eg targets, sequencing) • Developing project targets such as overall costs or timescale needed (eg project should take 20 weeks). • Dividing the project into activities and placing these activities into the right sequence, often a complicated task if overlapping. • Developing a framework for the procedures and structures, manage the project (eg decide, in principle, to have weekly team meetings, performance reviews etc).
Detailed planning	Work breakdown structure, resource requirements, network analysis for scheduling. (Covered in Chapter 5.)
Teambuilding	Build cohesion and team spirit.
Communication	The project manager must let superiors know what is going on, and ensure that members of the project team are properly briefed.
Co-ordinating project activities	Between the project team and users, and other external parties (eg suppliers of hardware and software).
Monitoring and control	The project manager should estimate the causes for each departure from the standard, and take corrective measures.
Problem-resolution	Even with the best planning, unforeseen problems may arise.
Quality control	There is often a short-sighted trade-off between getting the project out on time and the project's quality.

2.4   The project management process helps project managers maintain control of projects and meet their responsibilities.

The responsibilities of a project manager

2.5   A project manager has responsibilities to both management and to the project team.

Responsibilities to management

- Ensure resources are used efficiently – strike a balance between cost, time and results
- Keep management informed with timely and accurate communications
- Manage the project to the best of his or her ability
- Behave ethically, and adhere to the organisation's policies
- Maintain a customer orientation (whether the project is geared towards an internal or external customer) - customer satisfaction is a key indicator of project success

Responsibilities to the project and the project team

- Take action to keep the project on target for successful completion
- Ensure the project team has the resources required to perform tasks assigned
- Help new team members integrate into the team
- Provide any support required when members leave the team either during the project or on completion

The skills required of a project manager

2.6 To meet these responsibilities a project manager requires a wide range of skills. The skills required are similar to those required when managing a wider range of responsibilities. The narrower focus of project management means it is easier to make a judgement as to how well these skills have been applied.

Type of skill	How the project manager should display the type of skill
Leadership and team building	Be **enthusiastic** about what the project will achieve.
	Be **positive** (but realistic) about all aspects of the project.
	Understand where the project fits into the **'big picture'.**
	Delegate tasks appropriately – and not take on too much personally.
	Build team spirit through encouraging **co-operation.**
	Do not be restrained by organisational structures – a high tolerance for ambiguity (lack of clear-cut authority) will help the project manager.
Organisational	Ensure all project **documentation** is clear and distributed to all who require it.
	Use project **management tools** to analyse and monitor project progress.
Communication	**Listen** to project team members.
	Use **persuasion** to coerce reluctant team members or stakeholders to support the project.
	Ensure management is kept **informed** and is never surprised.
Technical	By providing (or at least providing access to) the **technical expertise** and experience needed to manage the project.
Personal	Be **flexible**. Circumstances may develop that require a change in plan.
	Show **persistence**. Even successful projects will encounter difficulties that require repeated efforts to overcome.
	Be **creative**. If one method of completing a task proves impractical a new approach may be required.
	Patience is required even in the face of tight deadlines. The 'quick-fix' may eventually cost more time than a more thorough but initially more time-consuming solution.

Leadership styles and project management

2.7 As in other forms of management, different project managers have different styles of leadership. There is no 'best' leadership style, as individuals suit and react to different styles

BPP
PUBLISHING

in different ways. The key is adopting a style that suits both the project leader and the project team.

2.8 Managers will usually adopt a style from the range shown in the following diagram.

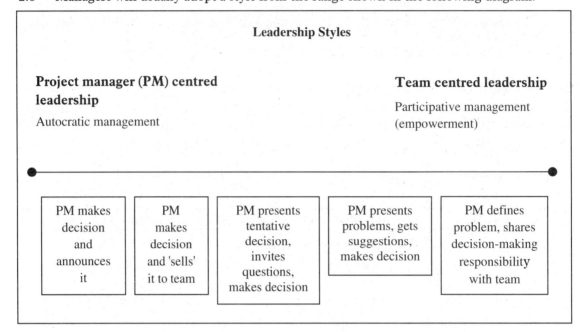

Leadership Styles

Project manager (PM) centred leadership
Autocratic management

Team centred leadership
Participative management (empowerment)

| PM makes decision and announces it | PM makes decision and 'sells' it to team | PM presents tentative decision, invites questions, makes decision | PM presents problems, gets suggestions, makes decision | PM defines problem, shares decision-making responsibility with team |

2.9 The leadership style adopted will affect the way decisions relating to the project are made. Although an autocratic style may prove successful in some situations (eg 'simple' or 'repetitive' projects), a more consultative style has the advantage of making team members feel more a part of the project. This should result in greater **commitment**.

2.10 Not all decisions will be made in the same way. For example, decisions that do not have direct consequences for other project personnel may be made with no (or limited) consultation. A **balance** needs to be found between ensuring decisions can be made efficiently, and ensuring adequate consultation.

2.11 The type of people that comprise the project team will influence the style adopted. For example, professionals generally dislike being closely supervised and dictated to. (Many non-professionals dislike this too!) Some people however prefer to follow clear, specific instructions and not have to think for themselves.

2.12 Project management techniques encourage **management by exception** by identifying, from the outset, those activities which might threaten successful completion of a project.

3 THE PROJECT TEAM

Building a project team

> **KEY TERM**
>
> The **Project Team** comprises the people who report directly or indirectly to the project manager.

3.1 Project success depends to a large extent on the team members selected. The ideal project team achieves project completion on time, within budget and to the required specifications - with the minimum amount of direct supervision from the project manager.

3.2 The team will comprise individuals with **differing skills and personalities**. The project manager should choose a balanced team that takes advantage of each team member's skills and compensates elsewhere for their weaknesses.

3.3 The project team will normally be drawn from existing staff, but highly recommended **outsiders with special skills** may be recruited. When building a team the project manager should ask the following questions.

(a) **What skills** are required to complete each task of the project?

(b) **Who** has the talent and skills to complete the required tasks (whether inside or outside the organisation)?

(c) Are the people identified **available, affordable**, and able to join the project team?

(d) What level of **supervision** will be required?

3.4 Although the composition of the project team is critical, project managers often find it is not possible to assemble the ideal team, and have to do the best they can with the personnel available. If the project manager feels the best available team does not possess the skills and talent required, the project should be **abandoned or delayed.**

3.5 Once the team has been selected each member should be given a (probably verbal) project briefing, outlining the overall aims of the project, and detailing the role they are expected to play. (The role of documentation is discussed later).

3.6 The performance of the project team will be enhanced by the following.
- Effective communication
- All members being aware of the team's purpose and the role of each team member
- Collaboration and creativity among team members
- Trusting, supportive atmosphere in group
- A commitment to meeting the agreed schedule
- Innovative/creative behaviour
- Team members highly interdependent, interface effectively
- Capacity for conflict resolution
- Results orientation
- High energy levels and enthusiasm
- An acceptance of change

3.7 Collaboration and interaction between team members will help ensure the skills of all team members are utilised, and should result in 'synergistic' solutions. Formal (eg meetings) and informal channels (eg e-mail links, a bulletin board) of **communication** should be set up to ensure this interaction takes place.

3.8 Team members should be responsible and accountable. The project manager should provide **regular updates** on project progress and timely **feedback** on team and individual performance.

3.9 Most **effective project managers** display the ability to:
- Select the right people
- Connect them to the right cause

BPP
PUBLISHING

- Solve problems that arise
- Evaluate progress towards objectives
- Negotiate resolutions to conflicts
- Heal wounds inflicted by change

Managing conflict

3.10 It is inevitable when people from wide-ranging backgrounds combine to form a project team that **conflict** will occasionally occur. Some conflicts may actually be **positive**, resulting in fresh ideas and energy being input to the project. Other conflicts can be **negative** and have the potential to bring the project to a standstill.

3.11 An open exchange of views between project personnel should be encouraged as this will help ensure all possible courses of action and their consequences are considered. The project manager should keep in touch with the relationships of team members and act as a conciliator if necessary.

3.12 Ideally, conflict should be harnessed for productive ends. Conflict can have **positive effects** such as those listed below.
- Results in better, well thought-out ideas
- Forces people to search for new approaches
- Causes persistent problems to surface and be dealt with
- Forces people to clarify their views
- Causes tension which stimulates interest and creativity

Negotiation techniques

3.13 When conflict occurs the project manager should avoid displaying bias and adopt a logical, ordered approach towards achieving resolution. The following principles should be followed.
- Focus on the problem, not the personalities
- Define the problem carefully
- Try to develop options that would result in mutual gain
- Look for a wide variety of possible solutions

Resolution techniques

3.14 Ideally the conflict will be resolved by the parties involved **agreeing** on a course of action. In cases where insufficient progress towards a resolution has occurred the project manager should attempt to bring about a resolution.

3.15 The project manager should employ the following **techniques** in an attempt to resolve the conflict.

(a) Work through the problem using the **negotiation techniques** described above.

(b) Attempt to establish a **compromise** - try to bring some degree of satisfaction to all parties through give and take.

(c) Try to **smooth out any differences** and downplay the importance of any remaining differences.

(d) **Emphasise areas of agreement.**

(e) If all else fails, and resolution is vital, the project manager should force the issue and **make a decision**. He or she should emphasise to all parties that their commitment to the project is appreciated, and that the conflict should now be put behind them.

Case example

BUSINESS DAY SURVEY - PROJECT MANAGEMENT - STAFF ARE THE KEY TO SUCCESS

People who have left the comfort of their traditional management environment are often the most important ingredient in successful project management.

You can have the best tools and techniques, the most advanced systems and methods and most innovative structure, but ultimately it is the committed project team of people who choose to make it happen, says Mark Wright, MD of Scott Wilsons project management division. The faster the markets change and the technology advances, the greater need there will be for successful project management implementation to satisfy goals.

As the project management profession continues to evolve, globalisation is often seen as a threat. But it need not be seen as such, says David Sparrow, managing partner of global operations for EC Harris, an international capital project and facilities consultancy company. The reality is that through globalisation, various world-class processes are exposed to the local market. Similarly, clients are globalising and changing to remain competitive, he says.

Project managers need to be focused on client needs and thus the technical consultancy skill is now just a mere tool that needs to be applied in innovative ways. Trevor Lowen, GM of business development for Axis Interim Management, says the problem most organisations have is the lack of project management experience within their ranks. He says the use of interim management is creating a growing project management resource for business.

Interim management is the provision of short-term senior managers, industry or functional specialists to companies to undertake an assignment which they lack the resources to undertake themselves. The launch of a new product is an example of project work undertaken by interim managers.

Business Day (South Africa) Nov 1999

A computerised information system project team

3.16 In a modern organisation it may be that the IS department has a very limited number of staff. An **hierarchical structure** of manager, analysts, programmers, etc may prove to be **very inflexible** in terms of getting individual projects done. For instance, someone who officially has the 'status' of 'Project Manager' may find that he or she has no projects to manage at a particular time but may have four or five projects to manage at another time.

3.17 This situation is likely to arise frequently because much of the work of a dedicated IS department is **project-based**. One project may require a considerable amount of programming from scratch, while the next is largely 'tweaking' an existing system, requiring analyst skills, and someone who can motivate staff and control progress but very little programming.

3.18 A solution adopted increasingly in organisations is to organise the IS department according to a **flat** structure that recognises that multi-talented individuals will adopt **different roles at different times** rather than occupying a particular 'status' whether or not there is any work for someone of that status to do. Staff are selected from a pool of available staff and perform different roles depending upon demand.

3.19 To operate such a system the organisation needs to devise a **remuneration system** that recognises **skills** and work done rather than status.

 BPP
PUBLISHING

3.20 We will cover the systems development process in depth later in this text. In the context of explaining the roles of analysts and programmers, developing a computer system can be divided into two parts.

(a) **Designing** a program or programs that will do the data processing work that the user department wants, and to the user's specification (for example about response times, accuracy etc).

This involves deciding what hardware there should be, what the input and files should be, how output should be produced, and what programs there should be to do this work.

This is the task of the **systems analyst**.

(b) **Writing the software** – this is the job of the programmer.

Systems analysts

3.21 In general terms, the tasks of the systems analyst are as follows.

3.22 **Systems analysis** - involves carrying out a methodical study of a **current system** (manual or computerised) to establish:

(a) What the current system **does**.

(b) Whether it does what it is **supposed to do**.

(c) What the user department would **like it to do,** and so what the required objectives of the system are.

3.23 **Systems design** - having established what the proposed system objectives are, the next stage is to design a system that will **achieve these objectives**.

3.24 **Systems specification** - in designing a new system, it is the task of the systems analyst to **specify** the system in detail.

3.25 This involves identification of inputs, files, processing, output, hardware, costs, accuracy, response times and controls.

3.26 The system design is spelled out formally in a document or manual called the **systems specification** (which includes a program specification for each program in the system).

3.27 The analyst will be responsible for **systems testing**.

3.28 Once installed, the analyst will keep the system under **review**, and control system **maintenance** with the co-operation of **user** departments.

Programmers

3.29 Programmers write the programs. This involves:

(a) Reading the **system specification** and understanding it.

(b) Recognising what the processing requirements of the program are, in other words, **defining the processing problem in detail**.

(c) Having defined and analysed the processing problem, **writing the program** in a programming language.

(d) Arranging for the program to be **tested**.

(e) Identifying **errors** in the program and getting rid of these 'bugs' - ie **debugging** the program.

(f) Preparing full documentation for each program within the system.

Case example

Call centre software implementation – Project Team Structure

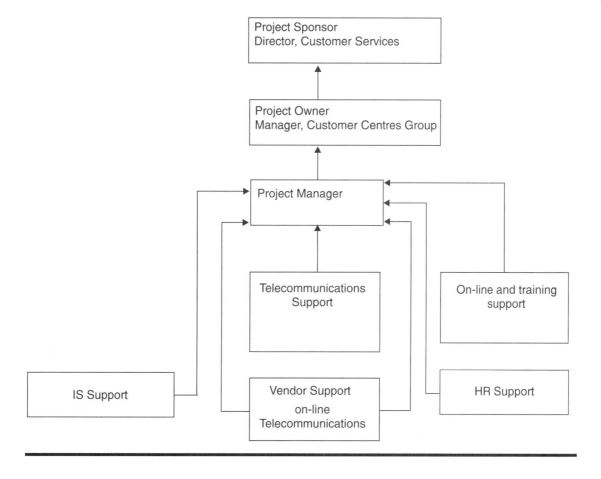

Controlling the team

3.30 The project manager is responsible for overall control of the project team.

3.31 There are two types of control strategies related to supervision.

(a) **Behaviour control** deals with the behaviour of team members. In other words, control is exercised through agreed procedures, policies and methodologies.

(b) **Output control** is where management attention is focused on results, more than the way these were achieved.

3.32 Handy writes of a **trust-control dilemma** in which the sum of trust + control is a constant amount:

$$T + C = Y$$

where   T= the trust the superior has in the subordinate, and the trust which the subordinate feels the superior has in him;

         C= the degree of control exercised by the superior over the subordinate;

         Y= a constant, unchanging value.

Any increase in C leads to an equal decrease in T; that is, if the manager retains more 'control' or authority, the subordinate will immediately recognise that he or she is being trusted less. If the superior wishes to show more trust in the subordinate, this can only be done by reducing C, that is by delegating more authority.

Span of control

3.33 Span of control or 'span of management', refers to the number of subordinates responsible to a person.

3.34 Classical theorists suggest:

(a) There are physical and mental limitations to a manager's ability to control people, relationships and activities.

(b) There should be tight managerial control from the top of an organisation downward. The span of control should be restricted to allow maximum control.

3.35 Project managers may control very large teams. On large projects management layers will be required between the overall project manager and team members. The appropriate span of control will depend on:

(a) **Ability of the manager**. A good organiser and communicator will be able to control a larger number. The manager's workload is also relevant.

(b) **Ability of the team members**. The more experienced, able, trustworthy and well-trained subordinates are, the easier it is to control larger numbers.

(c) **Nature of the task**. It is easier for a supervisor to control a large number of people if they are all doing routine, repetitive or similar tasks.

(d) The **geographical dispersal** of the subordinates, and the **communication system** of the organisation.

Flat management structures

3.36 The span of control has implications for the 'shape' of a project team and of an organisation overall. An organisation with a narrow span of control will have more levels in its management hierarchy – the organisation will be narrow and **tall**. A tall structure reflects tighter supervision and control, and lengthy chains of command and communication.

3.37 A team or organisation of the same size with a wide span of control will be wide and **flat**. The flat organisation reflects a greater degree of delegation - the more a manager delegates, the wider the span of control can be.

3.38 The wide range of people and skills required to successfully complete a systems development project has led to the acceptance of flat management structures being the most appropriate for this task.

3.39 The justification is that by empowering team members (or removing levels in hierarchies that restrict freedom), not only will the job be done more effectively but the people who do the job will get more out of it.

3.40 Project team members must be **flexible** to be able to respond quickly to specific and varied customer demands. Team members must therefore be committed.

3.41 The following steps may help increase commitment.

(a) Develop **identification** with the team and the project by means of:

- Communications
- Participation
- Team member ideas
- Financial bonuses

(b) Ensure that people **know what they have to achieve** and are aware of how their performance will be measured against agreed targets and standards.

(c) Introduce a **reward system**, which relates at least partly to individual performance.

(d) Treat team members **as human beings,** not machines.

4 PROJECT STAKEHOLDERS

KEY TERM

Project stakeholders are the individuals and organisations who are involved in or may be affected by project activities.

4.1 We have already looked at the role of the **Project Manager** and the **Project Team**. Other key stakeholders are defined as follows.

KEY TERMS

Project sponsor is accountable for the resources invested into the project and responsible for the achievement of the project's business objectives. The sponsor may be owner, financier, client etc., or their delegate.

Project support team is a term used to designate the personnel working on a project who do not report to the project manager administratively.

Users are the individual or group that will utilise the end product, process (system), or service produced by the project.

Risk manager. For large projects it may be necessary to appoint someone to control the process of identifying, classifying and quantifying the risks associated with the project.

Quality manager. For large projects it may be necessary to appoint someone to write the quality plan and develop quality control procedures.

4.2 Project stakeholders should all be **committed towards a common goal** – successful project completion. The Project Plan (covered in Chapter 5) should be the common point of reference that states priorities and provides cohesion.

4.3 However, the individuals and groups that comprise the stakeholders all have different roles. A **stakeholder matrix** is a useful tool for identifying and clarifying the role of stakeholders. An example follows.

Case example

STAKEHOLDER ANALYSIS - CALL CENTRE IMPLEMENTATION PROJECT

Stakeholder	Reason for Involvement	Importance2			Nature of Communic-ations	Current Attitude[1]				Detail of Attitude	Required Attitude[1]		Required Outcome	Knowledge	Previous Communications
		H	M	L		H	S	A	R		H	S			
Call Centre Team Managers	Will be significant user of system	✔			Awareness & Training	✔				Positive	✔		High commitment, understanding context and of need to upgrade	Awareness of the broad concept but low understanding of detail	Limited (some mention in team meetings), Internal newsletter article
User Group	Vehicle for communication of project details to other key stakeholders	✔			Awareness, consultation and work group	✔				Largely positive, not fully engaged, gap in understanding of role (lack of willingness to train own people)	✔		High knowledge of project, use of position to relay information to Users and Owners	High	Active involvement in process through user group meetings, Internal newsletter article
Group / Div Managers and Directors	Need to be aware of developments, impacts and potential for their area		✔		Awareness	✔		✔		Varying from ambivalence to positive / supportive		✔	Awareness of impact and potential	Low	Internal newsletter article
Users	Will be significant user of system	✔			Awareness & Training	✔			✔	Likely to be positive, maybe some resistance to need for greater structure	✔		Acceptance of system along with high technical knowledge and understanding of reasons for the change	Should be reasonably high (through user group reps)	Regular updates from UG reps, visits from IRT, informal discussion w/ CCC people as part of normal business, Internal newsletter article
Owners	Will be significant user of system and system output; increased accountability reliant on system use	✔			Awareness & Training, consultation through user group	✔				Likely to be positive (as they can see the benefits)	✔		Acceptance of system, high technical knowledge, impact on other areas	Should be reasonably high (through user group reps & direct dealings)	Regular updates from UG reps, visits from IRT, informal discussion w/ CCC people as part of normal business, Internal newsletter article
Wider Organisation	Support for direction / use of CCC; possible potential for use of system by others		✔		Awareness	✔		✔		Largely ambivalent, positive for those that see potential		✔	Awareness of the broad concept of integrated incident management	Very low	Internal newsletter article

Notes
1. H = High commitment, S = supportive, A = ambivalent, R = resistant
2. H = High commitment, M = medium, L = low

Managing stakeholder disputes

4.4 The first step is to establish a **framework** to predict the potential for disputes. This involves **risk management,** since an unforeseen event (a risk) has the potential to create conflict, and **dispute management**: the matching of dispute procedures with minimum impacts on costs, goodwill and progress.

4.5 One approach to dispute management strategy is to organise affairs in a way that minimises exposure to the risk of disputes. This means employing effective management techniques throughout all areas of operation. (Risk management is covered in Chapter 5.)

Dispute resolution processes

4.6 **Resolution** is the solution of a conflict. **Settlement** is an arrangement which brings an end to the conflict, but does not necessarily address the underlying causes.

4.7 Wherever there is a potential for conflict, a **process to resolve** it should be established before the conflict occurs.

4.8 We have already discussed negotiation and resolution techniques in the context of project team conflict. Many of the principles discussed previously can be applied to stakeholder conflicts, although the relative positions of the stakeholders involved can complicate matters. Conflict between project stakeholders may be resolved by:

- **Negotiation** (perhaps with the assistance of others)
- **Partnering**
- **Mediation**
- A third party neutral may judge or intervene to **impose a solution**

4.9 On very large projects a **Disputes Review Board** (DRB) may be formed. This may comprise persons directly involved in the project engaged to maintain a 'watching brief' to identify and attend upon disputes as they arise. Usually there is a procedure in place which provides for the DRB to make an 'on the spot' decision before a formal dispute is notified so that the project work can proceed, and that may be followed by various rights of review at increasingly higher levels.

4.10 In practice, disputes are often resolved by the acceptance of the view of the party that has financial responsibility for the project. In such a situation mediation and negotiation may only deliver an outcome which is a reflection of the original power imbalance.

BPP
PUBLISHING

Chapter roundup

- A **project** is an undertaking that has a beginning and an end and is carried out to meet established goals within cost, schedule and quality objectives.

- **Project management** is the combination of systems, techniques, and people used to control and monitor activities undertaken within the project.

- A project will be deemed successful if it is completed at the specified level of **quality**, **on time** and within **budget**.

- The person who takes ultimate responsibility for ensuring the desired result is achieved on time and within budget is the **project manager**.

- Project **success** depends to a large extent on the **team members** selected.

- **Project stakeholders** are the individuals and organisations who are involved in, or may be affected by, project activities.

- Wherever there is a potential for conflict a **process to resolve** it should be established before the conflict occurs.

- Most conflicts that arise during a project should be able to be resolved using **negotiation** and **resolution** techniques.

Quick quiz

1   What is a successful project?

2   List four areas a project manager should be skilled in.

3   Who is the project sponsor?

4   Project management techniques encourage management by exception. TRUE or FALSE?

5   List four ways a dispute between project stakeholders could be settled.

Answers to quick quiz

1   One that is completed on time, within budget and to specification.

2   [Four of] Leadership, team building, organisational, communication, technical, personal.

3   The project sponsor may be the owner, financier, client etc., or their delegate. The sponsor is accountable for the resources invested into the project and responsible for the achievement of the project's business objectives.

4   TRUE, see paragraph 2.14.

5   Negotiation (perhaps with the assistance of others)
    Partnering
    Mediation
    A third party neutral may judge or intervene to impose a solution

The material covered in this Chapter is tested in Question 1(b)(i) in the Exam Question Bank.

Chapter 5

PROJECT PHASES AND MANAGEMENT TOOLS

Topic list	Syllabus reference
1 The project life cycle	1(g)
2 Management tools and techniques	1(f), 1(g), 1(h)
3 Project management software	1(i)
4 Documentation and reports	1(f), 1(g), 1(h)
5 Risk management	1(d)
6 Information systems projects – common problems	1(h), 3(i)

Introduction

In this chapter we study the stages a project moves through from initiation to completion. Be aware that other books may refer to **project stages** with different names or may include more or fewer stages. This does not mean one description is incorrect. The principles behind the process and techniques are more important than the labels used.

Later in the chapter we study the various **management tools and techniques** used in project management.

Study guide

Part 1.4 – Organising information systems; structural issues

- Discuss the meaning and need for a risk management process

Part 1.6 – Project initiation

- Define the content and structure of the terms of reference
- Describe the typical contents of a Project Quality Plan and explain the need for such a plan

Part 1.7 – Project planning

- Assist in splitting the project into its main phases
- Participate in the breakdown of work into lower-level tasks
- Assist in the estimation of the time taken to complete these lower-level tasks
- Define dependencies between lower-level tasks
- Construct and interpret a project network
- Construct and interpret a Gantt Chart

Part 1.8 – Project monitoring and control

- Describe methods of monitoring and reporting progress
- Define the reasons for slippage and how to deal with slippage when it occurs
- Discuss the reasons for changes during the project and the need for a project change procedure
- Reflect the effects of progress, slippage and change requests on the project plan
- Discuss the particular problems of planing and controlling Information Systems projects

Study guide (continued)

Part 1.9 – Software support for project management

- Define the meaning of a project management software package and give a brief list of representative products

- Describe a range of features and functions that a project management software package may provide

- Explain the advantages of using a project management software package in the project management process

Part 3.27 – Relationship of management, development process and quality

- Explain the time/cost/quality triangle and its implications for information systems projects

Exam guide

Ensure you are able to apply project management tools and techniques. Network analysis and Gantt charts are highly examinable.

1 THE PROJECT LIFE CYCLE

1.1 A successful project relies on two activities – **planning** first, and then **doing**. These two activities form the basis of every project.

1.2 Projects can be divided into several phases to provide better management control. Collectively these phases comprise the **Project Life Cycle**.

KEY TERM

Project Life Cycle. The major time periods through which any project passes. Each period may be identified as a phase and further broken down into stages.

1.3 Although the principles of the project life cycle apply to all projects, the number and name of the phases identified will vary depending on what the project aims to achieve, and the project model referred to.

1.4 When studying Project Management it is convenient to give generic names to the phases of the **Project Life Cycle**. Remember though, in 'real' situations (or in examination questions!) the model can be modified to suit circumstances.

1.5 The diagram below shows a generic model of the **five main phases of a project**.

The phases of a project

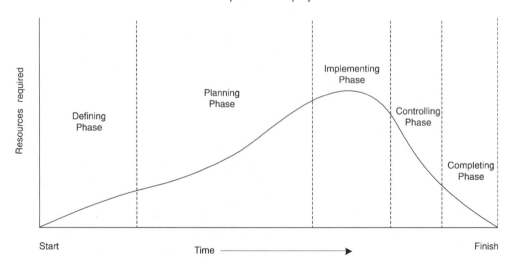

1.6 As shown on the diagram, resource use (such as funds and staff hours required) is low at the start of the project, higher towards the end and then drops rapidly as the project draws to a close.

1.7 The cost of making changes to the project increases the further into the life cycle the project has progressed.

Project phases and stages

1.8 The phases of a project can be broken down into a number of **stages**. Again, the number of stages identified varies depending on type of project and the conventions of the organisation undertaking the project.

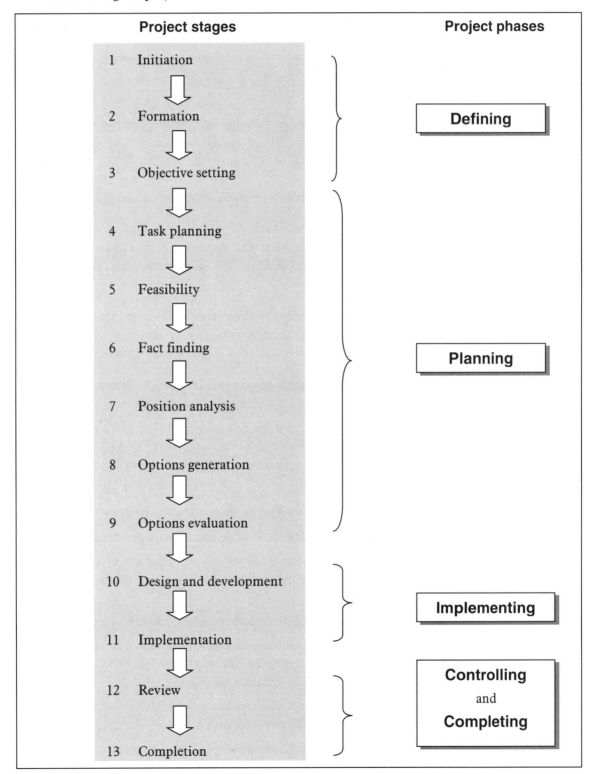

Project stages	Project phases
1 Initiation	
2 Formation	**Defining**
3 Objective setting	
4 Task planning	
5 Feasibility	
6 Fact finding	**Planning**
7 Position analysis	
8 Options generation	
9 Options evaluation	
10 Design and development	**Implementing**
11 Implementation	
12 Review	**Controlling** and **Completing**
13 Completion	

1.9   We now will look at each of these phases and stages.

Defining Phase

> **KEY TERM**
>
> The **defining phase** of a project is concerned with deciding whether a project should begin and committing to do so.

Initiation stage

> **KEY TERM**
>
> **Project initiation** describes the beginning of a project at which point certain management activities are required to ensure that the project is established with clear reference terms and an appropriate management structure.

1.10   Projects originate from someone attempting to resolve a **problem,** or seeing an **opportunity** to do something new.

1.11   It is often not clear precisely what the problem is. The project team should study, discuss and **analyse** the problem, from a number of different aspects (eg technical, financial).

1.12   Not all ideas will result in viable projects. A 'reality test' should be applied to all ideas. This is not a detailed feasibility study, and is intended to eliminate only concepts that are **obviously not viable.** For example, a small construction company should not waste resources investigating the possibility of submitting a tender to build the second channel tunnel.

1.13   At the start of a project, a **Project Initiation Document (PID)** may be drawn up, setting out the **terms of reference** for the project. Typical contents might include.

(a)   The **business objectives.** Projects should not be undertaken simply for their own sake: the business advantages should be clearly identified and be the first point of reference when progress is being reviewed, to make sure that the original aim is not lost sight of.

(b)   **Project objectives.**

(c)   The **scope** of the project: what it is intended to cover and what it is not.

(d)   **Constraints,** such as maximum amount to be spent and interim and final deadlines.

(e)   The **ultimate customer** of the project, who will resolve conflicts as they occur (for example between two different divisions who will both be using the new system) and finally accept it.

(f)   The **resources** that will be used – staff, technical resources, finance.

(g)   An **analysis of risks** inherent in the project and how they are to be avoided or reduced (for example, the consequences of replacing the old sales ledger system and only discovering after the event that the new one does not work).

(h)   A preliminary **project plan** (targets, activities and so on) and details of how the project is to be organised and managed (see the next section).

(i)   **Purchasing and procurement policy,** perhaps specifying acceptable suppliers and delivery details.

Formation stage

1.14   The formation stage involves selecting the personnel who will be involved with the project. First to be selected is usually the **Project Manager** (whose role was discussed in Chapter 4). and the **Project Board**.

1.15   The project manager should **select and build the project team**. This process was explained in Chapter 4.

Objective setting stage

1.16   Before specific objectives can be set it is necessary to establish more general **project goals**. Clear goals and objectives give team members **quantifiable targets** to aim for. This should improve motivation and performance, as attempting to achieve a challenging goal is more inspiring than simply being told 'do your best.'

1.17   The **overall project goal** or project definition will be developed. On complex projects it is likely that the goal will require be written in stages, with each definition being more detailed and refined than before. The project goal might be defined in a:
    *   Contract
    *   Product specification
    *   Customer's specification

KEY TERMS

A **goal** is a result or purpose that is determined for a project. Goals are broader than objectives.

An **objective** is a specific project outcome required – including required resources and timing.

1.18   Objectives are developed from broad goals. In an accounting software installation project a project goal could be 'to produce timely and accurate management accounting reports.' An objective of the same project could be 'to have the nominal ledger system live and fully operational by November 1 200X.'

1.19   Project objectives should be **SMART**:

    *   **S**pecific - so all involved are working towards the same end
    *   **M**easurable - how will success be measured
    *   **A**greed upon - by all team members and stakeholders
    *   **R**ealistic - to motivate goals and objectives must be achievable
    *   **T**ime-bound - a date must be allocated to provide focus and aid priority setting
    *   Allocated - in terms of responsibility

Planning Phase

KEY TERM

The **planning phase** of a project aims to devise a workable scheme to accomplish the overall project goal.

Task planning stage

1.20 After the project team is in place and project goals and objectives have been set, the project should be broken down into **manageable tasks**. This process is often referred to as **Work Breakdown Structure (WBS)**. A brief overview of the process follows. We cover WBS in greater detail later in this chapter.

KEY TERMS

A **task** is an individual unit of work that is part of the total work needed to accomplish a project.

An **activity** is a set of tasks that are carried out in order to create a deliverable.

A **deliverable** is another name for a required outcome (eg product, service, document etc) from a project.

1.21 By breaking the project down into a series of manageable tasks it is easier to determine the skills needed to complete the project. A **task list** should be produced showing what tasks need to be done and the work sequences necessary.

1.22 Building a task list for a complex project can be an involved and lengthy process. It can be difficult deciding what constitutes a task, and where one task ends and another begins.

1.23 Tasks should be:

  (a) **Clear**. Eg Design the layout of the fixed asset depreciation schedule.

  (b) **Self-contained**. No gaps in time should be apparent on work-units grouped together to form a task. All work-units within a task should be related.

Feasibility and fact finding stage

1.24 Once all the tasks have been defined a basic **network diagram** can be developed, together with a **complete list of resources** required. Network diagrams are covered later in this chapter.

1.25 A more realistic judgement as to the **overall feasibility** of the project can now be made. Any earlier feasibility decisions have been based on educated guesses and/or 'common-sense', it is only now that project feasibility can be established with any certainty.

1.26 For complex projects, a detailed **feasibility study** may be required to establish if the project can be achieved within acceptable **cost and time constraints**.

KEY TERM

A **feasibility study**, as its name suggests, is a formal study to decide what type of system can be developed which meets the needs of the organisation. Practice will vary between different organisations.

1.27 We cover the feasibility study in detail in Chapter 7, in the context of a systems development project.

1.28 Fact finding may be performed substantially during the feasibility study.

1.29 The activities carried out will differ depending on the nature of the project. For information systems projects the fact finding exercise would take the form of a systems investigation. This is covered in detail in Chapter 6.

Position analysis, options generation and options evaluation stages

1.30 Once the current position has been clearly established options can be generated with the aim of utilising the internal strengths identified.

1.31 The general management technique of **SWOT analysis** can be applied to establish the current position, generate available options and evaluate those options.

> **KEY TERM**
>
> **SWOT analysis** is a process that aims to determine:
>
> What **Strengths** do we have? (How can we take advantage of them?)
>
> What **Weaknesses** do we have? (How can we minimise them?)
>
> What **Opportunities** are there? (How can we capitalise on them?)
>
> What **Threats** might prevent us from getting there? (eg Technical obstacles.)

1.32 A **strengths and weaknesses analysis** should identify:

(a) Strengths the organisation has that the project may be able to exploit.

(b) Organisational weaknesses that may impact on the project. Strategies will be required to improve these areas or minimise their impact.

1.33 The **strengths** and **weaknesses** analysis has an **internal** focus. The identification of shortcomings in skills or resources could lead to a decision to purchase from outsiders or to train staff.

1.34 An **external appraisal** is required to identify **opportunities** which can be exploited by the company and also to anticipate environmental **threats** (a declining economy, competitors' actions, government legislation, industrial unrest etc) against which the company must protect itself.

1.35 The internal and external appraisals of SWOT analysis will be brought together.

(a) Major **strengths** and profitable opportunities can be **exploited** especially if strengths and opportunities are matched with each other.

(b) Major **weaknesses** and threats should be **countered,** or a contingency strategy or corrective strategy developed.

1.36 The elements of the SWOT analysis can be summarised and shown on a **cruciform chart.** The following chart relates to a project that proposes to install a new computerised accounting system.

1.37 EXAMPLE: NEW COMPUTERISED ACCOUNTING SYSTEM

STRENGTHS	WEAKNESSES
£1 million of funds allocated	Workforce has very limited experience of computerised systems
Willing and experienced workforce	Seems to be an expectation that the new system will 'do everything'

THREATS	OPPORTUNITIES
The software vendor is rumoured to be in financial trouble and may 'disappear'	Chance to introduce compatible systems in other departments at a later date
System failure, particularly at month or year end, would be costly	Later integration with e-commerce functions is possible

Potential strategy.

Significant benefits can be obtained from the project, which should be able to achieve its aims within the £1 million budgeted.

Assurances should be sought from the software vendor as to their future plans and profitability. Contractual obligations should be obtained in regard to this. If the rumours are justified, either another supplier should be approached or the possibility of employing the original vendor's staff on a contract basis could be explored. *(This is an example of an alternative strategy coming out of the SWOT analysis.)*

The end users of the system must be involved in all aspects of system design. Training of staff must be thorough and completed before the system 'goes live'. Management and users must be educated as to what the system will and will not be able to do.

A contingency plan should be in place for repairing or even replacing hardware at short notice.

Implementing Phase

> **KEY TERM**
>
> The **implementing phase** is concerned with co-ordinating people and other resources to carry out the project plan.

Design and development stage

1.38 The design and development stage is where the actual product, service or process that will be the end result of the project is worked on.

1.39 The activities carried out in this stage will vary greatly depending on the type of project. For example, in a software implementation this is when the programming of the software would take place, in a construction project the building design would be finalised.

Implementation stage

1.40 After the process, service or product has been developed it will be implemented or installed so it is available to be used.

1.41 If the project involves a new system or process, a period of parallel running alongside the existing system or process may be carried out. This enables results to be checked, and any last-minute problems to be ironed out before the organisation is fully reliant on the new system or process.

Controlling Phase

> **KEY TERM**
>
> The **controlling phase** is concerned with ensuring project objectives are met by monitoring and measuring progress and taking corrective action when necessary.

Review stage

1.42 Actual performance should be reviewed against the objectives identified in the project plan. If performance is not as expected, control action will be necessary.

Completing Phase

> **KEY TERM**
>
> **Completion** involves formalising acceptance of the project and bringing it to an orderly end.

Completion stage

1.43 Following installation and review there should be a meeting of the Project Board to:

- Check that all products are complete and delivered
- Check the status of any outstanding requests for change
- Check all project issues have been cleared
- Approve the project completion report
- Arrange for a post-implementation review

2 MANAGEMENT TOOLS AND TECHNIQUES

The Project Budget

> **KEY TERM**
>
> **Project budget.** The amount and distribution of resources allocated to a project.

2.1 Building a project budget should be an orderly process that attempts to establish a realistic estimate of the cost of the project. There are two main methods for establishing the project budget; **top-down** and **bottom-up**.

2.2 **Top-down budgeting** describes the situation where the budget is imposed 'from above'. Project Managers are allocated a budget for the project based on an estimate made by senior management. The figure may prove realistic, especially if similar projects have been undertaken recently. However the technique is often used simply because it is quick, or because only a certain level of funding is available.

2.3 In **bottom-up budgeting** the project manager consults the project team, and others, to calculate a budget based on the tasks that make up the project. Work breakdown structure (WBS) is a useful tool in this process. WBS is explained later in this section.

2.4 The budget may express all resources in monetary amounts, or may show money and other resources - such as staff hours. A monetary budget is often used to establish the current cost variance of the project. To establish this we need:

(a) **The Actual Cost of Work Performed (ACWP)**. This is the amount spent to date on the project.

(b) **The Budgeted Cost of Work Scheduled (BCWS)**. The amount that was budgeted to be spent to this point on scheduled activities.

(c) **The Budgeted Cost of Work Performed (BCWP)**. This figure is calculated by pricing the work that has actually been done – using the same basis as the scheduled work.

BCWP – ACWP = The **cost variance** for the project.
BCWP – BCWS = The **schedule variance** for the project.

2.5 During the project actual expenditure is tracked against budget on either a separate **Budget Report,** or as part of a regular **Progress Report.** We will be looking at project documentation and reports later in this chapter.

Work breakdown structure (WBS)

> **KEY TERM**
>
> **Work breakdown structure** is the analysis of the work of a project into different units or tasks. WBS:
>
> (a) Identifies the work that must be done in the project.
> (b) Determines the resources required.
> (c) Sequences the work done, to allocate resources in the optimum way.

2.6 **Work breakdown structure** is used as a starting point for many project management functions including budgeting and **scheduling**. As a simple example of WBS, **wiring** a house can be **sub-divided** into connecting the mains, fitting light sockets and power points etc. Dealing with the foundations involves digging, filling, area marking, damp proofing and disposal of soil.

2.7 The process of work breakdown continues until the smallest possible sub-unit is reached. Digging the foundations for example would be analysed so that the number of labour hours needed, and hence the cost, could be determined. *Lock* recommends giving each sub-unit of work a code number to enable resources to be obtained and the work to be planned.

2.8 WBS can be used in devising estimates. From the WBS it is possible to compile a complete list of **every task** that is going to attract expenditure.

2.9 Collating the various costs identified with each task has several benefits:

(a) Provides a useful **cost analysis** for various business functions.
(b) Assists **cost control**.
(c) Provides evidence, in any dispute with the client, that the costs are reasonable.

2.10 Estimates (and therefore budgets) cannot be expected to be 100% accurate. Business **conditions may change,** the project plan may be amended or estimates may simply prove to be incorrect.

2.11 Any **estimate** must be accompanied by some **indication of expected accuracy**.

2.12 Estimates can be **improved** by:

- **Learning** from past mistakes
- Ensuring sufficient design **information**
- Ensuring as **detailed a specification as possible** from the customer
- Properly **analysing the job** into its constituent units

2.13 The overall level of cost estimates will be influenced by:

(a) **Project goals**. If a high level of quality is expected costs will be higher.

(b) **External vendors**. Some costs may need to be estimated by outside vendors. To be realistic these people must understand exactly what would be expected of them.

(c) **Staff availability**. If staff are unavailable, potentially expensive contractors may be required.

(d) **Time schedules**. The quicker a task is required to be done the higher the cost is likely to be – particularly with external suppliers.

2.14 Budgets should be presented for approval and **sign-off** to the stakeholder who has responsibility for the funds being used.

2.15 It may be decided that a project costs more than it is worth. If so, scrapping the project is a perfectly valid option. In such cases the budgeting process has highlighted the situation before too much time and effort has been spent on an unprofitable venture.

Gantt charts

2.16 A Gantt chart, named after the engineer Henry Gantt who pioneered the procedure in the early 1900s, is a horizontal bar chart used to plan the **time scale** for a project and to estimate the amount of **resources** required.

2.17 The Gantt chart displays the **time relationships** between tasks in a project. Two lines are usually used to show the time allocated for each task, and the actual time taken.

2.18 A simple Gantt chart, illustrating some of the activities involved in a network server installation project, follows.

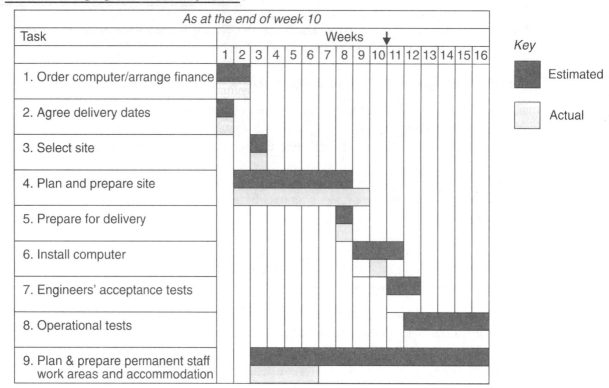

	As at the end of week 10																
Task	Weeks																
	1	2	3	4	5	6	7	8	9	10	11	12	13	14	15	16
1. Order computer/arrange finance																
2. Agree delivery dates																
3. Select site																
4. Plan and prepare site																
5. Prepare for delivery																
6. Install computer																
7. Engineers' acceptance tests																
8. Operational tests																
9. Plan & prepare permanent staff work areas and accommodation																

Key: Estimated / Actual

2.19 The chart shows that at the end of the tenth week Activity 9 is running behind schedule. More resources may have to be allocated to this activity if the staff accommodation is to be ready in time for the changeover to the new system.

2.20 Activity 4 had not been completed on time, and this has resulted in some disruption to the computer installation (Activity 6), which may mean further delays in the commencement of Activities 7 and 8.

2.21 A Gantt chart does not show the interrelationship between the various activities in the project as clearly as a **network diagram** (covered later in this chapter). A combination of Gantt charts and network analysis will often be used for project planning and resource allocation.

Network analysis

2.22 **Network analysis,** also known as **Critical Path Analysis** (CPA), is a useful technique to help with planning and controlling large projects, such as construction projects, research and development projects and the computerisation of systems.

KEY TERMS

Network analysis requires breaking down the project into tasks, arranging them into a logical sequence and estimating the duration of each.

This enables the series of tasks that determines the minimum possible duration of the project to be found. These are the **critical activities**.

2.23 CPA aims to ensure the progress of a project, so the project is completed in the **minimum amount of time**.

2.24 It pinpoints the tasks which are **on the critical path**, ie those parts which, if delayed beyond the allotted time, would **delay the completion** of the project as a whole.

2.25 The technique can also be used to assist in **allocating resources** such as labour and equipment.

2.26 Critical path analysis is quite a simple technique. The events and activities making up the whole project are represented in the form of a **diagram**.

2.27 Drawing the diagram or chart involves the following steps.

Step 1. Estimating the time needed to complete each individual activity or task that makes up a part of the project.

Step 2. Sorting out what activities must be done one after another, and which can be done at the same time, if required.

Step 3. Representing these in a network diagram.

Step 4. Estimating the critical path, which is the longest sequence of consecutive activities through the network.

2.28 The duration of the whole project will be fixed by the time taken to complete the largest path through the network. This path is called the **critical path** and activities on it are known as **critical activities**.

2.29 Activities on the critical path **must be started and completed on time**, otherwise the total project time will be extended. The method of finding the critical path is illustrated in the example below.

2.30 Network analysis shows the **sequence** of tasks and how long they are going to take. The diagrams are drawn from left to right.

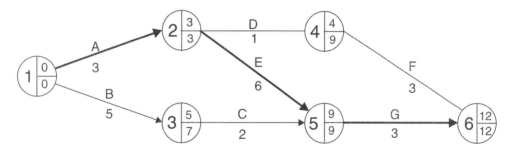

(a) **Events** (eg 1 and 2) are represented by circles. **Tasks** (eg A) connect events.

(b) The **critical path** is represented by drawing an extra line or a thicker line between the tasks on the path. It is the **minimum amount of time** that the project will take.

(c) It is the convention to note the earliest start date of any task in the *top* right hand corner of the circle.

(d) We can then work **backwards** identifying the **latest** dates when tasks have to start. These we insert in the bottom right quarter of the circle.

2.31 The **critical path** in the diagram above is AEG. Note the **float time** of five days for Activity F. Activity F can begin any time between days 4 and 9, thus giving the project manager a degree of flexibility.

Activity-on-node presentation

2.32 The method of drawing network diagrams explained here closely follows the presentation that you would see if you used the **Microsoft Project** software package. It is easier and clearer than old-fashioned method of using divided circles.

2.33 EXAMPLE: ACTIVITY ON NODE

Suppose that a project includes three activities, C, D and E. Neither activity D nor E can start until activity C is completed, but D and E could be done simultaneously if required.

This would be represented as follows.

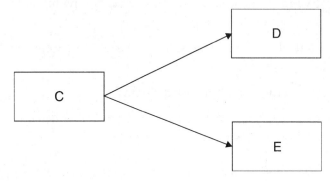

2.34 Note the following.

(a) An **activity** within a network is represented by a rectangular box. (Each box is a **node**.)
(b) The '**flow**' of activities in the diagram should be from **left to right**.
(c) The diagram clearly shows that **D and E must follow C.**

2.35 A second possibility is that an activity cannot start until two or more activities have been completed. If activity H cannot start until activities G and F are both complete, then we would represent the situation like this.

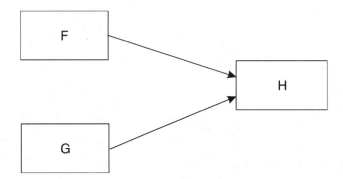

2.36 In some conventions an extra node is introduced at the start and end of a network. This serves absolutely no purpose (other than to ensure that all the nodes are joined up), so we recommend that you do not do it. Just in case you ever see a network presented in this way, both styles are shown in the next example.

2.37 EXAMPLE: STARTS AND ENDS

Draw a diagram for the following project. The project is finished when both D and E are complete.

Activity	Preceding activity
A	-
B	-
C	A
D	B & C
E	B

2.38 SOLUTION

Microsoft Project style

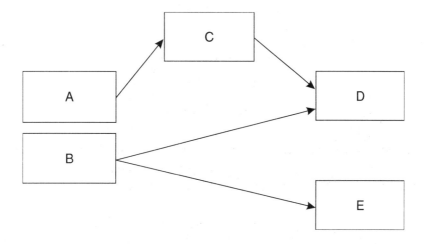

With start and end nodes

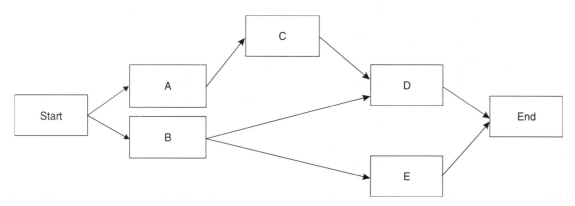

2.39 Any network can be analysed into a number of different paths or routes. A path is simply a sequence of activities which can take you from the start to the end of the network. In the example above, there are just three routes or paths.

(a) A C D.

(b) B D.

(c) B E.

2.40 The time needed to complete each individual activity in a project must be estimated. This **duration** is shown within the node as follows. The reason for and meaning of the other boxes will be explained in a moment.

Task A	
ID	6 days

2.41 EXAMPLE: THE CRITICAL PATH

Activity	*Immediately preceding activity*	*Duration (weeks)*
A	-	5
B	-	4
C	A	2
D	B	1
E	B	5
F	B	5
G	C, D	4
H	F	3
I	F	2

(a) What are the paths through the network?

(b) What is the critical path and its duration?

2.42 SOLUTION

The first step in the solution is to draw the network diagram, with the time for each activity shown.

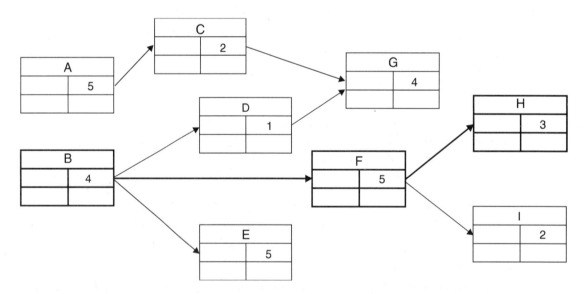

2.43 We could list the paths through the network and their overall completion times as follows.

Path	*Duration (weeks)*	
A C G	(5 + 2 + 4)	11
B D G	(4 + 1 + 4)	9
B E	(4 + 5)	9
B F H	(4 + 5 + 3)	12
B F I	(4 + 5 + 2 + 0)	11

2.44 The critical path is the longest, **BFH**, with a duration of 12 weeks. This is the **minimum time needed** to complete the project.

2.45 The **critical path** is indicated on the diagram by drawing **thick** (or **double-line**) arrows, as shown above. In Microsoft Project the arrows and the nodes are highlighted in **red**.

2.46 **Listing paths** through the network in this way should be easy enough for small networks, but it becomes a **long and tedious task** for bigger and more complex networks. This is why **software packages** are used in real life.

2.47 Conventionally it has been recognised as useful to calculate the **earliest and latest times for activities to start or finish**, and show them on the network diagram. This can be done for networks of any size and complexity.

2.48 Project management software packages offer a much larger variety of techniques than can easily be done by hand. Microsoft Project allows **each activity** to be assigned to any one of a variety of types: 'start as late as possible', 'start as soon as possible', 'finish no earlier than a particular date', 'finish no later than a particular date', and so on.

2.49 In real life, too, activity times can be shortened by working **weekends and overtime**, or they may be constrained by **non-availability of essential personnel**. In other words with any more than a few activities the possibilities are mind-boggling, which is why software is used.

2.50 Nevertheless, a simple technique is illustrated in the following example.

2.51 EXAMPLE: EARLIEST AND LATEST START TIMES

One way of showing earliest and latest **start** times for activities is to divide each event node into sections. This is similar to the style used in Microsoft Project except that Project uses real dates, which is far more useful, and the bottom two sections can mean a variety of things, depending what constraints have been set.

These sections record the following things.

(a) The **name** of the activity, for example Task A. This helps humans to understand the diagram.

(b) An **ID number** which is unique to that activity. This helps computer packages to understand the diagram, because it is possible that two or more activities could have the same name. For instance two bits of research are done at different project stages might both be called 'Research'.

(c) The **duration** of the activity.

(d) The **earliest start time**. Conventionally for the first node in the network, this is time 0.

(e) The **latest start time**.

(**Note**. Don't confuse start times with the '**event**' times that are calculated when using the **activity-on-arrow** method, even though the approach is the same.)

Task D	
ID number: 4	Duration: 6 days
Earliest start: Day 4	Latest start: Day 11

Earliest start times

2.52 To find the earliest start times, always start with activities that have no predecessors and give them an earliest starting time of 0. In the example we have been looking at, this is week 0.

Then work along each path from **left to right** through the diagram calculating the earliest time that the next activity can start.

For example, the earliest time for activity C is week $0 + 5 = 5$. The earliest time activities D, E and F can start is week $0 + 4 = 4$.

To calculate an activity's earliest time, simply look at the box for the **preceding** activity and add the bottom left figure to the top right figure.

If **two or more** activities precede an activity take the **highest** figure as the later activity's earliest start time: it cannot start before all the others are finished!

Latest start times

2.53 The latest start times are the latest times at which each activity can start **if the project as a whole is to be completed in the earliest possible time**, in other words in 12 weeks in our example.

Work backwards from **right to left** through the diagram calculating the latest time at which the activity can start, if it is to be completed at the latest finishing time. For example the latest start time for activity H is $12 - 3 =$ week 9 and for activity E is $12 - 5 =$ week 7.

2.54 Activity F might cause difficulties as two activities, H and I, lead back to it.

(a) Activity H must be completed by week 12, and so must start at week 9.
(b) Activity I must also be completed by week 12, and so must start at week 10.

Activity F takes 5 weeks so its latest start time F is the either $9 - 5 =$ week 4 or $10 - 5 =$ week 5. However, if it starts in week 5 it not be possible to start activity H on time and the whole project will be delayed. We therefore take the **lower** figure.

2.55 The final diagram is now as follows.

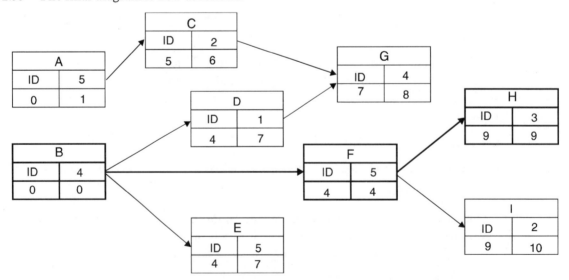

2.56 **Critical activities** are those activities which must be started on time, otherwise the total project time will be increased. It follows that each event on the critical path must have the same earliest and latest start times. The critical path for the above network is therefore **B F H**.

Criticisms of critical path/network analysis

2.57 (a) It is not always possible to devise an effective WBS for a project.

(b) **It assumes a sequential relationship** between activities. It assumes that once Activity B starts after Activity A has finished. It is not very good at coping with the possibility that an activity 'later' in the sequence may be relevant to an earlier activity.

(c) There are **problems in estimation**. Where the project is completely new, the planning process may be conducted in conditions of relative ignorance.

(d) Although network analysis plans the use of resources of labour and finance, it **does not appear to develop plans for contingencies, other than crashing time**.

(f) CPA **assumes a trade-off between time and cost.** This may not be the case where a substantial portion of the cost is **indirect overheads** or where the direct labour proportion of the total cost of limited.

2.58 EXAMPLE: GANTT CHARTS AND RESOURCES

This example is provided as an illustration of the use of Gantt charts to manage resources efficiently.

A company is about to undertake a project about which the following data is available.

Activity	Preceded by activity	Duration Days	Workers required
A	–	3	6
B	–	5	3
C	B	2	4
D	A	1	4
E	A	6	5
F	D	3	6
G	C, E	3	3

There is a multi-skilled workforce of nine workers available, each capable of working on any of the activities.

Draw the network to establish the duration of the project and the critical path. Then draw a Gantt chart, using the critical path as a basis, assuming that jobs start at the earliest possible time.

2.59 SOLUTION

Here are the diagrams.

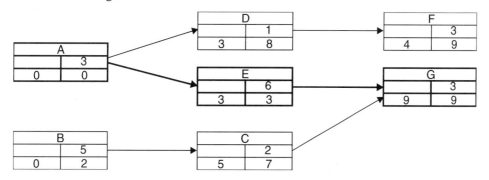

BPP
PUBLISHING

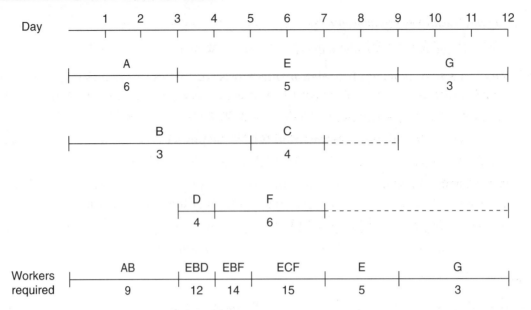

2.60 It can be seen that if all activities start at their earliest times, as many as 15 workers will be required on any one day (days 6-7) whereas on other days there would be idle capacity (days 8-12).

2.61 The problem can be reduced, or removed, by using up spare time on non-critical activities. Suppose we **deferred the start** of activities D and F until the latest possible days. These would be days 8 and 9, leaving four days to complete the activities by the end of day 12.

2.62 The Gantt chart would be redrawn as follows.

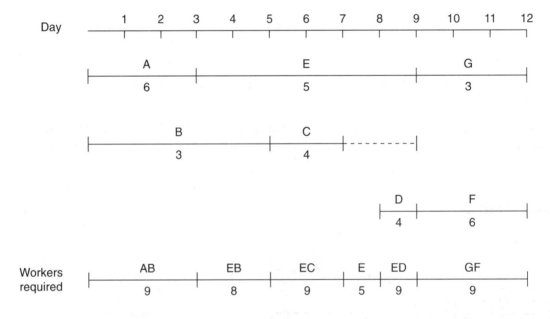

Project evaluation review technique (PERT)

2.63 **Project evaluation and review technique (PERT)** is a technique for allowing for uncertainty in determining project duration. Each task is assigned a best, worst, and most probable completion time estimate. These estimates are used to determine the average completion time. The average times are used to establish the critical path and the standard deviation of completion times for the entire project.

2.64 PERT is a modified form of network analysis designed to account for **uncertainty**. For each activity in the project, optimistic, most likely and pessimistic estimates of times are made, on the basis of past experience, or even guess-work. These estimates are converted into a mean time and also a standard deviation.

2.65   Once the mean time and standard deviation of the time have been calculated for each activity, it should be possible to do the following.

(a)   Estimate the **critical path** using expected (mean) activity times.

(b)   Estimate the **standard deviation of the total project time**.

Exam focus point

PERT is not mentioned in the syllabus, so we have not included a worked example. Just be aware that it exists and that it is designed to build in an allowance for time uncertainty.

Resource histogram

2.66   A useful planning tool that shows the amount and timing of the requirement for a resource (or a range of resources) is the resource histogram.

KEY TERM

A resource histogram shows a view of project data in which resource requirements, usage, and availability are shown against a time scale.

2.67   A simple resource histogram showing programmer time required on a software development program is shown below.

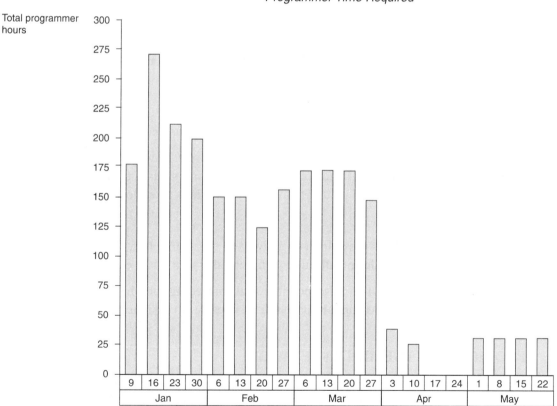

Programmer Time Required

2.68   Some organisations add another bar (or a separate line) to the chart showing resource availability. The chart then shows any instances when the required resource hours exceed the available hours. Plans should then be made to either obtain further resource for these peak times, or to re-schedule the work plan. Alternately the chart may show times when the available resource is excessive, and should be re-deployed elsewhere. An example follows.

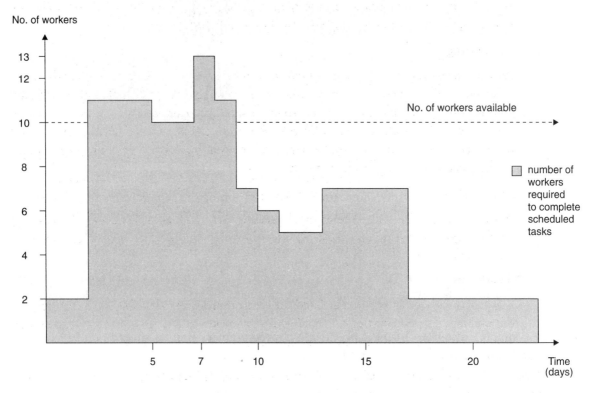

2.69   The number of workers required on the seventh day is 13. Can we re-schedule the non-critical activities to reduce the requirement to the available level of 10? We might be able to re-arrange activities so that we can make use of the workers available from day 9 onwards.

Float times and costs

2.70   **Float time** is the time built in to allow for unforeseen circumstances.

(a)   **Total float** on a job is the time available (earliest start date to latest finish date) *less* time needed for the job. If, for example, job A's earliest start time was day 7 and its latest end time was day 17, and the job needed four days, total float would be:

$(17 - 7) - 4 = 6$ days

(b)   **Free float** is the delay possible in an activity on the assumption that all preceding jobs start as early as possible and all subsequent jobs also start at the earliest time.

(c)   **Independent float** is the delay possible if all preceding jobs have finished as late as possible, and all succeeding jobs have started as early as possible.

3   PROJECT MANAGEMENT SOFTWARE

3.1   Project management techniques are ideal candidates for computerisation. Project management software packages have been available for a number of years. Microsoft Project and Micro Planner X-Pert are two popular packages.

3.2   Software might be used for a number of purposes.

(a)   **Planning**

Network diagrams (showing the critical path) and Gantt charts (showing resource use) can be produced automatically once the relevant data is entered. Packages also allow a sort of 'what if?' analysis for initial planning, trying out different levels of resources, changing deadlines and so on to find the best combination.

(b)   **Estimating**

As a project progresses, actual data will become known and can be entered into the package and collected for future reference. Since many projects involve basically similar tasks (interviewing users and so on), actual data from one project can be used to provide more accurate estimates for the next project. The software also facilitates and encourages the use of more sophisticated estimation techniques than managers might be prepared to use if working manually.

(c)   **Monitoring**

Actual data can also be entered and used to facilitate monitoring of progress and automatically updating the plan for the critical path and the use of resources as circumstances dictate.

(d)   **Reporting**

Software packages allow standard and tailored progress reports to be produced, printed out and circulated to participants and senior managers at any time, usually at the touch of a button. This helps with co-ordination of activities and project review.

3.3   Most project management packages feature a process of identifying the main steps in a project, and breaking these down further into specific tasks.

3.4   A typical project management package requires four **inputs**.

(a)   The length of **time** required for each activity of the project.
(b)   The **logical relationships** between each activity.
(c)   The **resources** available.
(d)   **When** the resources are available.

3.5   The package is able to analyse and present this information in a number of ways. The views available within Microsoft Project are shown in the following illustration – on the drop down menu.

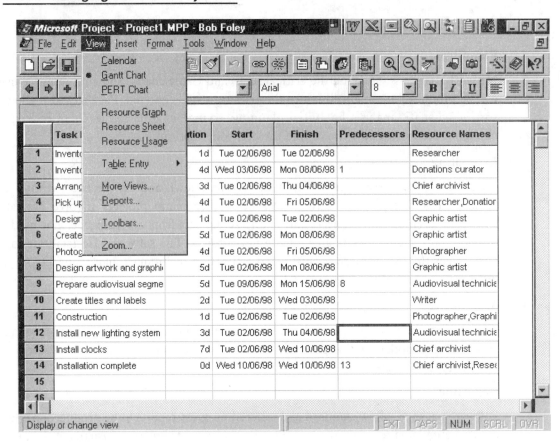

3.6 The advantages of using project management software are summarised on the following table.

Advantage	Comment
Enables quick re-planning	Estimates can be **changed many times** and a new schedule produced almost instantly. Changes to the plan can be reflected immediately.
Document quality	Well-presented plans give a **professional** impression and are easier to understand.
Encourages constant progress tracking	The project manager is able to compare **actual** progress against **planned** progress and investigate problem areas promptly.
What if? analysis	Software enables the effect of various scenarios to be calculated quickly and easily. Many project managers conduct this type of analysis using **copies** of the plan in separate computer files – leaving the actual plan untouched.

3.7 Two **disadvantages** of project management software are:

(a) Some packages are difficult to use.

(b) Some project managers become so interested in producing perfect plans that they spend too much time producing documents and not enough time managing the project.

4 DOCUMENTATION AND REPORTS

4.1 We will now look at the main **documents and reports** used in project management. The name allocated to documents will vary across different organisations. What is constant is the need for clear and relevant documentation that helps monitor and control the project.

4.2 Remember that reports are **not a substitute for one-on-one communication**. Too many (or too lengthy) reports will result in **information overload**.

4.3 When outlining possible content of documents some duplication of items occurs. This does not mean that information should be repeated, but that the information may appear in one or other of the documents depending on the format adopted by the organisation.

4.4 It is likely that the Project Initiation Document will evolve until it is ultimately incorporated into the Project Management Plan, sometimes referred to as the Project Quality Plan.

The Project Plan

4.5 The project manager should also develop a **Project Plan**. In some organisations what is described here as the Project Plan would be called the **Project Management Plan**. In other organisations the Project Plan refers only to the project schedule, usually in the form of a network diagram.

> **KEY TERM**
>
> The **Project Plan** is used to guide both project execution and project control. It outlines how the project will be planned, monitored and implemented.

4.6 The **project plan** should include:

- Project objectives and how they will be achieved and verified
- How any **changes** to these procedures are to be **controlled**
- The **management and technical procedures**, and **standards**, to be used
- Details of the **quality** strategy
- The **budget** and **time-scale**
- **Safety**, health and environmental policies
- Inherent **risks** and how they will be managed

4.7 An example of a simple **Project Plan / Project Management Plan** is shown over the page. This plan was produced by an American organisation - the Project Management Institute (PMI) - to manage a project to produce formal project management principles.

4.8 The Project Plan **evolves** over time. A high level plan for the whole project and a detailed plan for the current and following stage is usually produced soon after project start-up. At each subsequent stage a detailed plan is produced for the following stage and if required, the overall project plan is revised

4.9 An important element of the overall Project Plan is the Project Quality Plan.

> ### KEY TERM
>
> The **Project Quality Plan** outlines the quality strategy to be followed and links this to any formal quality management approach the organisation has chosen to follow.

4.10 There is no generally accepted format for a quality plan - in fact **the distinction between a project management plan and a quality plan is becoming increasingly blurred**.

4.11 Key elements of a quality plan include:

- The formal stages of the project
- Standards to be used throughout the project
- Controls that aim to ensure quality
- Checks to ensure quality

4.12 We look at quality assurance in the systems development process in Chapter 9.

Case example

Project Management Plan	
Project Name	The full name of this project is 'Project Management Principles.'
Project Manager	The project manager is Joe Bloggs. The project manager is authorised to (1) initiate the project, (2) form the project team and (3) prepare and execute plans and manage the project as necessary for successful project completion.
Purpose / Business Need	This project addresses a need for high-level guidelines for the project management profession through the identification and presentation of project management principles. The project sponsor and accepting agent is the Project Management Institute (PMI) Standards Program Team (SPT). The principal and beneficial customer is the membership of PMI. Principles are needed to provide high-level context and guidance for the profession of project management. These Principles will provide benefit from the perspectives of practice, evaluation, and development.
Product Description and Deliverables	The final deliverable of this project is a document containing a statement of project management Principles. The text is to be fully developed and ready for publication. As a research and development project, it is to be approached flexibly in schedule and resource requirements, with an initially proposed publication date of June 2001.
Project Management	The project team will use project methodology consistent with PMI Standards. The project is to be managed with definitive scope and acceptance criteria fully established as the project progresses and the product is developed.
Assumptions, Constraints and Risks	The project faces some increased risk that without a clearly prescribed definition of a Principle, standards for product quality will be more difficult to establish and apply. To mitigate this risk, ongoing communication between the project team and the project sponsor on this matter will be required.
Resources	The PMI Standards Program Team (SPT) is to provide the project team with the following. **Financial.** SPT will provide financial resources as available. The initial amount for the current year is $5,000. The project manager must not exceed the allocated amount, and notify the SPT when 75% of the allocation has been spent. **Explanation of Standards Program.** SPT will provide guidance at the outset of the project, updates as changes occur, and clarifications as needed. **Personnel / Volunteers.** SPT will recruit volunteer team members from within the membership of PMI through various media and liaisons. The project team is to consist of no less than ten members, including the project manager. General qualifications to be sought by SPT in recruiting will be:

	Mandatory • Acceptance of project plan • Demonstrated capability for strategic, generalised or intuitive thinking • Capability to write clearly on technical subject matter for general audiences • Capability to work co-operatively with well developed interpersonal skills • Be conversant in English and be able to use telephone and Internet email telecommunications **As possible** • Time availability (Team members may contribute at different levels. An average of approximately five to ten hours per month is desired.) • Diversity (Team members collectively may represent diverse nationalities, types of organisations or corporate structure, business sectors, academic disciplines, and personal experience) • Travel (As determined mutually by the project sponsor and manager, some travel for face-to-face meetings may be requested)
Approach	The project will progress through the following phases. **Phase 1: Team formation** – Recruit and orient volunteer team members. Establish procedures and ground rules for group process and decision-making. **Phase 2: Subject Matter Clarification** – Identify and clarify initial scope and definitions of project subject matter. **Phase 3a: Exploration** – Begin brainstorming (through gathering, sharing, and discussion) of data and views in unrestricted, non-judgmental process. **Phase 3b: Selection** – Conclude brainstorming (through evaluation and acceptance or rejection) of collected data and views. As the conclusion to this phase, the SPT will review as an interim deliverable the selection made by the project team. **Phase 4: Development** – Conduct further research and discussion to develop accepted subject matter. **Phase 5: Articulation** - Write a series of drafts to state the accepted and developed subject matter as appropriate for the project business need and product description. **Phase 6: Adoption** – Submit product to SPT for the official PMI standards approval and adoption process. Revise product as needed. **Phase 7: Closeout** – Perform closure for team and administrative matters. Deliver project files to SPT.
Communication and Reporting	The project manager and team will communicate with and report to the PMI Standards Program Team as follows. **Monthly Status Reports** – Written monthly status and progress reports are to include: • Work accomplished since the last report • Work planned to be performed during the next reporting period • Deliverables submitted since the last report • Deliverables planned to be submitted during the next reporting period • Work tasks in progress and currently outside of expectations for scope, quality, schedule or cost • Risks identified and actions taken or proposed to mitigate • Lessons Learned • Summary statement for posting on PMI Web site **Monthly Resource Reports** – Written monthly resource reports are to include: **Financial resources** • Total funds allocated • Total funds expended to date • Estimated expenditures for the next reporting period • Estimated expenditures for entire project to completion

	Human resources • List of all volunteer team members categorised by current involvement (i.e., active, new (pre-active), inactive, resigned) • Current number of new and active volunteer team members • Estimated number of volunteer team members needed for project completion **Milestone and Critical Status Reports** – Additional status reports are to be submitted as mutually agreed upon by SPT and the project manager and are to include at least the following items. • Milestone Status Reports are to include the same items as the Monthly Status reports, summarised to cover an entire project phase, period since the last milestone report, or entire project to date. • Critical Status Reports are to focus on work tasks outside of expectations and other information as requested by SPT or stipulated by the project manager.
Acceptance	The project manager will submit the final product and any interim deliverables to the Standards Program Team (SPT) for formal acceptance. The SPT may (1) accept the product as delivered by the project team, or (2) return the product to the team with a statement of specific requirements to make the product fully acceptable. The acceptance decision of the SPT is to be provided to the project manager in writing.
Change Management	Requests for change to this plan may be initiated by either the project sponsor or the project manager. All change requests will be reviewed and approved or rejected by a formal proceeding of the Standards Program Team (SPT) with input and interaction with the project manager. Decisions of the SPT will be documented and provided to the project manager in writing. All changes will be incorporated into this document, reflected by a new version number and date.

Plan Acceptance	**Signature and Date**
By PMI Standards Program Team	———————————————————— 12 July 1999 Fred Jones - PMI Technical Research & Standards Manager
By Project Manager	———————————————————— 20 July 1999 Joe Bloggs - PMI Member

4.13 The contents of the plan will vary depending on the complexity of the project. The contents page and introduction from a detailed Project Plan relating to a software implementation project at a call centre, are shown below.

Case example

Extract from a call centre software implementation - Project Plan

SECTION 1

INTRODUCTION

1.a   **Purpose of the Project Plan**

The purpose of this Plan is to define the working relationship between Project Team (PT) and the Manager, Customer Centres Group (MCCG). It details the level of service to be provided by Project Team to the client and the associated cost. If the nature of the project changes, or if situations develop which indicate a need for modification, then this plan will be altered accordingly in consultation with the Client. This Plan details key process steps (milestones), the methods for delivering these steps, and responsibilities of the project manager, project owner (client), and project team representatives.

1.b   **Project Objective**

To develop and fully support a call centre environment that promotes the achievement of '80% of all incoming calls resolved at the first point of contact.'

1.c   **Project Deliverable**

To deliver to the MCCG, fully commissioned and operational system upgrades as defined within this project plan, including an appropriately skilled call centre team, by 15 April 2001 at an estimated Project Team cost of £123,975.

> *Note*: Only the contents page and introduction of this comprehensive plan are reproduced here.

Progress report

> **KEY TERM**
>
> A **progress report** shows the current status of the project, usually in relation to the planned status.

4.14   The frequency and contents of progress reports will vary depending on the length of the project and the progress being made.

4.15   The report is a **control tool** intended to show the discrepancies between where the project is, and where the plan says it should be.

4.16   A common form of progress uses two columns – one for **planned** time and expenditure and one for **actual**.

4.17   Any additional content will depend on the format adopted. Some organisations include only the 'raw facts' in the report, and use these as a basis for discussion regarding reasons for variances and action to be taken, at a project review meeting.

4.18 Other organisations (particularly those involved in long, complex projects) produce more comprehensive progress reports, with more explanation and comment.

4.19 The report should monitor progress towards key **milestones.**

> **KEY TERM**
>
> A **milestone** is a significant event in the project, usually completion of a major deliverable.

4.20 Another way of monitoring progress that could be included in a progress report is a milestone slip chart.

4.21 The milestone slip chart compares planned and actual progress towards project milestones. Planned progress is shown on the X-axis and actual progress on the Y-axis. Where actual progress is slower than planned progress **slippage** has occurred.

4.22 A milestone slip chart is shown below.

Milestone slip chart

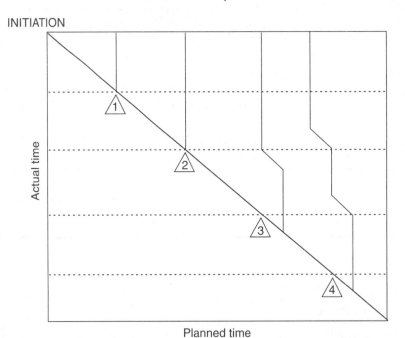

4.23 On the chart above milestones are indicated by a triangle on the diagonal planned progress line. The vertical lines that meet milestones 1 and 2 are straight – showing that these milestones were achieved on time.

4.24 At milestone 3 some slippage has occurred. The chart shows that no further slippage is expected as the progress line for milestone 4 is the same distance to the right as occurred at milestone 3.

4.25 We look at ways of dealing with slippage later in this chapter.

4.26 The progress report should also include an updated budget status – perhaps showing the cost and schedule variance explained earlier in this chapter.

4.27   The following example shows a progress report format used in a system implementation.

Case Example

PROJECT STATUS REPORT

e.g

Project title: Software Implementation   **To date: 11 May 2000**

OVERALL STATUS	Behind **XX** days	On target	Ahead.........days

KEY MILESTONES

	Plan	Actual
1. Project scope and plans signed off		
2. SLA / contract signed off		
3. Acceptance criteria signed off		
4. Training plan signed off		
5. Business processes signed off		
6. User training complete (on existing 'test' system)		
7. Pilot system established		
8. Pilot system reviewed		
9. Go live date confirmed		
10. Go live		

IMPACT OF SLIPPAGES

M/s	Details / planned remedial action	Date

KEY RISKS

Ref	Description	Management actions	Date

KEY ISSUES

Ref	Description	Resolve by date

FINANCIAL STATUS

$ 000's	"a" Initial budget	"b" Curr budget (inc app'd changes	"c" Actual spend to date	"d" R/cast - to complete	"e" Var	Reason
Capital						
Fixed						
Variable						
Ongoing						
Fixed						
Variable						
Total						

Note: Var = (c+d) - b

Other comments (notable achievements / major changes / planned absences etc.):

Project Manager:...

Project Sponsor...

BPP PUBLISHING

Completion report

> **KEY TERM**
>
> The **completion report** summarises the results of the project, and includes client sign-off.

4.28 On project completion the project manager will produce the **Completion Report.** The main purpose of the completion report is to document (and gain client sign-off for) the end of the project.

4.29 The report should include a **summary** of the project outcome. The completion report should contain:

(a) Project objectives and the outcomes achieved.

(b) The final project budget report showing expected and actual expenditure (If an external client is involved this information may be sensitive - the report may exclude or 'amend' the budget report).

(c) A brief outline of time taken compared with the original schedule.

4.30 The completion report will also include provision for any **on-going issues** that will need to be addressed after completion. Such issues would be related to the project, but not part of the project. (If they are part of the project the project is not yet complete!) An example of an on-going issue would be a procedure for any 'bugs' that become apparent **after** a new software program has been tested and approved.

4.31 Responsibilities and procedures relating to any such issues should be laid down in the report.

4.32 The manager may find it useful to distribute a provisional report and request **feedback**. This should ensure the version presented for client sign-off at the completion meeting is acceptable to all parties.

4.33 A more detailed review of the project and the system follows a few months after completion, the post-completion audit.

The post-completion audit

> **KEY TERM**
>
> The **post-completion audit** is a formal review of the project that examines the lessons that may be learned and used for the benefit of future projects.

4.34 The audit looks at all aspects of the project with regard to two questions.

(a) Did the end result of the project meet the **client's expectations**?

- The actual **design** and **construction** of the end product
- Was the project achieved **on time**?
- Was the project **completed within budget**?

(b) Was the **management of the project** as successful as it might have been, or were there bottlenecks or problems? This review covers:

(i) Problems that might occur on future projects with similar characteristics.

(ii) The performance of the team individually and as a group.

In other words, any project is an opportunity to learn how to manage future projects more effectively.

4.35 The post-completion audit should involve **input from the project team**. A simple questionnaire could be developed for all team members to complete, and a reasonably informal meeting held to obtain feedback. On what went well (and why), and what didn't (and why).

4.36 This information should be formalised in a report. The **post-completion audit report** should contain the following.

(a) A **summary** should be provided, emphasising any areas where the structures and tools used to manage the project have been found to be **unsatisfactory**.

(b) A **review** of the end result of the project should be provided, and compared against the results expected. Reasons for any significant **discrepancies** between the two should be provided, preferably with suggestions for how any future projects could **prevent these problems recurring**.

(c) A **cost-benefit review** should be included, comparing the forecast costs and benefits identified at the time of the feasibility study with actual costs and benefits.

(d) **Recommendations** should be made as to any steps which should be taken to **improve** the project management procedures used.

4.37 Lessons learnt that relate to the way the **project was managed** should contribute to the smooth running of future projects.

4.38 A starting point for any new project should be a **review** of the documentation of any **similar projects** undertaken in the past.

4.39 In information systems projects the post-completion audit may be conducted as part of the post-implementation review (covered later in this Text). Strictly speaking, a **post-completion audit** would **include** a detailed review of the **project management process**, while the **post-implementation review** is concerned mainly with the **resulting system**.

5 RISK MANAGEMENT

5.1 The identification of risks involves an overview of the project to establish what could go wrong, and the consequences.

- What are the sources of risk?
- What is the likelihood of the risk presenting itself?
- To what extent can the risk be controlled?
- What are the consequences of that risk presenting itself?
- To what extent can those consequences be controlled?

BPP PUBLISHING

5.2   The likelihood and consequences of risks can be plotted on a matrix.

Risk Assessment Matrix

Potential impact			
High	M	**H**	**VH**
Med	L	M	**H**
Low	VL	L	M
	Low	Med	High

Threat Likelihood

5.3   Developing a **contingency plan** that contains strategies for risks that fall into the VH quadrant should have priority, followed by risks falling into the two H quadrants. Following the principle of **management by exception**, the most efficient way of dealing with risks outside these quadrants may be to do nothing unless the risk presents itself.

5.4   Dealing with **conflicts arising from a risk** involves four strategies:

(a)   **Avoidance**: the factors which give rise to the risk are removed.

(b)   **Reduction**: the potential for the risk cannot be removed but analysis has enabled the identification of ways to reduce the incidence and / or the consequences.

(c)   **Transference**: the risk is passed on to someone else - or is perhaps financed by an insurer.

(d)   **Absorption**: the potential risk is accepted in the hope or expectation that the incidence and consequences can be coped with if necessary.

6   INFORMATION SYSTEMS PROJECTS – COMMON PROBLEMS

6.1   It is not uncommon for information systems projects to be years late, wildly over budget, and produce a system that does not meet user requirements.

6.2   A number of factors can combine to produce these expensive disasters.

Project managers

6.3   IS project managers were often **technicians,** not managers. Technical ability for IS staff is no guarantee of management skill - an individual might be a highly proficient analyst or programmer, but **not a good manager**.

6.4 The project manager has a number of **conflicting requirements**.

   (a) The **systems manager**, usually the project manager's boss, wants the project **delivered on time**, to specification and within budget.

   (b) **User** expectations may be misunderstood, ignored or unrealistic.

   (c) The project manager has to plan and supervise the work of **analysts** and **programmers** and these are rather different roles.

6.5 The project manager needs to develop an **appropriate management style**. What he or she should realise is the extent to which the project will fail if users are not consulted, or if the project team is unhappy. As the project manager needs to encourage participation from users, an excessively authoritarian style is not suitable.

Other factors

6.6 Other factors can be identified.

   (a) The project manager may accept **an unrealistic deadline** - the timescale is fixed early in the planning process. User demands may be accepted as deadlines before sufficient consideration is given to the realism of this.

   (b) **Poor or non-existent planning** is a recipe for disaster. Unrealistic deadlines would be identified much earlier if a proper planning process was undertaken.

   (c) A lack of **monitoring** and **control**.

   (d) Users **change their requirements**, resulting in costly changes to the system as it is being developed.

   (e) **Poor time-tabling and resourcing**. It is no use being presented on day 1 with a team of programmers, when there is still systems analysis and design work to do. The development and implementation of a computer project may take a considerable length of time (perhaps 18 months from initial decision to operational running for a medium-sized installation); a proper plan and time schedule for the various activities must be drawn up.

6.7 A project is affected by a number of factors, often in **conflict** with each other.

   (a) **Quality** of the system required, in terms of basic system requirements.

   (b) **Time,** both to complete the project, and in terms of the opportunity cost of time spent on this project which could be spent on others.

   (c) **Costs** and resources allocated to the project.

6.8 The balance between the constraints of time, cost and quality will be different for each project.

   (a) If a system aims to provide competitive advantage then time will tend to be the dominant factor.

   (b) If safety is paramount (eg an auto-pilot system) then quality will be most important.

   (c) If the sole aim of a project is to meet administrative needs that are not time dependent, then cost may be the dominant factor.

6.9   The relationship can be shown as a triangle.

The Time/Cost/Quality Triangle

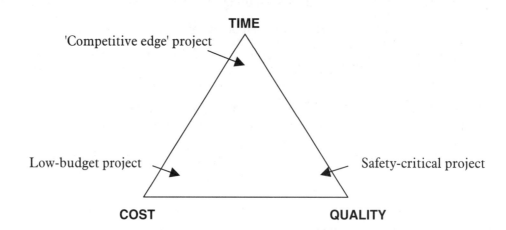

6.10   The balance of time, cost and quality will influence decision making throughout the project – for example whether to spend an extra £5,000 to fix a problem completely or only spend £1,000 on a quick fix and implement a user work-around?

Dealing with slippage

6.11   When a project has slipped behind schedule there are a range of options open to the project manager. Some of these options are summarised in the following table.

Action	Comment
Do nothing	After considering all options it may be decided that things should be allowed to continue as they are.
Add resources	If capable staff are available and it is practicable to add more people to certain tasks it may be possible to recover some lost ground. Could some work be subcontracted?
Work smarter	Consider whether the methods currently being used are the most suitable – for example could prototyping be used.
Replan	If the assumptions the original plan was based on have been proved invalid a more realistic plan should be devised.
Reschedule	A complete replan may not be necessary – it may be possible to recover some time by changing the phasing of certain deliverables.
Introduce incentives	If the main problem is team performance, incentives such as bonus payments could be linked to work deadlines and quality.
Change the specification	If the original objectives of the project are unrealistic given the time and money available it may be necessary to negotiate a change in the specification.

Project change procedure

6.12 Some of the reactions to slippage discussed above would involve changes that would significantly affect the overall project. Other possible causes of changes to the original project plan include:

- The availability of new technology
- Changes in personnel
- A realisation that user requirements were misunderstood
- Changes in the business environment
- New legislation eg Data protection

6.13 The **earlier** a change is made the **less expensive** it should prove. However, changes will cost time and money and should not be undertaken lightly.

6.14 When considering a change **an investigation** should be conducted to discover:

(a) The consequences of **not** implementing the proposed change.

(b) The impact of the change on **time, cost** and quality.

(c) The expected costs and benefits of the change.

(d) The risks associated with the change, and with the status-quo.

6.15 The process of ensuring that proper consideration is given to the impact of proposed changes is known as **change control.**

6.16 Changes will need to be implemented into the project plan and communicated to all stakeholders.

Case example

WHY CAN'T WE BUILD SOFTWARE LIKE WE BUILD BUILDINGS?

Introduction

The software development industry has a reputation for poor project performance. This makes many organisations reluctant to undertake large development projects.

The Project Manager's Responsibility

The project manager plays the same role within a software development as they would in a construction project: their aim is to finish the job within time and cost to the quality required.

Get the Right Person for the Job

Just imagine that you have built a garden shed and a passer-by compliments you on your achievement. The passer-by then asks since you've made such a good job of the shed would you build a new three-bedroom house. After all, it will utilise the same materials, just more of them. It's not very likely is it?

Yet many people learned how to use a PC-based database development application such as Microsoft Access, Dbase, or Paradox, and then went on to build 'commercial' systems. In many cases these were not designed to be commercial systems, they just started as a useful place to store information, then grew until they became a vital source of information.

Appropriate Methodology

Every size of building project requires its own set of processes to most cost effectively complete. Software is no different. Applying skyscraper standards to a house will be expensive and result in over-engineering. When setting up a software development project the same rules apply. Select the right methodology and ensure that your developer is experienced with this methodology.

Reusable Components

When building, there is little point in designing non-standard sizes into a building then trying to fit standard components into the design. These components are often as simple as the garage or interior doors, but could well include items which cannot easily be built on site, such as sealed unit double glazing.

In the software industry, the reuse of code or objects is a relatively recent development. As with buildings, if you are going to use existing components, the design must be created in such a way as to accommodate them. In the early years of software development these components would be simple subroutines which could be copied into the code to perform simple tasks such as date verification. More recently the advent of commercially successful component infrastructures such as CORBA, the Internet, ActiveX or Java Beans, has triggered a whole industry of off-the-shelf components for various domains, allowing you to buy and integrate components rather than developing them all in-house. Reusability shifts software development from programming software (a line at time) to composing software (by assembling components) just as a modern builder does not fabricate their own material but assembles the delivered components.

Responsibility of the Project Manager

The project manager is key to the success of any project and must be able to manage both people and other resources. The key role of the manager is not simply in monitoring progress but is in fixing things when they go wrong. This is the case in both industries.

Create the Environment

The project manager can create a little bit of 'project magic' by establishing a project environment which allows project participants to operate effectively and co-operatively. This type of project environment is significantly more effective than an aggressive environment.

Issue Resolution

In the building industry, the issues that arise are more likely to be physical in nature. If a team is gathered around a hole in the ground or a piece of building which doesn't quite fit, they can start to suggest solutions by measuring, drawing or simply explaining what they think will fix it.

In the software industry, the issues that arise are more likely to be abstract. However, the need for the sponsor to understand the problem is just as important. Any explanation that can be given in terms which mere mortals can understand is worth far more than the exact technical definition, especially if the Sponsor is required to make a decision on how to resolve the issue.

Conclusion

The use of modern methodologies and modelling techniques allows much of the risk of software development to be reduced. The rigorous use of CASE tools applies standards which are as close to regulations the software industry has at present. The development environments, frameworks and object libraries of software developers are gaining in sophistication to a point where many of the risks are already written out of a new development.

It may take a few years to come to terms with the international implications of electronic commerce over the Internet. The changes in taxable revenue of having a business process independent of location will have far-reaching effects. This is likely to be the next challenge of the technology industry.

Adapted from a paper prepared by Synergy International 1999

Chapter roundup

- A project typically passes through five **phases**: defining, planning, implementing, controlling and completing.

- The number and sequence of stages of a project will vary across organisations.

- Various **tools and techniques** are available to plan and control projects.

- Project **documentation** plays an important part in project control and communication.

- The mind-map following the quick quiz summarises the project management process.

Quick quiz

1   List five typical stages of a project.

2   What would you expect a Project Initiation Document to contain?

3   What is Work Breakdown Structure?

4   What is the purpose of a Gantt chart?

5   What is the project quality plan used for?

6   Why do many project managers prefer to use project management software?

7   Briefly outline the relationship between quality, cost and time in the context of an information systems project.

8   What should the risk management process achieve?

Answers to quick quiz

1   Defining, Planning, Implementing, Controlling, Completing.

2   Contents could include: Project objectives, the scope of the project, overall budget, final deadlines, the ultimate customer, resources, risks inherent in the project, a preliminary project plan (targets, activities and so on) and details of how the project is to be organised and managed.

3   Work Breakdown Structure (WBS) is the process of breaking down the project into manageable tasks.

4   A Gantt chart displays the time relationships between tasks in a project. It is a horizontal bar chart used to estimate the amount and timing of resources required.

5   The Project Quality Plan is used to guide both project execution and project control. It outlines how the project will be planned, monitored and implemented.

6   A project management software package saves time and produces high quality output. As with all software, it is dependant on the quality of the data fed into the package - the length of time required for each activity of the project, the logical relationships between each activity, the resources available and when the resources are available.

7   The quality of information system produced is dependant upon (among other things) the time available to develop the system and the resources (ie cost) available to the project. Insufficient time and / or resources will have an adverse effect on the quality of system produced.

8   The risk management process should identify and quantify the risks associated with the project, and decide on how the risks should be managed.

The material covered in this Chapter is tested in Questions 1(b)(ii), 4(d), 4(e), 10(b) and 14 in the Exam Question Bank.

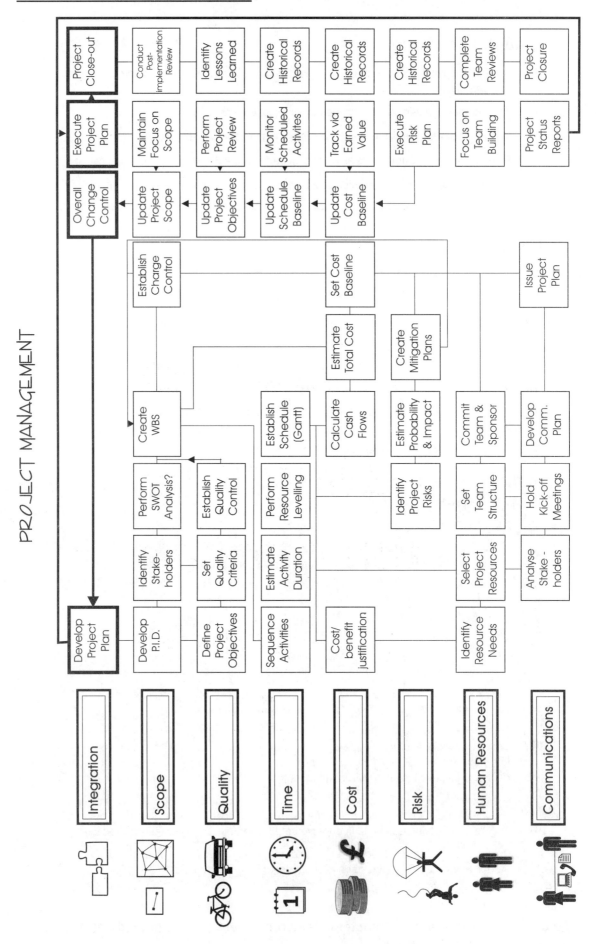

Part B
Designing information systems

Chapter 6

THE INFORMATION SYSTEMS DEVELOPMENT PROCESS

Topic list	Syllabus reference
1 Systems development lifecycles	2(a), 3(i)
2 The waterfall approach	2(a)
3 The spiral approach	2(a)
4 Systems development methodologies	2(a)
5 Software support for the systems development process	2(f), 2(i)
6 User involvement	2(a)

Introduction

In this chapter we consider the approaches to systems development which may be used on Information Systems projects. These approaches are often referred to as lifecycle models. The two approaches we look at in detail are those identified in the ACCA Study Guide; the waterfall approach and the spiral approach.

Later we look at how methodologies can assist the development process. The chapter concludes by exploring the impact of software development tools.

Study guide

Part 2.10 – The information system development process

- Define the participants in the systems development process

- Describe the waterfall approach to systems development and identify its application in a representative systems development methodology

- Describe the spiral approach to systems development and identify its application in a representative systems development methodology

- Discuss the relative merits of the waterfall and spiral approaches including an understanding of hybrid approaches that include elements of both

Part 2.15 – External design

- Explain how prototyping may be used in defining external design

Part 2.18 – Software support for the systems development process

- Define a CASE tool and give a brief list of representative products
- Describe a range of features and functions that a CASE tool may provide
- Explain the advantages of using a CASE tool in the systems development process
- Define a Fourth Generation Language and give a brief list of representative products
- Describe a range of features and functions that a Fourth Generation Language may provide
- Explain how a Fourth Generation Language contributes to the prototyping process

BPP PUBLISHING

1 SYSTEMS DEVELOPMENT LIFECYCLES

KEY TERM

The term '**systems development lifecycle**' describes the stages a system moves through from inception until it is discarded or replaced.

1.1 In the context of information systems projects a **distinction** can be made between the **project lifecycle** and the **systems development lifecycle**. As a project has a definite end it is unlikely that **ongoing maintenance** would be included in the scope of a project, but falls within our definition of the system development lifecycle.

1.2 In the early days of computing, systems development was **piecemeal**, involving automation of existing procedures rather than forming part of a planned strategy. The development of systems was **not properly planned**. The consequences were often poorly designed systems, which cost too much to make and which were not suited to users' needs.

1.3 This led to the development of systems development lifecycle models. Among the first models was that developed by the National Computing Centre in the 1960s. This **disciplined approach** to systems development identified several stages of development.

Stage	Comment
Identification of a problem or opportunity	This involves an analysis of the organisation's information requirements.
Feasibility study	This involves a review of the existing system and the identification of a range of possible alternative solutions. A feasible (technical, operational, economic, social) solution will be selected – or a decision not to proceed made. We look at the feasibility study in greater detail later in Chapter 7.
Systems investigation	A fact finding exercise which investigates the existing system to assess its problems and requirements and to obtain details of data volumes, response times and other key indicators.
Systems analysis	Once the workings of the existing system have been documented, they can be analysed. This process examines why current methods are used, what alternatives might achieve the same, or better, results, and what performance criteria are required from a system.
Systems design	This is a technical phase which considers both computerised and manual procedures, addressing, in particular, inputs, outputs, program design, file design and security. A detailed specification of the new system is produced.

Stage	Comment
Systems implementation	This stage carries development through from design to operations. It involves acquisition (or writing) of software, program testing, file conversion or set-up, acquisition and installation of hardware and 'going live'.
Review and maintenance	This is an ongoing process which ensures that the system meets the objectives set during the feasibility study, that it is accepted by users and that its performance is satisfactory.

1.4   In the early 1970s a similar systems development lifecycle model was published by *Royce* - the waterfall model. The sequential approach described by the National Computing Centre and the waterfall model is sometimes referred to as the '**traditional approach**'.

2   THE WATERFALL MODEL

2.1   *Royce's* waterfall model (like the National Computing Centre model) breaks the systems development process into sequential stages – with the output from a stage forming the input to the following stage. The model is shown below.

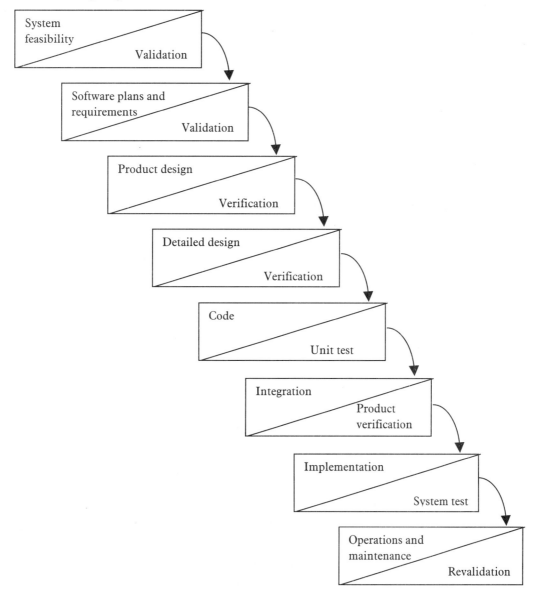

2.2 As shown on the diagram, each stage is divided into two parts – the actual work associated with the stage followed by a procedure to check what has been done. **Verification** in this context is concerned with ensuring required specifications have been met ('Have we built the system in the correct way?'). **Validation** is concerned with ensuring the system is fit for its operational role ('Have we built the correct product?').

2.3 The term 'waterfall model' is now used to describe any system development model that is made up of a number of sequential stages – regardless of the name given to the stages. It works reasonably well where the system requirements are well understood by users and developers.

Drawbacks of the waterfall approach

2.4 The waterfall approach is an efficient means of computerising existing procedures within easily defined processing requirements. It produces systems modelled on the manual systems they are replacing.

2.5 Sequential models restricted user input throughout much of the process. This often resulted in substantial and costly modifications late in the development process. It becomes increasingly difficult and expensive to change system requirements the further a system is developed.

2.6 Time overruns were the norm. The sequential nature of the process meant a hold-up on one stage would stop development completely – contributing to time overruns. Time pressures and lack of user involvement often resulted in a poor quality system and blame for the developers.

2.7 Operations and maintenance are treated as if the activity had a distinct start and end. Maintenance is in fact on-going and open-ended. *Birrel* and *Ould* devised **The 'b' model** to address this issue.

The 'b' model

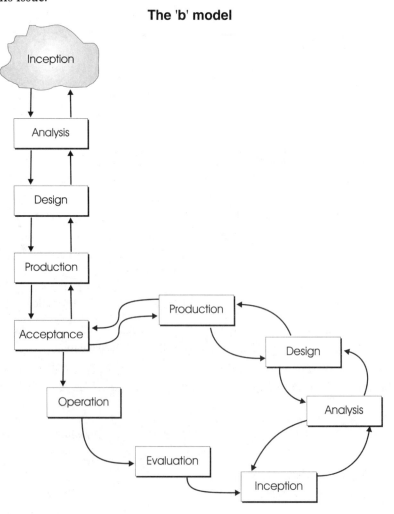

2.8 The 'b' model shows that enhancements or changes to the system (ie system maintenance) are made through a series of cycles that follow the same sequence as the original system development. Each change will go through the stages of feasibility, analysis, design production and operation.

3 THE SPIRAL MODEL

3.1 When developing systems where requirements are difficult to specify it is unrealistic to follow a sequential process which relies on getting things correct at each stage of development before starting subsequent activities. In these more complex situations the spiral approach is appropriate.

3.2 The spiral model represents an evolutionary approach to systems development. It involves carrying out the same activities over a number of cycles in order to clarify requirements and solutions.

3.3 The first spiral model was developed by *Boehm*. The model is shown below.

Boehm's spiral model

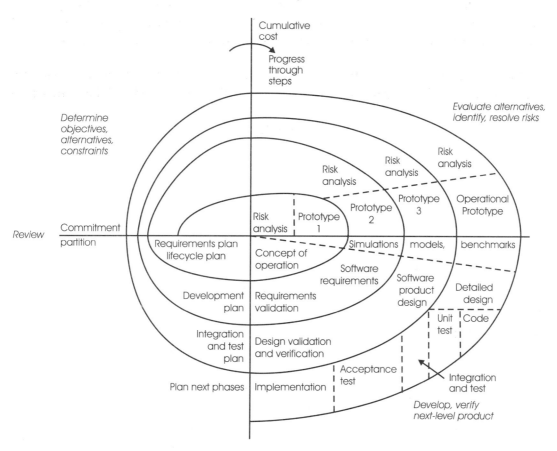

3.4 The development process starts at the centre of the spiral. At the centre requirements are not well defined. System requirements are refined with each rotation around the spiral. The longer the spiral, the more complex the system and the greater the cost.

3.5 The model is divided into four quadrants.

(a) Top left

- Objectives determined
- Risks identified and resolved

    (b) Top right

- Alternatives evaluated
- Risks identified and resolved

    (c) Bottom right

- System development
- Covers the activities described in the waterfall model (including implementation)

    (d) Bottom left

- The next phase in the development process is planned

3.6   Boehm's spiral model of system development includes the processes of objective setting and risk management that we have previously identified as key elements of project management.

3.7   The spiral approach aims to avoid the problems of the waterfall model (lack of user involvement, long delays). It is usually used in conjunction with prototyping which we look at later in this chapter.

4   SYSTEMS DEVELOPMENT METHODOLOGIES

4.1   Another way to facilitate systems development is to use a systems development methodology.

> **KEY TERM**
>
> A systems development **'methodology'** is a collection of procedures, techniques, tools and documentation aids which will help systems developers in their efforts to implement a new information system.

Characteristics of methodologies *Quality Assurance Process*

Defines

Characteristic	Comment
Separation of logical and physical	The initial focus is on business benefits – on what the system will achieve (the logical design).
	Physical design and implementation issues are looked at later.
User involvement	User's information requirements determine the type of data collected or captured by the system.
	Users are involved throughout the development process.
Diagramatic documentation	Diagrams rather than text-based documentation are used as much as possible to ensure the focus is on what the system is trying to achieve – and to aid user understanding of the process.
Data driven	Most structured methods focus on data items regardless of the processes they are related to.
	The type of data within an organisation is less likely to change than either the processes which operate on it or the output information required of it.
Defined structure	Most methodologies prescribe a consistent structure to ensure a consistent and complete approach to the work. For example, the Structured Systems Analysis and Design Method (**SSDAM**) suggests five modules: Feasibility, Requirements Analysis, Requirements Specification, Logical Systems Specification and Physical Design.

4.2 *Jayaratna* (*Understanding and Evaluating Methodologies*, 1994) estimates that there are **over 1,000 brand named methodologies** in use in the world. The Structured Systems Analysis and Design Method (**SSDAM**) was originally designed for use by the UK Government in 1980 – but is now widely used in many areas of business.

4.3 All methodologies seek to facilitate the '**best**' solution. But 'best' may be interpreted in a number of ways, such as **most rapid** or **least cost** systems. Some methodologies are highly **prescriptive** and require rigid adherence to stages whilst others are highly **adaptive** allowing for creative use of their components.

4.4 In choosing the **most appropriate methodology**, an organisation must consider the following questions.

- How **open** is the system?
- To what extent does the methodology facilitate **participation**?
- Does it generate **alternative solutions**?
- Is it **well documented, tried, tested and proven** to work?
- Can **component** 'tools' be selected and used as required?
- Will it benefit from **computer aided tools** and **prototyping**?

4.5 Ultimately it is important to remember that whilst methodologies may be valuable in the development their use is a matter of great skill and experience. They **do not, by themselves, produce good systems solutions**.

Advantages and disadvantages

4.6 The **advantages** of using a methodology are as follows.

(a) Detailed **documentation** is produced.

(b) **Standard methods** allow less qualified staff to carry out some of the analysis work, thus **cutting the cost** of the exercise.

(c) Using a standard development process leads to **improved system specifications**.

(d) Systems developed in this way are **easier to maintain and improve**.

(e) **Users are involved** with development work from an early stage and are required to sign off each stage.

(f) The emphasis on **diagramming** makes it easier for relevant parties, including users, to **understand** the system than if purely narrative descriptions were used.

(g) The structured framework of a methodology **helps with planning**. It defines the tasks to be performed, sets out when they should be done and identifies an end product. This allows control by reference to actual achievements rather than to estimates of progress.

(h) A logical design is produced that is **independent of hardware and software**.

(i) Techniques such as data flow diagrams, logical data structures and entity life histories **allow information to be cross-checked** between diagrams and ensure that the system delivered does what is required. These techniques are explained in this Chapter 7.

4.7 The use of a methodology in systems development also has **disadvantages**.

(a) It has been argued that methodologies are ideal for analysing and documenting processes and data items at an operational level, but are perhaps **inappropriate for information of a strategic nature** that is collected on an ad hoc basis.

(b) Some are a little **too limited in scope**, being too concerned with systems design, and not with their impact on actual work processes or social context of the system.

(c) Arguably, methodologies encourage excessive documentation and **bureaucracy** and are just as suitable for documenting bad design as good.

5 SOFTWARE SUPPORT FOR THE SYSTEMS DEVELOPMENT PROCESS

5.1 There are a number of software tools that can be used to facilitate systems development process. We will examine three of the most widely used software tools – CASE tools, fourth generation languages and prototypes.

Computer aided software engineering (CASE)

5.2 CASE techniques aim to automate the document production process, and to ensure automation of some of the design operation.

> **KEY TERM**
>
> A **CASE tool** is a software package that supports the construction and maintenance of logical system models. The more sophisticated tools facilitate software prototyping and code generation.

5.3 There are two types of CASE tool: analysts' workbenches and programmers' workbenches.

Analysts' workbenches

5.4 These are software which perform several analysis tasks.

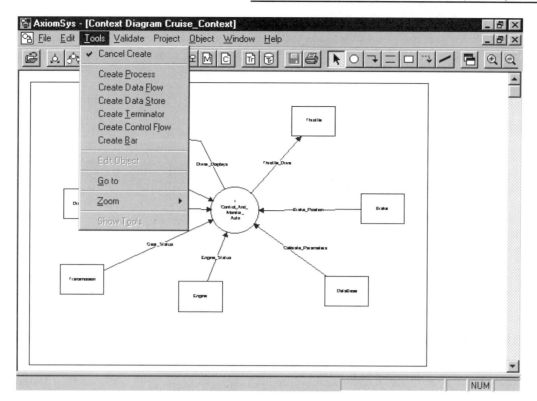

(a) **Create design diagrams on screen**

High quality documentation can be produced, and **very easily updated**. Maintenance of complex models such as data flow diagrams and entity-relationship models is made easy. The diagramming facilities are used with a mouse, in a manner similar to most graphics packages.

Tool-kits come with a bank of **pre-designed symbols** including those used in flowcharts and data flow diagrams and, like graphics packages, allow on-screen editing.

(b) **Check adherence to design and development standards**

Standards define how development will be carried out. A CASE tool will **not allow designers to break rules** (such as not linking a data store directly to an external entity) that they could easily break accidentally if working manually.

(c) **Consistencies and relationships**

CASE tools can verify that diagrams are **consistent** with each other and that the **relationships** are correct.

(d) **Documentation**

CASE tools can help generate **specimen input and output documentation** (ie from the data flows identified in the diagrams).

(e) **Data dictionaries**

CASE tools can create a logical data dictionary from the items identified. Entries will be made for entities, data flows, data stores, processes, external entities and individual data items and the dictionary can be **easily maintained**, checked for **consistency, cross-referenced** and analysed. For example it will be possible to produce a listing of all the data flows where a particular data item is used, or cross reference the entities of the entity relationship diagram to the data stores of the DFD.

Programmers' workbenches

5.5 These provide similar features to ensure **consistency of coding** during the later stages of the design cycle.

(a) There is usually a **code-generator facility** to automate the production of code in a high level language from, say, Structured English.

(b) **Diagnostic aids** enable subroutines to be tested independently of other programs.

(c) A library of **subroutines** is also provided. These are **often-repeated procedures** which can be incorporated into programs.

Advantages of CASE

5.6 Advantages of CASE include the following.

(a) The drudgery is taken out of **document preparation** and **re-drawing of diagrams** is made easier.

(b) **Accuracy of diagrams** is improved. Diagram drawers can ensure consistency of terminology and maintain certain standards of documentation.

(c) **Prototyping** (see later in this section) is made easier, as re-design can be effected very quickly and the models are always consistent with the actual system.

(d) **Blocks of code can be re-used**. Many applications incorporate similar functions and processes; blocks of software can be retained in a library and used (or modified) as appropriate.

5.7 Two examples of CASE tools are **Teamwork** from Cadre and **Select SSADM Professional** from Select Software Tools. Teamwork is designed for use with the UNIX operating system while Select SSADM Professional is a low-cost, PC/Windows-based application.

Fourth generation languages (4GLs)

Background

5.8 A **programming language** is neither the 'normal' written language of humans, nor is it usually the machine code language of computers.

(a) A computer can only deal with data and program instructions which are in **binary form** (the 1 and 0 corresponding to the on and off states of a transistor). Every program must be in a computer's **machine code** before the computer can interpret it.

(b) A program in a programming language, however, can be translated into **machine code**. Programming languages are **easier for humans to use**, being more condensed and displaying a logic that humans can understand.

5.9 **Assembly languages** were a subsequent development from machine code. They are also machine specific, but the task of learning and writing the language is made easier than with machine language because they are **written in symbolic form**. Instead of using machine code operation numbers, the programmer is able to use easily learned and understood operation mnemonics (for example, ADD, SUB and MULT).

5.10 Machine code and assembly languages are sometimes known collectively as **low-level languages**.

5.11 To overcome the low-level language difficulty of machine dependency, high-level (or machine independent) languages were developed. Such programming languages, with an extensive vocabulary of words and symbols are used to instruct a computer to carry out the necessary procedures, regardless of the type of machine being used. Some examples of **high-level languages,** also known as **third-generation languages** are **COBOL, Pascal, C, C++** and **Java.**

4GLs

5.12 A fourth generation language is a programming language that is easier to use than languages like COBOL, PASCAL and C++. Well known examples include **Informix** and **Powerhouse.**

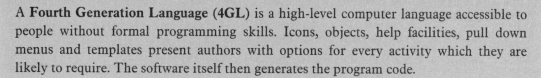

> **KEY TERM**
>
> A **Fourth Generation Language (4GL)** is a high-level computer language accessible to people without formal programming skills. Icons, objects, help facilities, pull down menus and templates present authors with options for every activity which they are likely to require. The software itself then generates the program code.

5.13 Most fourth generation systems use a mixture of text and graphics, often a **graphical user interface.** A fourth generation system should have the following features.

  (a) It should be **easy to learn** and use.
  (b) It should contain **on-line 'help'** facility for users.
  (c) It should be usable **interactively.**
  (d) It should be **'fault' tolerant** (ie any mistakes in data entry should be dealt with easily).
  (e) It should be suitable for **document design** work.

5.14 The basis of 4GLs is the recognition that **many of the functions** such as data input, sorting, searching, file management, report writing and the like are **quite similar** in operation even when these program segments are found in quite different applications programs.

Advantages and disadvantages of a fourth generation language

5.15 **Advantages**

  (a) It enhances **end-user computing,** so limiting the work of IS staff.

  (b) It taps user **creativity.**

  (c) It **diffuses IT** throughout the organisation.

  (d) It vastly increases programmer **productivity,** even though it uses more hardware resources.

5.16 **Disadvantages**

  (a) The information systems department might get overloaded by **training** requirements.

  (b) Programs written in a 4GL make **less efficient use of computer processing power** and memory. This can have the effect of slowing down the execution of a program to unacceptable levels.

BPP PUBLISHING

Case example: Informix

The following is an extract from marketing material on the Informix website.

The INFORMIX-4GL Product Family, comprised of INFORMIX-4GL Rapid Development System, INFORMIX-4GL Interactive Debugger, and INFORMIX-4GL Compiler, is a comprehensive fourth-generation application development and production environment that provides power and flexibility without the need for third-generation languages like C or COBOL. INFORMIX-4GL version 4.1 provides more enhancements to the product line than any other release since 4GL was introduced in 1986 giving you more functionality than ever before!

Wouldn't you like to find a self-contained application development environment that:

- Provides rapid development and interactive debugging capabilities
- Offers high performance in the production environment
- Integrates all the functionality you could possibly need for building even the most complex applications
- Doesn't require the use of a third-generation language
- Allows you to easily maintain your applications for years to come
- Is based on industry-standard SQL
- Is easily portable?

Look no further. You've just described INFORMIX-4GL.

Whether you're building menus, forms, screens, or reports, INFORMIX-4GL performs all development functions, and allows for easy integration between them, eliminating the need for external development packages. Because our INFORMIX-4GL products are source-code compatible, portability is ensured.

5.17 Some other successful 4th-generation languages are SQL, Focus, and Iris Explorer.

Prototyping

5.18 The use of 4GLs, together with the realisation that users need to see how a system will look and feel to assess its suitability, have contributed to the increased use of **prototyping**.

KEY TERM

A **prototype** is a model of all or part of a system, built to show users early in the design process how it will appear.

5.19 As a simple example, a prototype of a formatted screen output from a system could be prepared using a graphics package, or even a spreadsheet model. This would describe how the screen output would appear to the user. The user could make suggested amendments, which would be incorporated into the next model.

5.20 Using prototyping software, the programmer can develop **a working model of application program quickly**. He or she can then **check with the data user** whether the prototype program that has been designed appears to **meet the user's needs,** and if it doesn't it can be amended.

The prototyping process

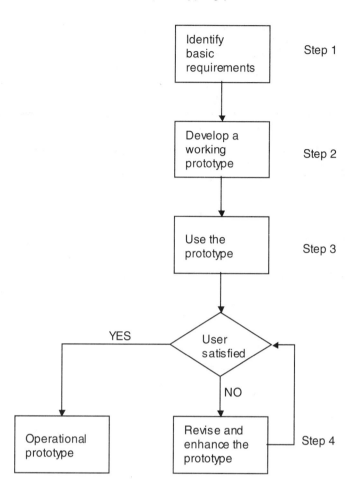

Advantages and disadvantages of prototyping

5.21 The **advantages** of prototyping.

(a) It makes it possible for programmers to present a 'mock-up' version of an envisaged system to users **before a substantial amount of time and money** have been committed. The user can judge the prototype before things have gone too far to be changed.

(b) The process facilitates the production of **'custom built' application software** rather than off-the-shelf packages which may or may not suit user needs.

(c) It makes **efficient use of programmer time** by helping programmers to develop programs more quickly. Prototyping may speed up the 'design' stage of the systems development lifecycle.

(d) A prototype does not necessarily have to be written in the language of what it is prototyping, so prototyping is not only a tool, but a **design technique**.

5.22 **Disadvantages** of prototyping.

(a) Many prototyping tools are **tied** to a particular make of **hardware**, or a particular **database system**.

(b) It is sometimes argued that prototyping tools are **inefficient** in the program codes they produce, so that programs are bigger and require more memory than a more efficiently coded program.

BPP
PUBLISHING

(c) Prototyping may help users to steer the development of a new system towards an **existing system**.

(d) Some believe prototyping tools encourage the production of **shoddy programs** at a high speed.

6 USER INVOLVEMENT

6.1 The importance of user involvement in the development process cannot be over-estimated. This section looks at a number of approaches intended to ensure that the required level of involvement is achieved.

Structured walkthroughs

6.2 Structured walkthroughs are a technique used (often in conjunction with SSADM) by those responsible for the design of some aspect of a system (particularly analysts and programmers) to present their design to interested **user groups** – in other words to 'walk' them through the design. Structured walkthroughs are **formal meetings**, in which the **documentation produced during development is reviewed and checked** for errors or omissions.

6.3 These presentations are used both to **introduce and explain** the new systems to users and also to offer the users the opportunity of **making constructive criticism** of the proposed systems, and suggestions for further amendments/improvements, before the final systems specification is agreed.

6.4 Users are involved in structured walkthroughs because their knowledge of the desired system is more extensive than that of the systems development personnel. Walkthroughs are sometimes referred to as **user validation**.

The importance of signing off work

6.5 At the end of each stage of development, the resulting output is presented to users for their approval. There must be a **formal sign-off** of each completed stage before work on the next stage begins.

6.6 This **minimises reworking**, as if work does not meet user requirements, only the immediately preceding stage must be revisited. More importantly, it clarifies responsibilities and leaves little room for later disputes.

(a) If the systems developers fail to deliver something that both parties formally agreed to, it is the **developers' responsibility** to put it right, at their own expense, and compensate the user for the delay.

(b) If users ask for something extra or different, that was not formally agreed to, the developers cannot be blamed and **the user must pay** for further amendments and be prepared to accept some delay.

Question 1

What, besides identification of mistakes (errors, omission, inconsistencies etc), would you expect the benefits of a walkthrough to be?

Answer

(a) Users become involved in the systems analysis process. Since this process is a critical appraisal of their work, they should have the opportunity to provide feedback on the appraisal itself.

(b) The output from the development is shown to people who are not systems development personnel. This encourages its originators to prepare it to a higher quality and in user-friendly form.

(c) Because the onus is on users to approve design, they are more likely to become committed to the new system and less likely to 'rubbish' it.

(d) The process focuses on quality of and good practice in operations generally.

(e) It avoids disputes about who is responsible for what.

Joint applications development

6.7 Joint Applications Development (JAD) describes the partnership between users and system developers.

6.8 JAD was originally developed by *IBM* to promote a more participative approach to systems development. The potential value to an organisation may be as follows.

(a) It creates a **pool of expertise** comprised of interested parties from all relevant functions.

(b) Reduced risk of systems being **imposed** by systems personnel.

(c) This **increases user ownership** and responsibility for systems solutions.

(d) Emphasises the **information needs of users** and their relationship to business needs and decision making.

6.9 There are a number of possible **risks** affecting the potential value of JAD.

(a) The relative **inexperience of many users** may lead to misunderstandings and possibly unreasonable expectations/demands on the system performance.

(b) The danger of **lack of co-ordination** leading to fragmented, individual, possibly esoteric information systems.

6.10 The shift of emphasis to applications development by end-users must be well managed and controlled. An organisation may wish to set up an **information centre** to provide the necessary support and co-ordination.

Rapid applications development

6.11 **Rapid Applications Development (RAD)** can be described as a quick way of building software. It combines a managed approach to systems development with the use of modern software tools such as **prototyping**. RAD also involves the **end-user** heavily in the development process.

6.12 RAD has become increasingly popular as the pace of change in business has increased. To develop systems that provide **competitive advantage** it is often necessary to build and implement the system quickly.

6.13 RAD can create **difficulties for the project manager** as RAD relies to a certain extent on a **lack of structure** and control.

User groups

6.14 User groups enable users to share ideas and experience relating to a particular product; usually a software package.

6.15 User groups can provide valuable insights and suggestions when system upgrades are being considered. We look at user groups in greater detail in Chapter 11.

Chapter roundup

- The term 'systems development lifecycle' describes the stages a system moves through from inception until it is discarded or replaced.

- Traditional lifecycle models such as *Royce's* waterfall model breaks the systems development process into sequential stages – with the output from a stage forming the input to the following stage.

- The spiral approach involves carrying out the same activities over a number of cycles in order to clarify requirements and solutions.

- A **methodology** is a collection of procedures, techniques, tools and documentation aids which are designed to help systems developers in their efforts to implement a new system. Methodologies are usually broken down into phases.

- A **CASE tool** may be used to support the construction and maintenance of a system model - often allowing the construction of a prototype.

- A **structured walkthrough** usually takes the form of a meeting in which the output from a phase or stage of development is presented to users for discussion and for formal approval.

- A **4GL** enables programs to be constructed more quickly, as English-like commands can be taken to produce high-level code.

- Prototyping enables programmers to write programs more quickly and allows the user to see a 'preview' of the system that is envisaged.

- **Joint Applications Development (JAD)** describes the partnership between users and developers.

- **Rapid Applications Development (RAD)** combines a less structured approach to systems development with the use of modern software tools such as prototyping.

Quick quiz

1 List the seven stages identified in the National Computing Centre systems development lifecycle model.

2 What is the key feature of the waterfall model?

3 What shortcoming of the waterfall model did the 'b' model address?

4 What is the key feature of the spiral model?

5 Define 'systems development methodology'.

6 What would a CASE tool be used for?

7 Explain one advantage of prototyping.

8 Distinguish between JAD and RAD.

Answers to quick quiz

1   Identification of a problem or opportunity, Feasibility study, Systems investigation, Systems analysis, Systems design, Systems implementation, Review and maintenance.

2   The waterfall model, like the National Computing Centre model, breaks the systems development process into sequential stages, with the output from a stage forming the input to the following stage.

3   The 'b' model recognised that operations and maintenance are on-going.

4   The spiral approach involves carrying out the same activities over a number of cycles in order to clarify requirements and solutions.

5   A systems development 'methodology' is a collection of procedures, techniques, tools and documentation aids which will help systems developers in their efforts to implement a new information system.

6   A CASE tool is used to aid with system design and program coding.

7   Prototyping makes it possible for developers to present a 'mock-up' version of the envisaged system without committing too much time and effort. Users can then suggest improvements which can be incorporated in the actual system.

8   Joint Applications Development (JAD) describes the partnership between users and system developers. **Rapid Applications Development (RAD) is** a quick way of building software. It combines a managed approach to systems development with the use of modern software tools such as **prototyping** and **object oriented design methods**. As RAD involves the **end-user** heavily in the development process it is one example of JAD.

The material covered in this Chapter is tested in Question 1(a) in the Exam Question Bank.

BPP PUBLISHING

Chapter 7

SYSTEM FEASIBILITY AND MODELLING

Topic list	Syllabus reference
1 The feasibility study	1(e)
2 Investment appraisal techniques	1(e)
3 Investigating user requirements	2(b)
4 Documenting and modelling techniques	2(c), 2(d), 2(e)
5 Other system design issues	2(c), 2(d), 2(e)

Introduction

We start this chapter with a closer look at the **purpose and objectives of a feasibility study**, before moving on to examine some **common techniques of systems investigation**, including the use of **interviews** and **questionnaires**.

In the second half of the chapter we demonstrate the recording and **documenting tools** used during the analysis and design of information systems.

Study guide

Part 1.5 – Feasibility study

- Explain the purpose and objectives of a feasibility study
- Evaluate the technical, operational, social and economic feasibility of the proposed project
- Describe and categorise the benefits and costs of the proposed project
- Apply appropriate investment appraisal techniques to determine the economic feasibility of a project
- Define the typical content and structure of a feasibility study report

Part 2.11 – Investigating and recording user requirements

- Define the tasks of planning, undertaking and documenting a user interview
- Identify the potential role of background research, questionnaires and special purpose surveys in the definition of requirements
- Explain the potential use of prototyping in the requirements definition
- Explain how requirements can be collected from current computerised information systems
- Discuss the problems users have in defining, agreeing and prioritising requirements

Part 2.12 – Documenting and modelling user requirements – processes

- Describe the need for building a business process model of user requirements
- Briefly describe different approaches to modelling the business processes
- Describe in detail the notation of one of these business process models
- Construct a business process model of narrative user requirements using this notation
- Explain the role of process models in the systems development process

Study guide (continued)

Part 2.13 – Documenting and modelling user requirements – static structures

- Describe the need for building a business structure model of user requirements
- Briefly describe different approaches to modelling the business structure
- Describe in detail the notation of one of these business structure models
- Construct a business structure model of narrative user requirements using this notation
- Explain the role of structure models in the systems development process

Part 2.14 – Documenting and modelling user requirements – events

- Describe the need for building a business event model of user requirements
- Briefly describe different approaches to modelling the business events
- Describe in detail the notation of one of these business event models
- Construct a business event model of narrative user requirements using this notation
- Explain the role of event models in the systems development process

Exam guide

It is likely that the examination will require you to model a process, structure or event. The purpose and conduct of a feasibility study are also likely exam topics.

1   THE FEASIBILITY STUDY

KEY TERM

A **feasibility study** is a formal study to decide what type of system can be developed which best meets the needs of the organisation.

The feasibility study team

1.1   A feasibility study team should be appointed to carry out the study (although individuals might be given the task in the case of smaller projects).

(a)   Members of the team should be drawn from the **departments affected by the project.**

(b)   At least one person must have a **detailed knowledge of computers and systems design** (in a small concern it may be necessary to bring in a systems analyst from outside.

(c)   At least one person should have a **detailed knowledge of the organisation** and in particular of the workings and staff of the departments affected. Managers with direct knowledge of how the current system operates will know what the **information needs** of the system are, and whether any proposed new system (for example an off-the-shelf software package) will do everything that is wanted. They are also most likely to be in a position to recognise **improvements that can be made in the current system.**

(d)   It is possible to hire **consultants** to carry out the feasibility study, but their **lack of knowledge about the organisation** may adversely affect the usefulness of their proposals.

(e)   Before selecting the members of the study group, the steering committee must ensure that they possess **suitable personal qualities,** eg the ability to be **objectively critical.**

(f) All members of the study group should ideally have some knowledge of information technology and systems design. They should also be encouraged to read as widely as possible and take an **active interest in current innovations.**

1.2 With larger projects it may well be worthwhile for a small firm to employ a **professional systems analyst** and then appoint a management team to work with the analyst.

Identifying and selecting IS projects

1.3 A planned approach is needed when identifying and selecting new information systems projects. The following actions should be considered.

(a) IS projects almost always utilise IT. IT is critical to the success of many organisations. This means that an **IT strategy** should form a **core part of the overall corporate strategy** and should be developed/updated whenever the organisation's strategy is reviewed or as otherwise necessary. IT needs can then be identified in the context of **overall business needs**.

(b) Because IT is critical, it requires adequate **representation at senior management level.** It is no longer suitable for IT to be under the control of the MD, FD or computer centre manager. It really needs a separate Board level person responsible, such as an **Information Director** or an **IS director**. This will help to ensure that IT is given adequate consideration at strategic level.

(c) The IT development can no longer function as a subsystem of accounting, administration or finance. It should be given **separate departmental or functional status** in the organisation with its own reporting lines and responsibilities.

(d) Once the IT department has been set up, its **funding** must be considered. A simplistic approach would be to treat it as an overhead; this is simple but inefficient. There are various approaches possible to the recovery of IT costs from user departments, and the IT department may even operate as a commercial concern providing services to third parties at a profit.

(e) A **strategic plan for the use of IT** should be developed. This should take in separate elements such as information technology and information systems. It should also acknowledge the importance of the organisation's information resource.

(f) If new computer systems are to be introduced regularly, the organisation may set up a **steering committee** to oversee **systems development**. A steering committee can also be set up for a one-off project. The role of the steering committee includes approving or rejecting individual projects and where appropriate submitting projects to the Board for approval. The composition and determination of terms of reference for the steering committee must be agreed.

(g) The **approach** of the organisation to individual projects must be decided. Will it follow the traditional **life cycle** or will it use a **methodology**? Commercial methodologies impose discipline and have a number of advantages.

(h) Procedures for **evaluating and monitoring performance** both during and after a project need to be put in place. Many methodologies require formal sign-off of each stage, but this does not obviate the need for good project management or for post-implementation evaluation.

(i) Details of the **systems development procedures** must be agreed. If a commercial methodology is used, much of this will be pre-determined, but, for example, decisions must be made on the approach to **feasibility studies**, methods of **cost-benefit analysis**, **design specifications** and conventions, **tools and techniques** which will be used, **reporting** lines, contents of standard **invitations to tender**, drawing up of **supplier conditions** and procedures for **testing and implementation**.

Conducting the feasibility study

1.4 Some of the work performed at the feasibility study stage may be similar to work performed later on in the development of the project. This is because some of the information necessary to decide whether to go ahead with a project or trying to define a problem is common to both phases.

1.5 **Reasons for having a feasibility study** include that new systems can:

(a) Be complicated and **cost** a great deal to develop.

(b) Be **disruptive** during development and implementation (eg staff and management time).

(c) Have **far reaching consequences** in a way an organisation conducts its business or is structured.

Terms of reference

1.6 The terms of reference for a feasibility study group may be set out by a steering committee, the information director or the board of directors, and might consist of:

(a) To **investigate** and report on an **existing system**, its procedures and costs.
(b) To define the **systems requirements**.
(c) To establish whether these requirements are being met by the **existing** system.
(d) To establish whether they could be met by an **alternative** system.
(e) To specify **performance criteria** for the system.
(f) To recommend the **most suitable system** to meet the system's objectives.
(g) To prepare a detailed **cost budget**, within a specified budget limit.
(h) To prepare a draft **plan for implementation** within a specified timescale.
(i) To establish whether the hoped-for **benefits** could be realised.
(j) To establish a detailed design, implementation and operating **budget**.
(k) To **compare** the detailed budget with the costs of the current system.
(l) To set the **date** by which the study group must **report back**.
(m) To decide which **operational managers** should be approached by the study group.

1.7 The remit of a feasibility study may be narrow or wide. The feasibility study team must engage in a substantial effort of fact finding. These facts may include matters relevant to the project which are not necessarily of a data processing nature.

Problem definition

1.8 In some circumstances the '**problem**' (for example the necessity for a real-time as opposed to a batch processed application) may be quite **exact**, in others it may be characterised as '**soft**' (related to people and the way they behave).

1.9 The problem definition stage should result in the production of a set of documents which define the problem.

(a) A set of **diagrams** representing, in overview:

(i) The current physical flows of data in the organisation (**documents**).

(ii) The activities underlying them (**data flows**).

(b) A description of all the people, jobs, activities and so on (**entities**) that make up the system, and their relationship to one another.

(c) The **problems/requirements** list established from the terms of reference and after consultation with users.

The problems/requirements list

1.10 The problems/requirements list or catalogue can cover, amongst other things, the following areas.

(a) The data **input** to the current system.

(b) The nature of the **output** information (contents, timing etc).

(c) Methods of **processing**.

(d) The expected **growth** of the organisation and so **future volumes** of processing.

(e) The systems **control** in operation.

(f) **Staffing** arrangements and organisational **structure**.

(g) The **operational costs** of the system.

(h) **Type of system** (batch, on-line).

(i) **Response times**.

(j) Current organisational **problems**.

Option evaluation

1.11 This stage involves suggesting a number of **options** for a new system, evaluating them and recommending one for adoption. It concludes with a final **feasibility study report**.

Step 1. Create the **base constraints** in terms of expenditure, implementation and design time, and system requirements, which any system should satisfy.

(a) **Operations** (for example faster processing, larger volumes, greater security, greater accuracy, better quality, real-time as opposed to other forms of processing).

(b) Information **output** (quality, frequency, presentation, eg GUIs, database for managers, EIS facilities).

(c) **Volume of processing**.

(d) **General system requirements** (eg accuracy, security and controls, audit trail, flexibility, adaptability).

(e) **Compatibility/integration** with existing systems.

Step 2. Create outlines of **project options**, describing, in brief, each option. The number will vary depending on the complexity of the problem, or the size of the application, but is typically between three and six.

Step 3. Assess the **impact** each proposal has on the work of the relevant user department and/or the organisation as a whole.

Step 4. **Review** these proposals with users, who should indicate those options they favour for further analysis.

System justification

1.12 A new system should not be recommended unless it can be justified. The justification for a new system would have to come from:

(a) An evaluation of the **costs and benefits** of the proposed system, and/or
(b) Other **performance criteria**.

Areas of feasibility

1.13 There are four key areas in which a project must be feasible if it is to be selected.

- Technical feasibility
- Operational feasibility
- Social feasibility
- Economic feasibility

Technical feasibility

1.14 The requirements, as defined in the feasibility study, must be technically achievable. This means that any proposed solution must be capable of being implemented using available **hardware, software and other equipment**. The type of requirement which might depend for success on technical feasibility might be one of the following.

(a) **Volume** of transactions which can be processed within a given time.
(b) **Capacity** to hold files or records of a certain size.
(c) **Response times** (how quickly the computer does what you ask it to).
(d) **Number of users** which can be supported without deterioration in the other criteria.

Operational feasibility

1.15 Operational feasibility is a key concern. If a solution makes technical sense but **conflicts with the way the organisation does business**, the solution is not feasible. Thus an organisation might reject a solution because it forces a change in management responsibilities, status and chains of command, or does not suit regional reporting structures, or because the costs of redundancies, retraining and reorganisation are considered too high.

Social feasibility

1.16 An assessment of social feasibility will address a number of areas, including the following.
- **Personnel** policies
- Redrawing of **job specifications**
- Threats to **industrial relations**
- Expected **skills requirements**
- **Motivation**

Economic feasibility

1.17 Any project will have economic costs and economic benefits. Economic feasibility has three strands.

(a) The **benefits must justify the costs**.

(b) The project must be the **'best' option** from those under consideration for its particular purpose.

(c) The project must **compete with projects in other areas of the business** for funds. Even if it is projected to produce a positive return and satisfies all relevant criteria, it may not be chosen because other business needs are perceived as more important.

Costs and benefits

1.18 **Cost-benefit analysis** before or during the development of information systems is complicated by the fact that many of the system cost elements are **poorly defined** (particularly for development projects) and that benefits can often be highly qualitative and subjective in nature.

The costs of a proposed system

1.19 In general the best cost estimates will be obtained for systems bought from an **outside vendor** who provides a cost quotation against a specification. Less concrete cost estimates are generally found with development projects where the work is performed by the organisation's own employees.

1.20 The costs of a new system will include costs in a number of different categories.

Cost	Example
Equipment costs	• Computer and peripherals • Ancillary equipment • The initial system supplies (disks, tapes, paper etc)
Installation costs	• New buildings (if necessary) • The computer room (wiring, air-conditioning if necessary)
Development costs	These include costs of measuring and analysing the existing system and costs of looking at the new system. They include software/consultancy work and systems analysis and programming. Changeover costs, particularly file conversion, may be very considerable.
Personnel costs	• Staff training • Staff recruitment/relocation • Staff salaries and pensions • Redundancy payments • Overheads
Operating costs	• Consumable materials (tapes, disks, stationery etc) • Maintenance • Accommodation costs • Heating/power/insurance/telephone • Standby arrangements, in case the system breaks down

Capital and revenue costs

1.21 The distinction between capital costs and revenue costs is important.

(a) The costs-benefit analysis of a system ought to include **cash flows and DCF**.

(b) The annual charge against profits shown in the financial accounts is of interest to **stakeholders.**

1.22 Capital items will be capitalised and then depreciated, and revenue items will be expensed as incurred as a regular annual cost.

1.23 In practice, **accounting treatment** of such development costs may **vary widely** between organisations depending on their accounting policies and on agreement with their auditors.

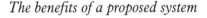

Question 1

Draw up a table with three headings: capital cost items, one-off revenue cost items and regular annual costs. Identify at least three items to be included under each heading. You may wish to refer back to the preceding paragraphs for examples of costs.

Answer

Capital cost items	'One-off' revenue cost items	Regular annual costs
Hardware purchase costs	Consultancy fees	Operating staff salaries/wages
Software purchase costs	Systems analysts' and programmers' salaries	Data transmission costs
Purchase of accommodation (if needed)	Costs of testing the system (staff costs, consumables)	Consumable materials
Installation costs (new desks, cables, physical storage etc)	Costs of converting the files for the new system	Power
		Maintenance costs
	Staff recruitment fees	Cost of standby arrangements
		Ongoing staff training

The benefits of a proposed system

1.24 The benefits from a proposed new system must also be evaluated. These ought to consist of benefits of several types.

   (a) **Savings** because the **old system** will no longer be operated. The savings should include:

   (i) Savings in **staff costs.**
   (ii) Savings in **other operating costs,** such as consumable materials.

   (b) Extra **savings** or revenue benefits because of the improvements or enhancements that the **new system** should bring:

   (i) Possibly **more sales revenue** and so additional contribution.

   (ii) **Better stock control** (with a new stock control system) and so fewer stock losses from obsolescence and deterioration.

   (iii) Further savings in **staff time,** resulting perhaps in reduced future staff growth.

   (c) Possibly, some one-off revenue benefits from the **sale of equipment** which the existing system uses, but which will no longer be required. Second-hand computer equipment does not have a high value, however! It is also possible that the new system will use **less office space,** and so there will be benefits from selling or renting the spare accommodation.

1.25 Some benefits might be **intangible,** or impossible to give a money value to.

   (a) Greater **customer satisfaction,** arising from a more prompt service (eg because of a computerised sales and delivery service).

   (b) Improved **staff morale** from working with a 'better' system.

(c) **Better decision making** is hard to quantify, but may result from better MIS, DSS or EIS.

2 INVESTMENT APPRAISAL TECHNIQUES

2.1 There are three principal methods of evaluating the economic viability of a project.

Method	Comment
Payback period	This method of investment appraisal calculates the length of time a project will take to recoup the initial investment; in other words how long a project will take to pay for itself. The method is based on **cash flows**.
Accounting rate of return	This method, also called **return on investment**, calculates the profits that will be earned by a project and expresses this as a percentage of the capital invested in the project. The higher the rate of return, the higher a project is ranked. This method is based on **accounting** results rather than cash flows.
Discounted cash flow (DCF)	This is a method which may be sub-divided into two approaches. (a) **Net present value (NPV)**, which considers all relevant cash flows associated with a project over the whole of its life and adjusts those occurring in future years to 'present value' by discounting at a rate called the 'cost of capital'. (b) **Internal rate of return (IRR)**, which involves comparing the rate of return expected from the project calculated on a discounted cash flow basis with the rate used as the cost of capital. Projects with an IRR higher than the cost of capital are worth undertaking.

2.2 Before looking at each of these methods in turn it is worth considering one **problem** common to all of them, that of **uncertainty**. Estimating **future** cash flows and other benefits cannot be done with complete accuracy, particularly as the future period under consideration may as long as five or even ten years.

2.3 It is therefore important that decision makers should consider how **variations** in the estimates **might affect their decision**.

The payback method

> **KEY TERM**
>
> The **payback period** is the length of time required before the total cash inflows received from the project is equal to the original cash outlay. In other words, it is the length of time the investment takes to pay itself back.

2.4 EXAMPLE: PAYBACK

The payback method has obvious disadvantages. Consider the case of two projects for which the following information is available.

	Project P £	Project Q £
Cost	100,000	100,000
Cash savings		
Year 1	10,000	50,000
2	20,000	50,000
3	60,000	10,000
4	70,000	5,000
5	80,000	5,000
	240,000	120,000

2.5 SOLUTION

Project Q pays back at the end of year two and Project P not until early in year four. Using the payback method Project Q is to be preferred, but this ignores the fact that the total profitability of Project P (£240,000) is double that of Q.

2.6 Despite the disadvantages of the payback method it is **widely used in practice**, though often only as a **supplement** to more sophisticated methods.

2.7 Besides being simple to calculate and understand, the argument in its favour is that its use will tend to **minimise** the effects of **risk** and **help liquidity**. This is because greater weight is given to **earlier cash flows** which can probably be **predicted more accurately** than distant cash flows.

Accounting rate of return

2.8 A project may be assessed by calculating the accounting rate of return (ARR) and comparing it with a pre-determined target level. Various formulae are used, but the important thing is to be **consistent** once a method has been selected. A formula for ARR which is common in practice is:

Accounting rate of return is calculated as follows

$$ARR = \frac{\text{Estimated average profits}}{\text{Estimated average investment}} \times 100\%$$

2.9 EXAMPLE: ARR

Caddick Limited is contemplating a computerisation project and has two alternatives. Based on the ARR method which of the two projects would be recommended?

	Project X	Project Y
Hardware cost	£100,000	£120,000
Estimated residual value	10,000	£15,000
Estimated life	5 years	5 years
Estimated future cost savings per annum before depreciation	£19,000	£21,800

2.10 SOLUTION

It is first necessary to calculate the average profits (net savings) and average investment over the life of the project (five years in this example).

	Project X £	Project Y £
Total savings before depreciation (eg £19,000 pa x 5 years)	95,000	109,000
Total depreciation	90,000	105,000
Total savings after depreciation	5,000	4,000
Average savings per annum (5 years so divide by 5)	1,000	800
Value of investment initially	100,000	120,000
Less eventual scrap value	(10,000)	(15,000)
	90,000	105,000
Average investment per annum (5 years so divide by 5)	18,000	21,000

2.11 The accounting rates of return are as follows. Project X would therefore be chosen.

$$\text{Project X} = \frac{£1,000}{£18,000} = 5.56\%$$

$$\text{Project Y} = \frac{£800}{£21,000} = 3.8\%$$

2.12 The return on investment is a measure of (accounting) profitability and its major **advantages** that it can be obtained from **readily available accounting data** and that its meaning is **widely understood**.

2.13 Its major **shortcomings** are that it is based on accounting profits rather than cash flows and that it fails to take account of the **timing** of cash inflows and outflows. For example, in the problem above cash savings in each year were assumed to be the same, whereas management might favour higher cash inflows in the **early years**. Early cash flows are less risky and they improve liquidity. This might lead them to choose a project with a lower ARR.

KEY TERM

Discounted cash flow or DCF is a technique of evaluating capital investment projects, using **discounting arithmetic** to determine whether or not they will provide a satisfactory return.

2.14 A typical investment project involves a payment of capital for fixed assets at the **start** of the project and then there will be profits coming in from the investment over a number of years. When the system goes live, there will be **running costs** as well. The benefits of the system should exceed the running costs, to give net annual benefits.

2.15 DCF recognises that there is a '**time value**' or interest cost and **risk** cost to investing money, so that the expected benefits from a project should not only pay back the costs, but should also yield a satisfactory return. Only **relevant** costs are recognised: accounting conventions like depreciation, which is not a real cash flow, are ignored.

2.16 £1 is now worth more than £1 in a year's time, because £1 now could be used to earn interest by the end of year 1. Money has a lower and lower value, the further from 'now' that it will be earned or paid. With DCF, this time value on money is allowed for by converting cash flows in future years to a smaller, **present value**, equivalent.

2.17 EXAMPLE: NPV

A DCF evaluation, using NPV analysis, of a proposed computer project might be as follows.

Project: new network system for administration department

Development and hardware purchase costs (all incurred over a short time)	£150,000
Operating costs of new system, expressed as cash outflows per annum	£55,000
Annual savings from new system, expressed as cash inflow	£115,000
Annual net savings (net cash inflows)	£60,000
Expected system life	4 years
Required return on investment	15% pa

2.18 SOLUTION

The calculation of NPV is performed as follows.

Year	Cost/Savings	Discount factor at 15%	Present value at 15%
	£		£
0	(150,000)	1.000	(150,000)
1	60,000	0.870	52,200
2	60,000	0.756	45,360
3	60,000	0.658	39,480
4	60,000	0.572	34,320
		Net present value of the project	21,360

2.19 In this example, the present value of the expected benefits of the project exceed the present value of its costs, all discounted at 15% pa, and so the project is financially justifiable because it would be expected to earn a yield greater than the minimum target return of 15%. Payback of the development costs and hardware costs of £150,000 would occur after 2½ years.

2.20 One disadvantage of the NPV method is that it involves complicated maths and this might make it **difficult to understand** for some people. More seriously, it is difficult in practice to determine the true **cost of capital.**

Internal rate of return (IRR)

2.21 The internal rate of return methods of DCF involves two steps.

(a) Calculating the **rate of return** which is expected from a project.
(b) **Comparing** the rate of return with the **cost of capital.**

2.22 If a project earns a higher rate of return than the cost of capital, it will be worth undertaking (and its NPV would be positive). If it earns a lower rate of return, it is not worthwhile (and its NPV would be negative). If a project earns a return which is exactly equal to the cost of capital, its NPV will be 0 and it will only just be worthwhile.

2.23 The manual method of calculating the rate of return is sometimes considered to be rather 'messy' and unsatisfactory because it involves some guesswork and approximation, but **spreadsheets** can do it with speed and precision.

Question 2

Draw up a table which identifies, for each of payback, ARR and NPV, two advantages and two disadvantages.

Answer

Method	Advantages	Disadvantages
Payback	(1) Easy to calculate (2) Favours projects that offer quick returns	(1) Ignores cash flows after payback period (2) Only a crude measure of timing of a project's cash flows.
ARR	(1) Easy to calculate (2) Easy to understand	(1) Doesn't allow for timing of inflows/outflows of cash (2) Subject to accounting conventions.
NPV	(1) Uses relevant cost approach by concentrating on cash flows (2) Represents increase to company's wealth, expressed in present day terms	(1) Not easily understood by laymen. (2) Cost of capital may be difficult to calculate.

The feasibility study report

2.24 Once each area of feasibility has been investigated a number of possible projects may be put forward. The results are included in a **feasibility report**. This should contain the following items.

- **Terms of reference**
- Description of **existing system**
- **System requirements**
- Details of the **proposed system(s)**
- **Cost/benefit analysis**
- **Development** and **implementation** plans
- **Recommendations** as to the preferred option

Question 3

You are the member of a feasibility study group with responsibility for preparing the first draft of the report so that this can be circulated to the other group members for their comments before your next meeting. List the sections of the report.

Answer

A typical report might include:

(a) Terms of reference.
(b) Description of existing system.
(c) System requirements.
(d) Details of the proposed system.
(e) Cost/benefit analysis.
(f) Development and implementation plans.
(g) Recommendations as to the preferred option.

3 INVESTIGATING USER REQUIREMENTS

3.1 The systems investigation is a detailed fact-finding exercise about the areas under consideration. It may be performed substantially **during the feasibility study**.

3.2 The project team has to determine the **inputs, outputs, processing methods and volumes of the current system**. It also examines **controls, staffing and costs** and reviews the **organisational structure**. It should also consider the **expected growth** of the organisation and its **future requirements**.

3.3 The stages involved in this phase of the study are as follows.

(a) **Fact finding** by means of questionnaires, interviews, observation, reading handbooks, manuals, organisation charts, or from the knowledge and experience of members of the study team.

(b) **Fact recording** using flowcharts, decision tables, narrative descriptions, organisation and responsibility charts.

(c) **Evaluation**, assessing the strengths and weaknesses of the existing system.

3.4 At this phase, when the team is trying to discover the details of a system with which they are generally quite unfamiliar, they will be interested in all sorts of facts about the organisation. After all, the **organisational context of the system will affect its operation**. Consequently, fact finding in a user department can cover a broad area, as demonstrated by a few examples, below. The emphasis in each area will be on the potential for **improvement**.

(a) **Plans and objectives.** Does the department have clear plans and objectives and are these consistent with the objectives of the organisation as a whole?

(b) **Organisation structure.** Is the structure geared towards achieving the department's objectives? Are responsibilities clearly delegated and defined?

(c) **Policies, systems and procedures.** How has the department established its current policies? Are they written down and formally reviewed? How does management ensure that policies are adhered to?

(d) **Personnel.** Are there adequate systems/procedures for job specifications and appraisals? Are there adequate systems for staff development and training?

(e) **Equipment and the office.** What is the general condition of office equipment? Is it used to full advantage?

(f) **Operations and control.** What exceptional cases are dealt with, and how are they dealt with? Are there bottlenecks in operations; if so, what can be done to ease them?

3.5 There are many items about which facts ought to be obtained, and so the systems investigators should begin by drafting a **checklist of points** before they start asking questions.

3.6 This 'top-down' approach **focuses first on management needs** and ignores operational needs until later on. Top management's needs in controlling the organisation are of great importance in systems design.

Interviews

3.7 **Interviews** with members of staff can be an effective method of fact finding. although they can be **time consuming** for the analyst, who may have several to conduct, and therefore expensive.

(a) In an interview, **nuances and attitudes not apparent from other sources** may be obtained.

(b) **Immediate clarification** can be sought to unsatisfactory/ambiguous responses.

(c) Interviews may be considered more appropriate by some senior managers who may **ignore a questionnaire**.

(d) If properly conducted, an interview should enable the investigator to **overcome the fears and resistance to change** that may be felt by employees, in addition to **finding out facts about their work**.

3.8 There are some helpful **guidelines** as to the approach and attitude to be adopted by the investigator who is conducting a fact-finding interview.

(a) The interviewer must appreciate that he or she is dealing with many different individuals with different attitudes and personalities. The approach should be adopted to suit the individual interviewee.

(b) The interviewer should be **fully prepared**, having details of the interviewee's name and job position, and a plan of questions to ask.

(c) **Employees ought to be informed** before the interview that a systems investigation is taking place, and its **purpose explained**.

(d) The interviewer must ask questions at the **level appropriate** to the employee's position within the organisation (for example top management will be concerned with policy, supervisors with functional problems).

(e) The interview should **not be too formal** a question and answer session, but should be allowed to develop into a **conversation** whereby the interviewee offers his opinions and suggestions.

(f) The interviewer must not **jump to conclusions** or confuse opinions with facts, accepting what the interviewee has to say (for the moment) and refraining from interrupting.

(g) The interviewer should gain the **interviewee's confidence** by explaining what is going on. This confidence may be more easily obtained by allowing the interview to take place on the interviewee's 'home ground' (desk or office). The purpose of note taking should also be explained.

(h) If possible, the interviewer may find it helps understanding to move **progressively** through the system, for example interviewing input personnel first, then supervisor then manager.

(i) The interviewer should refrain from making **off the record** comments during the course of the interview, for example about what is going to be recommended.

(j) The interview should be **long** enough for the interviewer to obtain the information required and to ensure an understanding of the system, but **short** enough to ensure that concentration does not wander.

(k) The interview should be **concluded** by a resumé of its main points and the interviewer should **thank** the interviewee for the time and trouble taken.

Question 4

Draw up a checklist of do's and don'ts for conducting fact-finding interviews.

Answer

A useful checklist for **guidance in conducting interviews** is suggested by Daniels and Yeates in *Basic training in systems analysis* as follows:

Do	Don't
Plan	Be late
Make appointments	Be too formal or too casual
Ask questions at the right level	Interrupt
Listen	Use technical jargon
Use the local terminology	Confuse opinion with fact
Accept ideas and hints	Jump to conclusions
Hear both sides	Argue
Collect documents and forms	Criticise
Check the facts back	Suggest
Part pleasantly	

Questionnaires

3.9 The use of questionnaires may be useful whenever a **limited amount of information is required from a large number of individuals,** or where the organisation is **decentralised** with many 'separate entity' locations.

3.10 Questionnaires may be used as the **groundwork for interviews** with some respondents being interviewed subsequently. Alternatively, interviews may be carried out in one site/department, and questionnaires designed on the basis of experience and used elsewhere.

3.11 Many respondents find questionnaires **less imposing than interviews** and may therefore express opinions better, thereby perhaps increasing their own motivation.

(a) **Employees ought to be informed** before receiving the questionnaire that a systems investigation is to take place, and **its purpose explained**. This will help to ensure a good proportion of responses and to encourage a sensible approach to completion by staff.

(b) Questions must be **designed to obtain exactly the information necessary** for the study. This is a **very difficult** task.

(c) Busy employees may consider it a **waste of time** to answer page after page of questions, and may be unwilling to do so, or may put the questionnaire in the 'pending' tray for a rainy day.

(d) Staff may prefer **anonymity,** but this will prevent follow-up of 'interesting' responses.

3.12 If a questionnaire is necessary, for example to establish the function of all employees within the organisation, the interviewer/analyst may design a form that enables individuals to list duties under various headings. The form **should be designed with the specific organisation in mind**.

3.13 It must be stressed that questionnaires, by themselves, are usually an **inadequate means of fact finding** in a systems development context, and should be followed up by an interview or observation. Whenever possible, questionnaires should be **designed** with the following in mind.

    (a)   They should **not contain too many questions** (people tend to lose interest quickly and become less accurate in their answers).

    (b)   They should be **organised in a logical sequence**.

    (c)   They should include an occasional question, the answer to which **corroborates the answers to previous questions**.

    (d)   Ideally, they should be designed so that each question can be answered by either **'yes' or 'no'** or a 'tick' rather than sentences or paragraphs.

    (e)   They should be **tested independently** before being issued to the actual individuals. The test answers should enable the systems analyst to establish the effectiveness of the questions and help determine the level of subsequent interviews and observations.

    (f)   They should take into account the **sensitivity** of individuals in respect of their job security, change of job definition etc.

Observation

3.14   Once the analyst has some understanding of the methods and procedures used in the organisation, he or she should be able to verify the findings and clarify any problem areas by an **observation of operations**.

3.15   Observation is a useful way of **cross-checking with the facts obtained by interview or questionnaire**. Different methods of recording facts ought to produce the same information, but it is not inconceivable that staff do their work in one way, whilst management believe that they do something different.

3.16   It should be noted that **staff may act differently from normal if they know that they are being observed**.

User workshops

3.17   User workshops are an important tool used to establish and record user requirements – particularly when JAD and/or RAD are being used. (Refer back to Chapter 6 if you need to refresh your knowledge of JAD and/or RAD.)

3.18   A workshop is a meeting with the emphasis on **practical exercises**.

3.19   Key users, meeting in workshops, analyse business functions and define the data associated with the system. An outline of the system is produced followed by the design of system procedures.

3.20   **Prototyping** may be used at such a workshop to prepare preliminary screen layouts.

3.21   Depending on the complexity of the system, the workshop may devise a **plan for implementation**. More complex systems may conduct a workshop early in the design stage and hold a later workshop with the aim of producing a **detailed system model**.

3.22   User workshops should be facilitated by a **facilitator**. The facilitator co-ordinates the workshop activities with the aim of ensuring the objectives of the session are achieved.

3.23   The facilitator would most likely be a systems analyst with excellent **communication** and leadership skills. The skills of the person in this role are critical to the success of the workshop.

3.24 Many user workshops also utilise a **scribe**. The scribe is an active participant who is responsible for producing the outputs of the workshop.

3.25 The scribe usually utilises a **CASE tool** (explained in Chapter 6).

Document review

3.26 The systems analyst must investigate the **documents** that are used in the system for input and output. One way of recording facts about document usage is the **document description form**, which is simply a standard form which the analyst can use to describe a document.

3.27 This may be a wide ranging investigation, using for example **organisation charts, procedures manuals and standard operational forms**.

3.28 One risk, however, is that **staff do not follow** documented policies and procedures or that these documents have **not been properly updated**, so this method is best used in tandem with one or more other techniques.

3.29 Document analysis can help the analyst estimate **file sizes, processing volumes** and related requirements.

Existing computerised systems

3.30 User requirements for a new computerised system can also be collected from existing computerised systems.

3.31 It is important to take into account changes in the way work is being carried out – it is unlikely that the new system will be performing an identical role to the old system.

3.32 With this in mind, areas where the existing system can provide useful information include:

- File structures
- Transaction volumes
- Screen design
- User satisfaction
- User complaints
- Help-desk/Information centre records
- Causes of system crashes
- Processor speed

4 DOCUMENTING AND MODELLING TECHNIQUES

4.1 The **systems analysis** process examines why **current methods** are used and what **alternatives** might achieve the same or better results.

4.2 A variety of fact-finding techniques are available to determine how a system operates, what document flows occur, what work processes are involved and what personnel are involved.

Data flow diagrams (DFD)

4.3 Data flow diagrams show the ways in which data is processed. The production of a data flow diagram is often the first step in a structured systems analysis, because it provides a **basic understanding of how the system works**.

4.4 **Four symbols** are used in data flow diagrams.

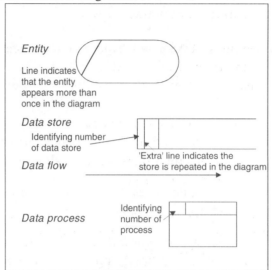

> **KEY TERM**
>
> An **entity** is a **source** or **destination** of data which is considered **external to the system** (not necessarily external to the organisation). It may be people or groups who provide data or input information or who receive data or output information.
>
> A **data store** is a point which receives a data flow and holds data.

4.5 Data stores are not restricted as to their **form**, and might be held in digital form, or on paper or microfiche.

> **KEY TERM**
>
> A **data flow** represents the movement or transfer of data from one point in the system to another.

4.6 A data flow may involve a document transfer or it may simply involve a notification that some event has occurred without any detailed information being passed. A data flow could be 'physically' anything - for example a letter, a telephone call, a fax message, a link between computers, or a verbal statement.

4.7 When a data flow occurs a copy of the data transferred may also be retained at the transmitting point.

> **KEY TERM**
>
> **Data processes** involve data being used or altered. The processes could be manual, mechanised or computerised.

4.8 An example of a process which simply **uses** the data would be an output operation, where the data held by the system is unchanged and it is merely made available in a different form, for example printed out.

4.9 A process which **alters** the data would be a mathematical computation or a process such as sorting in which the arrangement of the data is altered.

4.10 Systems vary widely in the amount of data processing which they perform. Some systems are dominated by the amount of data **movement** which they provide, whilst others are intensively concerned much more with **transforming** the data into a more useful form.

Levelled DFDs

4.11 The complexity of business systems means that it is impossible to represent the operations of any system by means of a **single** diagram.

4.12 At the top level, an overview of the different systems in an organisation can be given, or alternatively the position of a single system in the organisation shown. This might be achieved by means of a **context diagram**.

4.13 This is in turn 'exploded' by means of a more detailed data flow diagram, known as a Level-1 DFD. Further detail can be represented on a Level-2 DFD, and so on until all individual entities, stores, flows and processes are shown.

4.14 The diagram below illustrates how **levels of DFDs** are built up.

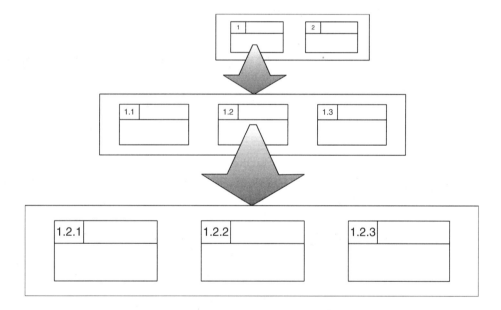

4.15 EXAMPLE: DATA FLOW DIAGRAM

The example used here is a system used for purchasing in a manufacturing company. Three data flow diagrams are shown; each is prepared to record a certain level of detail.

Level-0 DFD (context diagram)

4.16 A Level-0 DFD or **context diagram** summarises the inputs and outputs to the system at a high level.

4.17 The central box represents the system as a whole and (for simplicity in this case) one external entity is shown. (Usually the box would be *surrounded* by external entities who are dealt with in different ways by the system - the diagram would look like a spider.)

BPP PUBLISHING

4.18 Note that we are only showing **flows of data**. The physical resources (the goods supplied) *can* be shown (by means of broad arrows ⇨), but this tends to overcomplicate the diagram. Also no data stores are shown on the context diagram.

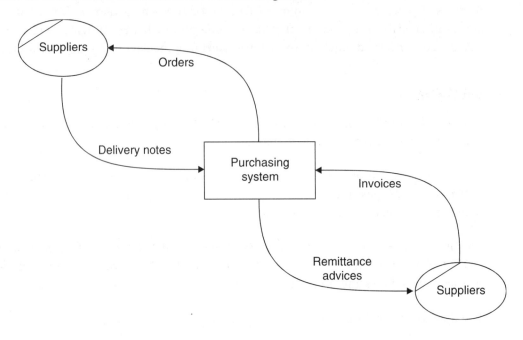

Level 1 DFDs

4.19 Within the purchasing system as a whole in this organisation there are two **subsystems**: the **Stores department** places requests for purchases and accepts delivery of the goods themselves; the **Purchasing department** places orders, and receives and pays invoices.

4.20 On the next page is shown a Level-1 DFD for the **purchasing department**.

4.21 This is not meant to depict an **ideal** system, if there is any such thing. You may be able to detect flaws or inefficiencies in the system shown on the next page. This is **irrelevant** at this stage since we are only trying to **describe** the system as it currently exists.

4.22 Also, for the sake of simplicity, we are only showing **purchasing department activities**. The supplier would send delivery notes to the Stores department who would carry out their own checks, prepare Goods Received Notice (GRNs), and have other data flows with other subsystems.

4.23 Note the following **important** points.

(a) Each process is **numbered**, but this is only for ease of identification: the numbers are **not** meant to show the **strict sequence of events**.

(b) The process box also has a heading showing where the process is carried out or who does it. The **description** of the process should be a **clear verb** like 'prepare', 'calculate', 'check' (**not** 'process', which is too vague).

(c) Arrows must **always** finish at or start from a **process**. (If you simply remember that data **cannot move** without intervention (processing) you should never get this wrong.)

(d) Rather than having data flow arrows criss-crossing all over the place it is often simpler to show a symbol **more than once** on the same diagram, wherever it is needed. When this is done **an additional line** is put within the symbol. The **supplier** entity and several of the **data stores** have extra lines for this reason.

(e) Data stores are given a reference number (again sequence is not important).

This is preceded by an M if it is a **manual** store and a D if it is a **computer** store.

(f) There may be **little reason to label arrows** that go **in and out of data stores,** because it will be clear enough from the description of the process. (See, for example, process 3 in the example DFD shown: is it really necessary to label the arrows 'invoice', 'invoice details', especially at this level?)

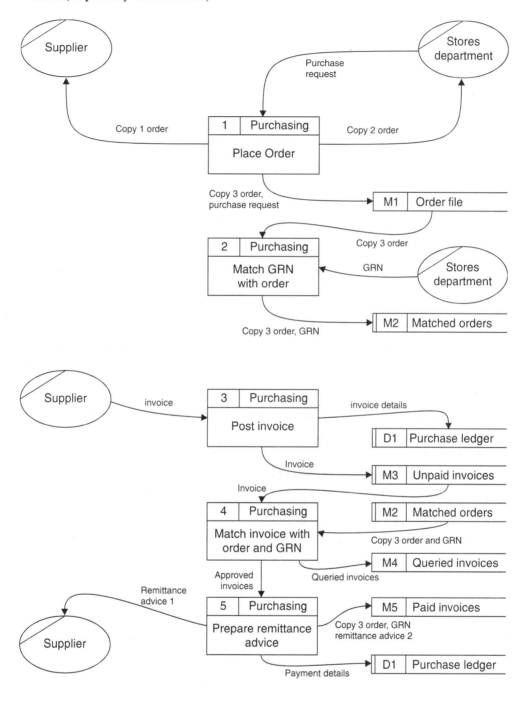

Level-2 DFDs

4.24 A separate DFD (Level-2) would then be prepared for **each of the numbered processes**.

4.25 This is known as **decomposing** a process. The diagram below, for example, shows the data flows for process 1, placing the order.

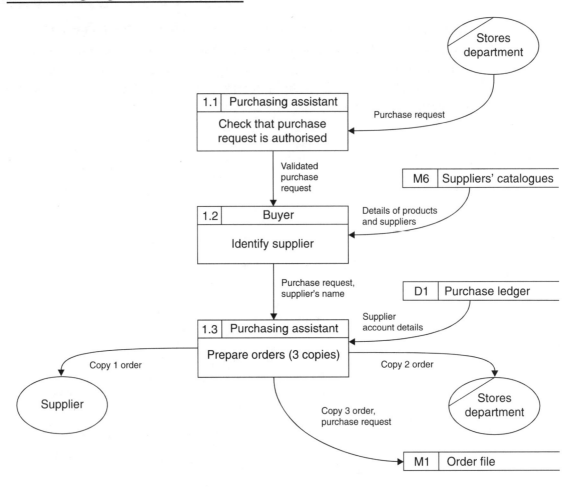

Question 5

Compare this diagram with the Level-1 DFD and note how it is possible to trace the same data flows from one level to the next.

4.26 In turn, box 1.1 could be **further decomposed** in a Level-3 DFD, with processes 1.1.1, 1.1.2 and so on, and box 1.2 could be decomposed into processes 1.2.1, 1.2.2 etc. In theory there is no limit to the number of lower levels, but **three levels is usually enough**.

Question 6

Study these diagrams carefully and then try to 'decompose' some of the other processes in the Level-1 DFD into Level-2 DFDs. For example try process 4 and show what might happen if an invoice does *not* match the GRN. You might also like to try to construct a Level-1 DFD for the Stores department.

Answer

There are no right answers, because we have not given you full details of the system: you will **need to make assumptions** based on your knowledge and experience of typical accounting systems. (Experienced systems analysts are likely to make mistakes when they first try to get a system down in DFD form: they will only get it right after discussion and agreement with **users**.)

Entity modelling

4.27 An **entity**, as we have seen, is an item (a person, a job, a business, an activity, a product or stores item etc) about which information is stored.

- In a sales ledger system a **customer** is an entity
- In a payroll system an **employee** is an entity

4.28 An **attribute** is a characteristic or property of an entity. For a customer, attributes include customer name and address, amounts owing, date of invoices sent and payments received, credit limit etc.

4.29 For any entity we can identify **relationships** between attributes and relationships between entities. Here are some simple examples. (The diagrams are sometimes called **Bachmann diagrams**.)

No relationship

4.30 There are **no relationships** in a printout of customer names. This is simply a list of records. Each address is an attribute.

One-to-one relationship

4.31 The relationship **employs** exists between *company* and *finance director*. There is one company which can only employ one finance director.

One-to-many relationship

4.32 The relationship **employs** also exists between *company* and *director*. The company employs more than one director.

Many-to-one relationship

4.33 This is really the same as the previous example, but **viewed from the opposite direction**. For example, many *sales managers* report to one *sales director*.

Many-to-many relationship

4.34 The relationship between *product* and *part* is **many-to-many**. A product is composed of many parts, and a part might be used in many products.

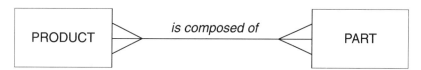

Breaking down relationships

4.35 Many-to-many relationships **cause difficulties** when designing the software to search for items and they should if possible be broken down so that they are eliminated.

4.36 The relationship depicted above could be amended by the insertion of a **new entity** called 'job sheet'. Thus a product is manufactured to job sheets and job sheets specify a part.

Entity relationship models (ERM)

> **KEY TERM**
>
> An **Entity Relationship Model (ERM)** (also known as an **entity model** or a **logical data structure**) provides an understanding of the logical data requirements of a system independently of the system's organisation and processes.

4.37 An **ERM** uses one-to-one, one-to-many and many-to-many relationships. These relationships can also be described by the notations: *1:1*, *1:m* and *m:m* respectively.

4.38 The correct classification of relationships is important. If the one-to-many relationship **customer order contains part numbers** is incorrectly described as one-to-one, the system designed on the basis of this ERM might allow an order to be entered with one item and one item only, thus necessitating the creation of a separate order for each part.

4.39 EXAMPLE: ERM

An example of a diagram relevant to a warehousing and despatch system is given below. This indicates that:

(a) A **customer** may make **many orders.**

(b) That an **order form** can contain **several order lines.**

(c) That each **line** on the order form can only detail **one product**, but that one product can appear on several lines of the order.

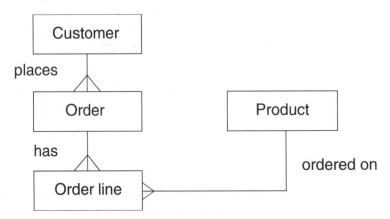

4.40 Another example of an entity model is given below. Note the structure of the accompanying narrative.

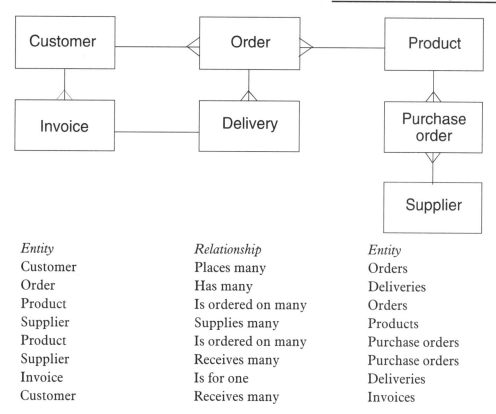

Entity	Relationship	Entity
Customer	Places many	Orders
Order	Has many	Deliveries
Product	Is ordered on many	Orders
Supplier	Supplies many	Products
Product	Is ordered on many	Purchase orders
Supplier	Receives many	Purchase orders
Invoice	Is for one	Deliveries
Customer	Receives many	Invoices

Entity life histories (ELH)

4.41 As we have seen, **Entity Relationship Models** take a **static** view of data. We will now look at a modelling tool that focuses on data processes.

> **KEY TERM**
>
> An **Entity Life History** (ELH) is a diagram of the *processes* that happen to an *entity*. Data items do not always remain unchanged - they may come into existence by a specific operation and be destroyed by another. For example, a customer order forms part of a number of processes, and is affected by a number of different events. An entity life history gives a **dynamic** view of the data.

4.42 At its simplest, an entity life history displays the following structure.

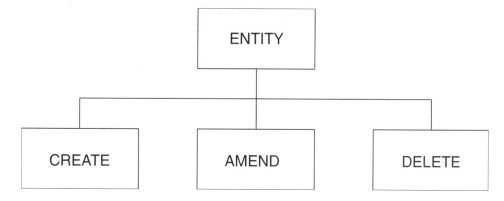

4.43 Entity life histories identify the various states that an entity can legitimately be in. It is really the **functions and events** which cause the state of the entity to change that are being analysed, rather than the entity itself.

4.44 The following conventions for ELHs are used.

(a) **Three** symbols are used. The main one is a **rectangular** box. Within this may be placed an **asterisk** or a **small circle**. as explained below.

(b) At the top level the first box (the **'root node'**) shows the **entity** itself.

(c) At lower levels the boxes represent **events** that affect the life of the entity.

d) The second level is most commonly some form of **'create, amend, delete'**, as shown above (or birth, life, death if you prefer). The boxes are read **in sequence** from left to right.

(e) If an event may affect an entity many times (**iteration**) this is shown by an asterisk in the top right hand corner of the box. A customer account, for example, will be updated many times.

(f) If events are alternatives (**selection**) - for example accept large order or reject large order - a small circle is placed in the top right hand corner.

4.45 Note the three types of process logic referred to above:
- Sequence
- Iteration
- Selection

4.46 Here is a very simple example.

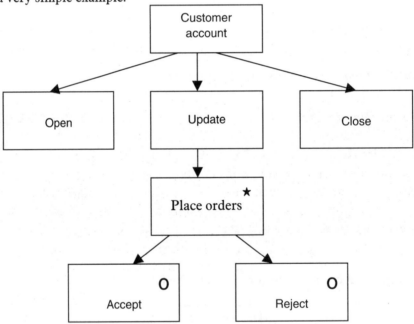

Structured English

4.47 A 'structured narrative' is a systems design tool which describes the logic of a process in a highly detailed narrative form.

4.48 This method uses **English** as the language but **severely limits the available vocabulary** and tries to follow the layout and logical operation of a computer program.

4.49 This tool is best suited for describing **specific activities** or functions, while the broader and more general concerns of system design are typically analysed by using data flow diagrams and decision tables.

4.50 There are several different kinds of Structured English, but they typically include the following features.

   (a) It is more **like spoken English** than normal programming languages and so is easier for programmers and non-programmers to understand.

   (b) It is much **more limited than normal speech,** as it has to follow a **strict logical order**.

   (c) There is a **variety of conventions** for writing it.

4.51 Structured English uses **keywords** (eg IF, ADD) which, by some conventions, are written in capitals and have a **precise logical meaning** in the context of the narrative.

4.52 The logical order in which instructions are performed is sometimes expressed in indentation. As with ELH, there are **three basic logical structures**.

   • Sequencing
   • Selection
   • Iteration

4.53 The **data elements** which are the subject of processing are, by some conventions, written in lower case and underlined.

4.54 For example, the calculation of gross pay from hours worked and rate of pay could be written in structured English.

> MULTIPLY <u>hours worked</u> by <u>pay rate</u> to get <u>gross pay</u>

5   OTHER SYSTEM DESIGN ISSUES

Requirements specification

5.1   This stage has several steps.

(a)   Detailed dataflow diagrams etc are drawn up, and the **proposed** system compared with the **current** system to ensure that all necessary processing will be performed. If necessary the DFDs are modified.

(b)   Specifications for **input** and **output** are prepared. These detail what appears on screen, or on documents. Prototyping could be used at this stage.

(c)   Relational data analysis (**normalisation**) is performed on the input and output descriptions. This is to identify any entities that might not have been noticed, or drawn in enough detail, in the existing **logical data structure.** (Normalisation is a way of **analysing and simplifying the relationships** between items of data.)

(d)   **Entity life histories** are drawn up, indicating what happens to each entity, ie what functions (processes) it is subjected to.

Logical design

5.2   In this stage, the **data and file structures** for the new system are designed.

Physical design

5.3   Physical design involves the following tasks.

(a)   **Initial physical design** - obtaining the design rules from the chosen system and applying them to the logical data design drawn up in the previous stages.

(b)   Further define the **processing** required. For instance requirements for **audit, security and control** are considered, such as **controls over access** to the system; controls **incorporated within programs** (eg data validation, error handling); and **recovery procedures,** in case processing is interrupted.

(c)   **Program specifications** are created. These provide in detail exactly what a particular program is supposed to achieve.

(d)   Program specifications are assessed for their **performance** when implemented. It should be possible to estimate the times that programs will take to run.

(e)   File and data specifications are **finalised**.

(f)   **Operating instructions** are drawn up (user documentation). These will include such items as error correction and detailed instructions for operators and users (eg the sort of screen format that will appear).

5.5   **Prototyping** may be used so that users can actually see what the system will look like and get a feel for how it will work.

Technical system options

5.6   The organisation will have to make choices concerning the specifications of the physical components of the new system.

5.7 There might be a number of options available so choices will need to be made regarding:

(a) **Hardware configuration -** for example mainframe, mini, PC; centralised or distributed processing; Internet connections.

(b) **Software -** use of an off the shelf package or a bespoke solution. This issue is covered in detail later in this Text.

5.8 **Performance objectives** for the system are then specified in detail so that these can be followed in the actual design of the system.

Chapter roundup

- The **feasibility study** is a formal study to decide what type of system can be developed which meets the needs of the organisation.

- There are four key areas in which a project must be feasible if it is to be selected. It must be justifiable on **technical, operational, social and economic** grounds.

- One of the most important elements of the feasibility study is the **cost-benefit analysis**. Costs include equipment costs, installation costs, development costs, personnel costs and running costs. Benefits are usually more intangible, but include cost savings, revenue benefits and qualitative benefits.

- There are three principal methods of evaluating the **economic viability** of a project: Payback, Accounting Rate of Return and Discounted Cash Flow.

- The Payback method calculates the length of time a project will take to recoup the initial investment.

- The Accounting Rate of Return (ARR) method, also called return on investment, expresses the profits that will be earned by a project as a percentage of the capital invested.

- Discounted Cash Flow (DCF) may be sub-divided into two approaches. Net Present Value (NPV) considers expected future cash flows but discounts future flows by the 'cost of capital'.

- Internal Rate of Return (IRR) compares the rate of return expected from the project calculated on a discounted cash flow basis with the rate used as the cost of capital. Projects with an IRR higher than the cost of capital are considered to be worth undertaking.

- Once each area of feasibility has been investigated a number of possible projects may be put forward. The results are included in a **feasibility report**.

- During the **systems investigation** the project team examines the inputs, outputs, processing methods and volumes, controls, staffing and costs of the current system. This may involve fact finding by means of questionnaires, interviews, observation and reviewing documents.

- **User workshops** may be used to devise a system model.

- **Dataflow diagrams** are used to record the ways in which data is processed.

- An **entity relationship model** provides an understanding of a system's logical data requirements independently of the system's processes.

- An **entity life history** shows the processes that happen to an entity.

- Structured English describes the **logic of a process** using simple keywords.

Quick quiz

1 List three reasons why an organisation considering the implementation of a new information system should undertake a feasibility study.

2 What four areas should a feasibility study ensure a project is feasible in?

3 List four methods used in systems investigations.

4   What four symbols are used in data flow diagrams?

5   List the three types of relationship an Entity Relationship Model (ERM) may portray.

6   What three types of process logic may an Entity Life History (ELH) show?

7   Distinguish between logical design and physical design.

Answers to quick quiz

1   A feasibility study should be undertaken when considering a new information system because new systems can:

Be complicated and cost a great deal to develop.

Be disruptive during development and implementation.

Have far-reaching consequences in a way an organisation conducts its business or is structured.

2   Technical, Operational, Social and Economic.

3   Questionnaires, interviews, observation and document review.

4   See paragraph 4.4.

5   One-to-one, one-to-many and many-to-many.

6   Sequence, iteration, selection.

7   Logical design is concerned with the nature of data or information viewed independently from the physical details of storage or output.

Physical design involves the physical aspects of data storage and presentation.

In general, the logical design is more relevant to the systems analyst while programmers will require details of physical design.

The material covered in this Chapter is tested in Questions 5, 7, 9, 10(a) and 11 in the Exam Question Bank.

Chapter 8

SOFTWARE DESIGN AND SELECTION

Topic list	Syllabus reference
1 Software vendor proposals	2(h)
2 Choosing software	2(f), 2(h)
3 Bespoke or off the shelf?	2(g)
4 Software contracts and licences	2(h), 3(b)

Introduction

In this chapter we look at the issues to be considered when **acquiring software** for information systems. The syllabus focuses on the issues surrounding **external design** – the parts of the system that the **user** interacts with.

Study guide

Part 2.15 – External design

- Define the characteristics of a 'user-friendly' system
- Describe the task of external design and distinguish it from internal design
- Select appropriate technology to support output design (also see Chapter 2)
- Design effective output documents and reports (also see Chapter 2)
- Select appropriate technology to support input design (also see Chapter 2)
- Design effective inputs
- Describe how the user interface may be structured for ease of use

Part 2.16 – Developing a system to fulfil requirements

- Define the bespoke software approach to fulfilling the user's information systems requirements
- Briefly describe the tasks of design, programming and testing required in developing a bespoke systems solution
- Define the application software package approach to fulfilling the user's information systems requirements
- Briefly describe the tasks of package selection, evaluation and testing required in selecting an appropriate application software package
- Describe the relative merits of the bespoke systems development and application software package approaches to fulfilling an information systems requirement

Part 2.17 – Software package selection

- Describe the structure and content of an Invitation to Tender (ITT)
- Describe how to identify software packages and their suppliers that may potentially fulfil the information systems requirements
- Develop suitable procedures for distributing an ITT and dealing with subsequent enquiries and bids
- Describe a process for evaluating the application software package, the supplier of the package and the bid received from the supplier
- Describe risks of the application software package approach to systems development and how these might be reduced or removed

Exam focus point

Throughout this chapter we have tried to keep references to hardware to a minimum. This is because the syllabus states 'Computer hardware will not be explicitly examined'.

We have referred to hardware requirements when we feel the information is required to fully understand the software issue being discussed.

1 SOFTWARE VENDOR PROPOSALS

1.1 Software may be purchased direct from a manufacturer, or through an intermediate supplier. Given that the expense is often considerable, the purchasing procedure must be carefully controlled.

Invitation to tender (ITT)

1.2 An organisation may issue an **Invitation To Tender** to a range of suppliers.

KEY TERM

An **Invitation To Tender** sets out the specification for the required system, explaining how it is to be used and setting out the timescale for implementation. It will set the performance criteria required of the new system.

1.3 The invitation to tender would give some **background information** about the company, together with an indication of the **purpose of the system** and with the details of requirements such as:

(a) The **volume of data** to be processed.

(b) The **complexity of processing** requirements (including interfaces with other systems).

(c) The **number of offices** or individual **people** who will want to access the computer system, and whether access needs to be instant or not.

(d) The **speed of processing** required, eg response times.

(e) **Inputs and outputs** desired.

(f) The type of **file processing** needed (ie whether the company require a real-time system).

(g) Estimated **life** of the system.

(h) Possible **upgrades** or expansion anticipated.

1.4 Details about the company should relate to its present **organisation structure**, the nature and **size** of its business and its plans for **future expansion**.

1.5 The invitation should also give details of general matters:

- **Contact** within company
- Any overall **financial constraints**
- **Form** that submissions are to take
- **Closing date** for submission of tenders
- **Address** to which tenders should be sent

1.6 **Responses** to an invitation to tender may vary from the sending of standard **brochures** and **price lists**, not tailored in any way to the organisation's needs, to offers to **visit** the organisation's site and provide a free **demonstration** of equipment and its capabilities.

Evaluating vendor proposals

1.7 Once vendor proposals have been obtained, they must be evaluated. Evaluation becomes very complicated if there is any doubt about system's **performance**, as this may necessitate a **test of the system**. The variety of responses may make a direct **comparison** of different tenders difficult.

1.8 The vendor will usually try to match the customer's profile with that of an **existing customer** to demonstrate that the system can handle such a workload. However, if the application is unusual or new, this will not be possible, and so a formal evaluation using **benchmarking** or **simulation tests** will be necessary.

Benchmark tests

1.9 There are several factors involved in measuring the capability of software. Software performance is also significantly affected by hardware performance. It is not an easy job to **compare the capability** of one software package against another similar package.

1.10 One way of comparing speed and capacity is to conduct **benchmark tests**.

> **KEY TERM**
>
> **Benchmark tests** test how long it takes a machine and program to run through a particular routine or set of routines.

1.11 There is some concern that some benchmark tests created by hardware manufacturers and **software producers** are designed to give the most **favourable** result to their products.

1.12 Benchmark tests are carried out to compare the performance of a piece of hardware or software against **pre-set criteria**. Typical criteria which may be used as benchmarks include **speed of performance** of a particular operation, acceptable volumes before a degradation in **response times** is apparent and the general **user-friendliness** of equipment. Benchmarks can cover subjective tests such as user-friendliness, although it may be harder to reach definitive conclusions.

1.13 The organisation might try out a series of different packages on its own existing hardware to see which performed the best according to various predefined criteria such as **speed** of response, ability to process different **volumes** of transactions, **reporting** capabilities and so on.

1.14 Once the performance of the software package under consideration has been evaluated, the acquiring organisation should consider other features of the proposal.

Supplier reliability

1.15 Reliability of suppliers should be considered in terms of **financial stability** (their help with the system they provide may be needed for many years to come), and **track record.**

1.16 If the supplier is a **major world player** such as Microsoft or Sage then there need be little doubt as to their reliability.

1.17 Suppliers of more specialised software or equipment may be much **smaller** and their products **less well tested** because they have a much smaller number of users.

Cost

1.18 Cost is obviously an important factor. By **shopping around**, a customer might be able to negotiate quite a large **discount** on the price from a supplier.

Utility software

1.19 A supplier may bundle a range of utility software and software tools with the main program. It might be worth checking what these are, and whether they vary between different suppliers.

Software maintenance and support

1.20 A software vendor will usually offer some support as part of the package. This may be in the form of a customer '**help-line**', or with more complex applications may involve contacting analysts that have been involved in the implementation. Support may be 'free' for a specified time and then be provided at a cost.

Training

1.21 Staff will require **training** to use the new system. There might be an agreement by the supplier to provide training for a specified number of the customer's employees for a specified period of time. Important questions that should be clarified are:

(a) **How many** will be trained?
(b) **How long** will they be trained for?

Keeping the package up-to-date

1.22 New improved versions of popular software packages are frequently brought on to the market. Occasionally, errors in existing packages are discovered and corrected. The vendor proposal for a software package should specify what **arrangements** there will be, if any, for the software supplier to provide the customer with any **changes or enhancements** to the software as they occur.

Key factors

1.23 The company might identify a number of **key factors** such as cost, security, support available and so on and **weight them** in order of importance.

1.24 The tender with the **highest overall score** would then be the most likely choice.

2 CHOOSING SOFTWARE

Software

2.1 Points to consider when choosing a suitable package.

Factor	Comment
User requirements	Does the package fit the **user's particular requirements**? This should cover such matters as report production, anticipated volume of data, data validation routines and any omissions which the user might compromise on.
	The package should be matched to the user.
Processing times	Are the **processing times** fast enough? If response times to enquiries is slow, the user might consider the package unacceptable.
Documentation	Is there full and clear **documentation** for the user? User manuals can be full of jargon and hard for a non-technical person to understand. They shouldn't be.
User-friendliness	Is the package easy to use? Is the software **user friendly** with menus and clear on-screen prompts for the keyboard operator? A user-friendly package will provide prompts and will be menu-driven, giving the operator a clear choice of what to do next. Some packages also provide extensive on-screen 'help' facilities.
Controls	What **controls** are included in the package (eg passwords, data validation checks, spelling checks, standard accounting controls and reconciliations, an audit trail facility etc)?
Up-to-dateness	How will the package be kept **up-to-date**? (eg what if a fault is discovered in the program by the software manufacturer? In an accounting package, what if the rate of VAT alters? etc).
Modification	Can the package be **modified** by the user - eg allowing the user to insert amendments to the format of reports or screen displays etc? Or will the software supplier agree to write a few tailor-made amendments to the software?
Other users	**How many other users** have bought the package, and how long has it been on the market? New packages might offer enhanced facilities, whereas well-established (but regularly updated) packages are more likely to be error-free.
Compatibility	Will the package **run** on the user's computer? Will additional peripheral equipment have to be bought - eg does the package need more hard disk space than is available?
	Also, does the software use file formats, field lengths and so on that are compatible with existing systems that will remain in use?

Factor	Comment
Support and maintenance	What **support** and **maintenance** service will the software supplier provide, in the event that the user has difficulty with the package?
Cost	A company should buy what it **needs for efficient operations** rather than the least-cost package available. The savings in purchase price would not be worth the trouble caused by trying to use an unsuitable package for a business application. However, the package must not **cost** so much that the costs are greater than the **benefits** of having it.

External design and internal design

2.2 Software package design can be broken down into external design and internal design.

> **KEY TERMS**
>
> **External design** refers to the elements of a software package that the user can see.
>
> **Internal design** refers to the elements of a software package the user does not see.

2.3 External design concerns the Human Computer Interface and screen layout.

2.4 Internal design is concerned with issues such as program and file structure.

The human-computer interface (HCI)

> **KEY TERM**
>
> The **Human-Computer Interface** is the set of commands or menus through which a user communicates with a program.

2.5 A command-driven interface is one in which you enter commands. A menu-driven interface is one in which you select command choices from various menus displayed on the screen.

2.6 A well-designed human-computer interface is one that takes account of the following factors.

(a) **Efficiency.** The system should be designed with the user in mind, so that menus and program groupings are arranged to match actual usage.

(b) **User-friendliness.** This covers on-line tutorials, on-screen help clear menus/icons and suitable dialogue boxes such as OK or Cancel.

(c) **Alternative options.** Although icons are user-friendly, they can hamper speed of operation. An experienced keyboard user will find it quicker, for example, to select 'Ctrl P' or similar than to click on a 'printer' icon then on a 'yes' button.

(d) **Ease of learning.** Common features across the HCIs of different packages should reduce training costs. A well designed system with a good HCI should be easy to learn.

Input design

2.7 People usually collect and input the data that the computer system will use, and in input design the **requirements of the system** must be balanced with the personal **capabilities of its users**. Input design is closely bound up with data collection and data capture. (The input devices we covered in Chapter 2 are relevant here.)

2.8 There are a number of considerations for input design.

(a) There should be no **unnecessary re-input** of data - for example, if standing file data includes a customer's name, address and code (account) number, it should only be necessary to input the unique **customer code.**

(b) What **volumes** of input are expected? **Large volumes** of input are more likely to require automated input procedures.

(c) What will be the **frequency** of input? Infrequent transaction data might suggest a random access system from keyboard terminals. With batched input, however, the frequency of input must be considered.

(d) In what **sequence** should batched data be input? For example, outstanding file maintenance ought to be input before transaction data, to ensure that the standing data is up-to-date before the transaction data is processed.

(e) **Where** will data be collected or captured for input? Where will it be converted into machine-sensible form?

(f) What should be the **input medium**?

(g) The **need for accuracy.** How extensive should built-in data validation checks be?

Screen design

2.9 The screen should display the information in a way that enables users to easily see and understand it.

2.10 The screen provides 'feedback' for the user, allowing the system to be flexible, interactive and conversational.

2.11 This **dialogue** between the system and the user is essential to the efficient running of a program. The term **conversational mode** describes a method of operation in which the operator carry's on a continual dialogue with the computer.

Menu selection

2.12 A menu is a **list of items to choose from**. For example, a main menu from an old (ie 1980s) DOS based sales ledger system follows.

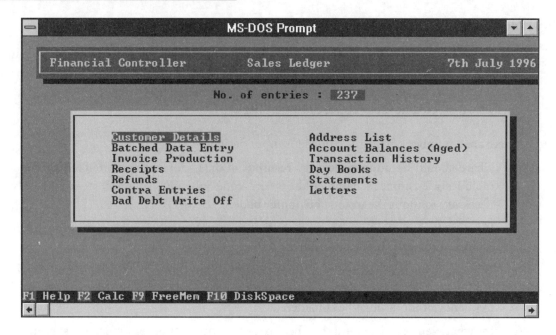

2.13 By selecting **Account Balances (Aged)**, the operator will be specifying that he or she wants to call up a list of account balances. **Another menu** may then be displayed, calling for the operator to narrow down the range of accounts.

2.14 A menu system is thus a **hierarchical** list of options.

Form filling

2.15 Form filling is a common way of laying out data input screens. Relevant data fields may be set up within an on-screen **skeleton** form. The input fields are arranged to facilitate ease of data entry.

2.16 **Screen formatting** for this purpose usually includes several features.

- **Different colours** for different screen areas
- **Flashing** items
- **Larger characters** for titles
- Paging or **scrolling** depending on the volume of information

2.17 Data is entered **automatically** in some fields when codes are entered. Other entries are made by **moving the cursor** from one field to the next and typing in the data.

2.18 A purchase ledger clerk wishing to raise a cheque may actually be confronted with a **proforma cheque** on screen. The cursor moves from line to line and the process is almost identical to the completion of a manual cheque.

Graphical user interfaces (GUI)

2.19 Graphical user interfaces (GUIs) were designed to make computers more 'user-friendly'.

2.20 A GUI involves the use of two design ideas and two operating methods which can be remembered by the abbreviation **WIMP**. This stands for 'Windows, Icons, Mouse, Pull-down menu' and is an environment which offers a **method of accessing the computer without using the keyboard**. Dialogue is conducted through images rather than typed text.

2.21 Graphical user interfaces have become the **principal means** by which humans communicate with machines.

Windows (the generic term rather than the operating system)

2.22　This basically means that the screen can be divided into sections, 'windows' of flexible size, which can be opened and closed. This enables **two or more documents to be viewed and edited** together, and sections of one to be inserted into another. For instance figures from an Excel spreadsheet can be pasted directly into a Word word-processing document.

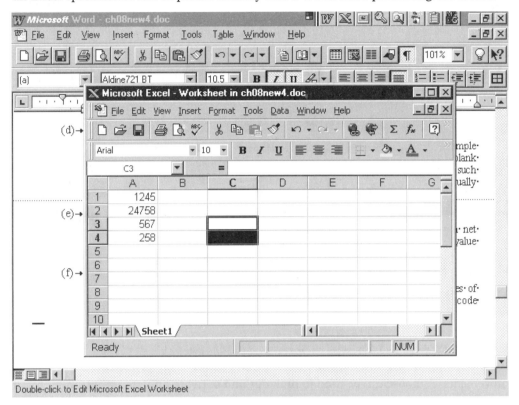

Icons

2.23　An icon is an image of an object used to represent a function or a file in an obvious way. For instance Windows based packages use a **picture of a printer** which is simply clicked to start the printing process. Another common icon is a **waste paper bin** to indicate the deletion of a document.

2.24　Both icons and windows are shown in the illustration over the page.

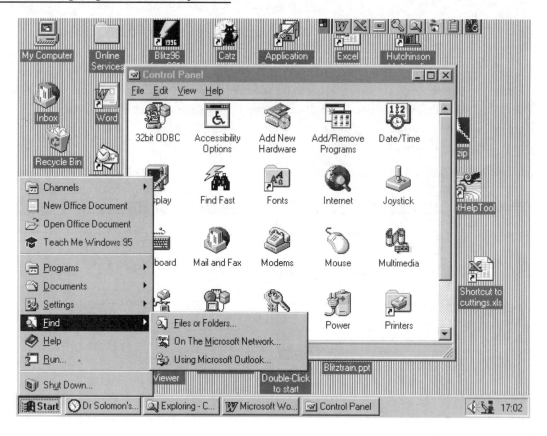

Mouse

2.25   As the mouse moves around on the desktop a *pointer* (cursor) on the screen mimics its movements. A mouse can be used to **pick out and activate an icon or button,** to **highlight** a block of text for deletion/insertion, or to **drag** data from one place on the screen to another. It also has buttons which are **clicked** to execute the current command.

Pull-down menu

2.26   A '**menu-bar**' will be shown across the top of the window. Using the mouse to move the pointer to the required item in the menu, the pointer '**pulls down**' a subsidiary menu - somewhat similar to pulling down a roller blind at a window. The pointer and mouse can then be used to **select** (input) the required item (output) on the pulled-down menu, which may lead to more menus.

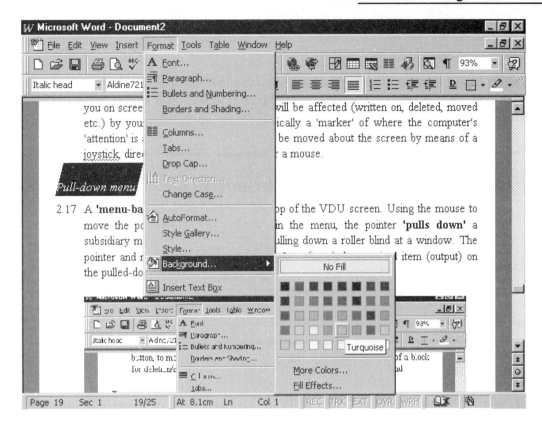

User-friendliness

2.27 The easier a package is to use, the more efficient it (and the user) will be. The following features all improve the user-friendliness of a system.

Ease of data entry

2.28 It must be easy for the user to input data into the system. This has several aspects.

(a) The **data entry screen** should be designed in a **logical order.** If an **input form** (source document) is used, the on-screen and off-screen order should be the same.

(b) The data entry screen should be **clearly designed,** so that, for example, input fields are highlighted, perhaps by **colour.** The position of the cursor should be clear.

Titles of fields should be **easy to read** and should **match** the titles used on **source** documents.

(c) **Default entries** should be provided for items such as the date (usually today's date) or the standard VAT rate.

The defaults will remain unless the user wishes to change them. This can speed up data entry considerably.

Intuitiveness

2.29 It should be possible for users to make **reasonable guesses about what they need to do.** Clear icons and menus help this process.

Consistent design

2.30 Most users will utilise many software packages. For example a spreadsheet and a word processing package.

183

2.31 This means that the more systems can **'look and feel' the same** the easier it will be for users to switch between packages.

2.32 One of the advantages of the **Windows** environment is that packages written for Windows are generally **similar in design**. This **reduces training time** and costs and makes **skills transferable**.

Question 1

Examine the menus and features of at least two software packages written for Microsoft Windows. You should notice many similarities.

Answer

Amongst the similarities are:

Common menu design eg drop-down menus, the File and Edit menus, Common function keys (F1 is 'help'). Common features eg Cut and Paste, use of toolbars, viewing options such as magnification, scroll bars etc.

On-screen help

2.33 It is increasingly common to find software pre-loaded onto computers without manuals being provided or to find that, when manuals *are* provided, they are rarely referred to. This is because packages invariably include **on-screen help**.

2.34 If a user requires help, he or she requests it at the touch of a **single key** (eg **F1**) or by clicking on **'Help'** on a **pull-down menu**. The help screen is usually **context specific**, so that, for example, if a particular dialogue box in a package is open, the system will offer help related to relevant functions and options. Problems can be resolved more quickly and productivity improved.

2.35 Help files are often written in **hypertext**, which provides **links** between topics. The user can click on words that are underlined and move directly to another topic.

Use of dialogue boxes and on-screen prompts

2.36 The more critical the potential effect of a command issued by the user, the more important it is that the user is not allowed simply to **start a process by mistake**.

2.37 Thus where commands such as **delete** a file, **format** a disk or **update** a ledger are being made, user-friendly software should issue a **warning** that such an operation is about to be carried out, *after* the initial command is entered.

2.38 This gives the user a **second chance** to confirm that the command was intended and that the computer is indeed required to carry out the specified process.

2.39 In turn this means that users will spend less time attempting to reverse the effects of **unintentionally-used commands**.

Escapability

2.40 An inexperienced user, or someone 'exploring' a package, might find himself in a situation they wish to back-track from.

2.41 Thus in Windows there is usually a '**Cancel**' button in each dialogue box. An alternative is often the '**Esc**' key.

Convenience

2.42 Many users find that they perform the **same series of actions** so frequently that it becomes tedious to click their way through menus and dialogue boxes. User-friendly software will recognise this and offer **fast alternatives**.

(a) '**Shortcut keys**' (typically pressing the Ctrl key together with one or more other keys) can be assigned to standard actions so that they are performed literally at the touch of a button.

(b) A series of actions can be 'recorded' as they are done in the form of '**macros**', which can then be activated using a shortcut key or user-defined button.

(c) We discuss end-user development in greater detail in Chapter 11.

3 BESPOKE OR OFF-THE-SHELF?

3.1 A key question regarding software is whether to develop a system specially or buy what is already available.

> **KEY TERM**
>
> **Bespoke software** is designed and written either 'in-house' by the IS department or externally by a software house.
>
> An **off-the shelf package** is one like Microsoft Word or Sage Line 50, that is sold to a wide range of users and intended to handle the most common user requirements.

Bespoke software

3.2 **Advantages** of having software specially written include the following.

(a) The company **owns** the software and may be able to **sell it** to other potential users.

(b) The company may be able to do things with its software that **competitors** cannot do with theirs. In other words it is a source of competitive advantage.

(c) The software can be written to **do everything** that the company requires it to do, both now and (with further enhancements in the face of changing business needs) in the future.

3.3 However, only **large organisations** are likely to have sufficiently complex processing requirements to justify employing full time computer programmers. Key **disadvantages** are.

(a) The software may **not** do what it should.

(b) There may be a **long delay** before the software is ready.

(c) The **cost** is considerable, compared with a ready-made package (the latter can be sold to lots of different users, not just one).

Off-the-shelf packages

3.4 **Advantages** of an off-the-shelf package

(a) It is **available now**.

(b) It is almost certainly **cheaper** because it is 'mass-produced'.

(c) It should have been written by software specialists and so should be of a **high quality**.

(d) A successful package will be **continually updated** by the software manufacturer, and so the version that a customer buys should be up-to-date.

(e) **Other users** will have used the package already, and a well-established package should be relatively **error-free**.

(f) Good packages are **well-documented**, with easy to follow user manuals. Good documentation is a key feature of successful software development.

(g) Some standard packages can be **customised** to the user's specific needs (but see below).

3.5 The **disadvantages** of ready-made packages are as follows.

(a) The computer user gets a **standardised solution** to a data processing task. A standard solution may not be well suited to the individual user's particular needs.

(b) The user is **dependent on the supplier** for maintenance of the package - ie updating the package, providing assistance in the event of problems for the user or even program errors cropping up. This is especially true if the general package is tailored in any way.

(c) Competitors may well use the same package and so there is **no competitive edge**.

Customised versions of standard packages

3.6 Standard packages can be **customised** so that they fit an organisation's specific requirements. This can either be done by **purchasing the source code** of the package and making modifications in-house or by paying the maker of the package to customise it.

3.7 **Advantages** of customisation are similar to those of producing a bespoke system, with the additional advantages that:

(a) Development time should be much **quicker**, given that most of the system will be written already.

(b) If the work is done in-house the organisation gains considerable **knowledge of how the software works** and may be able to 'tune' it so that it works more efficiently with the company's hardware.

3.8 **Disadvantages** of customising a standard package include the following.

(a) It may prove more **costly** than expected, because **new** versions of the standard package will **also** have to be customised. For instance upgrades to Sage Line 50, the most popular off-the-shelf accounting package in the UK, are released annually.

(b) Customisation may **delay delivery** of the software.

(c) Customisation may introduce **bugs** that do not exist in the standard version.

(d) If done **in-house**, the in-house team may have to **learn new skills**.

(e) If done by the **original manufacturer** disadvantages such as those for off-the-shelf packages may arise.

Add-ons and programming tools

3.9 Two other ways of trying to give a computer user more flexibility with packages are:

(a) The sale of 'add-ons' to a basic package, which the user can buy if they suit their particular needs.

(b) The provision of **programming tools**, such as fourth generation languages, with a package, which allows users to write amendments to the software (without having to be a programming expert).

4 SOFTWARE CONTRACTS AND LICENCES

4.1 We have already mentioned many of the matters that might typically be included in a software contract, such as:

(a) **Cost** and what it does and does not include.

(b) **Duration.**

(c) **Warranty** terms.

(d) **Support** available.

(e) Arrangements for **upgrades.**

(f) **Maintenance** arrangements (maintenance is discussed in more detail in Chapter 11).

4.2 If the software is being **specially written** there are likely to will be clauses about when the software is to be **delivered,** and who has **ownership** of the software and its source code once it has been delivered. **Performance criteria** (what the software will and will not do, how fast, for how many users etc) may also be specified.

4.3 Packaged software generally has a **licence,** the terms of which users are deemed to have agreed to the moment the package is unwrapped or a seal is broken.

4.4 A licence typically covers matters such as:

(a) **How many users** can use the software.

(b) Whether it can be **modified** without the manufacturer's consent.

(c) In what circumstances the licence is **terminated.**

(d) A limitation of **liability** (the writer of an accounting package, for instance, does not wish to be held liable if a user commits fraud). This is a complex area that is still developing. Not only the exclusion clause in the licence is relevant – the representations that the software supplier makes regarding the package's capabilities would also be taken into account in any legal dispute.

(e) The obligation to correct errors or **bugs** if they exist.

4.5 The unauthorised copying of software is referred to as **software piracy.**

4.6 When a user purchases software they are merely buying **the rights to use the software** in line with the terms and conditions within the licence agreement. The licence will be issued with the software, on paper or in electronic form. It contains the terms and conditions of use, as set out by the software publisher or owner of the copyright. A breach of the licence conditions usually means the owners' copyright has been infringed. In the UK, computer software is defined as a Literary Work in the Copyright, Designs and Patents Act (1988).

4.7 If an organisation is using illegal copies of software, the organisation may face a **civil suit**, and corporate officers and individual employees **may have criminal liability**. In the UK, remedies for civil copyright infringement may include damages to compensate the copyright owners for damage caused to their business, including reputation, and for loss of sales. Criminal penalties can include unlimited fines and two years' imprisonment or both.

4.8 The most common type of software piracy in a business setting is referred to as **Corporate Over-Use**. This is the installation of software packages on more machines than there are licences for. For example if a company purchases five single-user licences of a software program but installs the software on ten machines, then they will be using five infringing copies. Similarly, if a company is running a large network and more users have access to a software program than the company has licences for, this too is Corporate Over-Use.

4.9 A **grey area** is the installation of programs on portable or **laptop computers** for use off-site. Generally speaking, if a person has a program installed **on their desktop** in the office **and the same person** has the **same program on their laptop** for off-site use, then this **usually counts as one user** under the licence rather than two. However, the terms in different licences may differ.

4.10 To ensure they do not infringe copyright organisations should:

- Make sure they receive and **keep licences** - these are valuable documents
- **Track the number of users** with access to licensed programs
- Periodically check all computers for **unlicensed** software
- Buy from **reputable dealers**
- Get a **written quote** listing hardware/software specification and version
- Require an **itemised invoice** giving details of all hardware and software supplied

4.11 The Copyright, Designs and Patents Act 1998 specifically **allows the making of back-up copies** of software, but only providing it is for lawful use.

4.12 Shown below are extracts from a typical licence for an off-the-shelf package.

Case example: Licence for off-the-shelf package

1. **PROGRAM & LICENCE**

(i) The "Program" means the licensed software programs as stored on the computer disks or compact disks included in this box.

(ii) This Licence permits you to **install the Program on a single personal computer (or single network, where you have purchased this version**) and install data onto the Program for a single set of data at any one time (unless, and to the extent that, you have purchased the relevant licence for multiple users and/or multiple sets of data from X Co Ltd), whether for a company, partnership, group, person or otherwise, in the course of which you may make one copy of the Program in any computer readable format for back-up purposes. The copyright design right and any other intellectual property rights in the source and object codes of this Program vest exclusively in X Co Ltd ("X Co Ltd").

(iii) The **Program may not be copied** without the express consent in writing of X Co Ltd under such terms as it shall determine. In particular, **the Program shall not be installed onto any additional network** (where you have purchased such version) **or onto any additional personal computer** including any lap-top or portable computer **without an additional user licence**, available at separate cost from X Co Ltd.

(iv) THIS LICENCE IS PERSONAL TO YOU. **YOU MAY NOT TRANSFER** OR PART WITH POSSESSION OF THE PROGRAMS OR SEEK TO SUB-LICENSE OR ASSIGN THIS LICENCE OR YOUR RIGHTS UNDER IT.

YOU MUST NOT MODIFY OR MERGE (EXCEPT BY A X CO LTD APPROVED DEALER, OR OTHERWISE WITH THE WRITTEN CONSENT OF X CO LTD), REVERSE ENGINEER OR DECOMPILE THE PROGRAM. YOU MUST NOT COPY THE PROGRAM EXCEPT AS EXPRESSLY PROVIDED IN (II) ABOVE. ANY BREACH OF THIS SUB-CLAUSE (IV) WILL AUTOMATICALLY TERMINATE YOUR LICENCE.

(v)   X CO LTD DOES NOT WARRANT OR GUARANTEE THAT THE PROGRAM PERFORMS ANY PARTICULAR FUNCTION OR OPERATION WHICH MAY BE SUITABLE FOR YOUR REQUIREMENTS OTHER THAN MAY BE DISCLOSED IN RELEVANT DOCUMENTATION PUBLISHED BY X CO LTD.

Case example: Reports of corporate under licensing on the rise

Federation Against Software Theft reports 12% increase

Reports of corporate under licensing are on the rise according to the latest figures issued by industry watchdog, the Federation Against Software Theft (FAST). In the year 2000 the organisation received in excess of 380 reports of under licensing within the business community, an annual increase of 12%.

According to FAST the figures indicate a number of trends year on year not least the increased impact of the organisation's awareness campaigns. These campaigns, aimed at educating everyone within the workforce, have increasingly focused on the criminality of under licensing and the impact it can have on business.

Over the past couple of years FAST and other trade bodies associated with protecting copyright, have made it far easier to report the illegal use of software within the business community. This has included a new Hotline facility, greater anonymity for those reporting under licensing and even the ability to report via the FAST web site.

Commenting on the rise in reports made to the Federation, Geoff Webster, CEO said: 'We believe these figures reflect a positive change in attitude towards how organisations in general are viewing software piracy as a serious business issue. Particularly within large organisations, board level executives are realising that software piracy can have a huge financial impact on the business if not dealt with properly.'

He continued: 'It is an interesting point to note that while software piracy and under licensing is in general in decline, according to the latest figures from the Business Software Alliance (BSA), the number of reports is on the rise. This can to my mind solely be attributed to a general increase in awareness of the issue. FAST believes that its educational and enforcement roles are working in tandem and working effectively.'

FAST, January 2001

Chapter roundup

- When acquiring software an organisation may issue an **Invitation to Tender (ITT)** giving potential suppliers details about the proposed system.

- Suppliers' proposals need to be evaluated, perhaps using **benchmark tests,** and also on the basis of factors such as **reliability**, **warranty**, **support** and **training.**

- **Choice of software** depends on factors such as user requirements, user-friendliness, controls, compatibility and cost.

- A key question is whether software should be **specially written** (bespoke) or whether an **off-the-shelf** package is suitable.

- **Software contracts** include provisions relating to matters such as warranty, support and maintenance, ownership, and liability.

Quick quiz

1   Why would an organisation issue an Invitation To Tender (ITT)?

2   What is a benchmark test?

3   What does HCI stand for?

4   Why are Graphical User Interfaces favoured by most users?

5   What would you say is the main advantage of bespoke software?

6   What is the main disadvantage of bespoke software?

7   Define 'Corporate Over-Use'.

Answers to quick quiz

1   To invite tenders (offers to supply) for the system specified in the ITT.

2   A test of how long a machine and a program takes to run through a routine. Benchmark scores enable comparisons between systems.

3   Human-Computer Interface.

4   Because they are considered more user-friendly than text based interfaces.

5   As it is written for a specific purpose it should match user requirements very closely.

6   It's expensive when compared to off-the-shelf software.

7   The installation of software by more users than the organisation is licenced for.

The material covered in this Chapter is tested in Questions 2 and 8 in the Exam Question Bank.

Part C
Evaluating information systems

Chapter 9

IMPLEMENTATION AND QUALITY ISSUES

Topic list	Syllabus reference
1 Installation	3(f)
2 Testing	3(a), 3(e)
3 Training	3(f)
4 Documentation	3(f)
5 File conversion	3(a)
6 Changeover	3(f)
7 Quality assurance	3(d), 3(i)

Introduction

In the remaining three chapters of this Text we explore the issues surrounding systems **implementation** and **evaluation**. Some of the material in these chapters is similar to that covered earlier – eg performance testing is similar to benchmarking. The difference is that we are now dealing with a system that has been designed and is ready to be installed.

Study guide

Part 3.19 – Technical information system requirements

- Define and record performance and volume requirements of information systems
- Establish requirements for data conversion and data creation

Part 3.22 – Quality assurance in the management and development process

- Define the characteristics of a quality software product

- Define the terms quality management, quality assurance and quality control

- Describe the V model and its application to quality assurance and testing

- Explain the limitations of software testing

- Participate in the quality assurance of deliverables in requirement specification using formal static testing methods

- Explain the role of standards and their application in quality assurance

- Briefly describe the task of unit testing in bespoke systems development

Study guide (continued)

Part 3.23 – Systems and user acceptance testing

- Define the scope of systems testing

- Distinguish between dynamic and static testing

- Use a cause-effect chart (decision table) to develop an appropriate test script for a representative systems test

- Explain the scope and importance of performance testing and usability testing

- Define the scope and procedures of user acceptance testing

- Describe the potential use of automated tools to support systems and user acceptance testing

Part 3.24 – Implementation issues and implementation methods

- Plan for data conversion and creation

- Discuss the need for training and suggest different methods for delivering such training

- Describe the type of documentation needed to support implementation and comment on ways of effectively organising and presenting this documentation

- Distinguish between parallel running and direct changeover and comment on the advantages and disadvantages of each

Part 3.27 – Relationship of management, development process and quality

- Describe the relationship between the systems development process and quality assurance

Exam guide

The 'V' model is particularly suited to examination questions as it links the systems development process with testing and quality issues.

1 INSTALLATION

1.1 The main stages in the implementation of a computer system once it has been designed are as follows.

    (a) Installation of the **hardware and software.**
    (b) **Testing.**
    (c) **Staff training** and production of documentation.
    (d) **Conversion** of files and database creation.
    (e) **Changeover.**

1.2 The items in this list **do not** necessarily happen in a set **chronological order,** and some can be done at the same time - for example staff training and system testing can be part of the same operation.

1.3 The requirements for implementation **vary** from system to system.

Installation of equipment

1.4 Installing a **mainframe** computer or a large network is a major operation that is carried out by the manufacturer/supplier.

1.5 If just a few PCs are being installed in a small network, the customer may have to install the hardware.

1.6 Installing software used to be tedious and lengthy, taking perhaps half an hour for a package, but most new software is provided on CD-ROM and can be installed in minutes.

1.7 Software should be **registered** with the manufacturer, either by filling in a registration form and posting it or often by completing a form on screen and sending it in via the world wide web.

Installation of a mainframe

1.8 If a mainframe installation is to be successful it must be carefully planned. The particular problems of planning a large installation include the following.

Site selection

1.9 The site selected for the main computer might be in an existing or a new building. Factors in the choice of site are the need for the following.

(a) Adequate **space** for computer and peripherals, including servicing room.

(b) **Room for expansion**.

(c) **Easy access** for computer equipment and supplies (it should be unnecessary to knock holes in outside walls, as has happened, in order to gain access for equipment).

(d) **Nearness** to principal **user** departments.

(e) Space available for a **library**, **stationery** store, and **systems maintenance** staff.

(f) **Security**. How easy can access to the site be controlled?

Site preparation

1.10 The site preparation may involve consideration of certain potential problems.

(a) **Air conditioning** (temperature, humidity and dust).

(b) Special **electricity supplies**.

(c) **Raised floor** (or **false ceiling**) so that **cables** may pass easily from one piece of equipment to another.

(d) **Fire protection devices**.

(e) **Furnishings**.

Standby equipment

1.11 Standby equipment should be arranged, to ensure **continuity of processing** in the event of power or computer failure. Such equipment may include standby **generators** and standby **computers**.

2 TESTING

2.1 A system must be thoroughly tested before implementation, otherwise there is a danger that the new system will **go live with faults** that might prove costly. The scope of tests and trials will again **vary with the size** of the system.

2.2 Three types of testing can be identified: program testing, systems testing and acceptance testing.

Program testing

2.3 A **diagnostic routine**, or debugging routine, provides for outline program testing and error correction during program development. When a program does not operate correctly the cause of the error must be established. Diagnostic routines that step through the program line by line help this process.

2.4 Test data will be prepared of the type that the program will be required to process. This test data will deliberately include **invalid/exceptional items** to test whether the program reacts in the right way and generates the required management reports.

2.5 The anticipated results of extra space processing will be worked out in advance and then after processing the test program, there will be **item-for-item checking** against the actual computer output to test whether the program has operated as required.

2.6 Two types of program testing, unit testing and unit integration testing, are explained later in this chapter.

2.7 The testing of the whole system is referred to as **system testing.**

2.8 Two terms used in the context of testing are static testing and dynamic testing.

KEY TERMS

Static testing describes the process of evaluating a system or component based on its form, structure and content. The program or process is not executed or performed during static testing.

Dynamic testing is testing that is performed by executing a program.

2.9 Static testing techniques play a part in the requirement specification stage of system development. System modelling techniques (eg DFDs, flowcharts, ELHs, ERMs) are used to analyse, design and document a system. The system can then be compared with user requirements and redesigned as necessary. This process is also known as **static analysis**.

2.10 Static testing is also carried out after the program has been written. The code will be examined line by line, checking for syntax and logic errors.

2.11 Dynamic testing involves running the program and checking the results are as expected.

2.12 Tests can also be classified according to **what** they are testing – specifically performance and usability.

KEY TERMS

Performance testing is conducted to evaluate the compliance of a system or component with specified performance requirements.

Usability testing is conducted to evaluate how the operator interacts with the system.

2.13   The specific performance requirements which performance testing uses will vary depending on the nature of the system. Criteria should be chosen that ensure the system exceeds the requirements required for smooth and efficient day-to-day operation.

2.14   Possible **sources of performance requirements** include:

- Similar systems
- Operational information (eg transaction volumes)
- The current system specifications/performance
- User requirements

2.15   Usability testing is vital as a system may look great on paper and perform well when tested but provie inefficient when used by users in the required operating environment.

2.16   A key element in usability testing is the **user-friendliness** of the **Human Computer Interface (HCI)**. We covered the HCI in the previous chapter.

2.17   Various personnel will be involved in system tests.

(a)   The **IS project manager** will have overall responsibility for the project, and must ensure that the tests are planned and executed properly, and the system is fully documented.

(b)   **Systems analysts** must check with their tests that the system achieves the objectives set for it, and do not contain any errors.

(c)   **Programmers** must be on hand to de-bug any faults which the earlier program tests had not spotted.

(d)   The **computer operations manager** will be in charge of data preparation work and operations in the computer room.

2.18   Test data should be constructed to test **all conditions**. For example, dummy data records and transactions should be input which are designed to test all the data validation routines and the **links** between different parts of the system in the system.

2.19   Unusual, but feasible, transactions could be tested, to see how the system handles them - for example two wage packets in the same week for the same employee.

2.20   Many managers prefer to use **historical data** in trials, because it is then possible to check the output of the new system against the output that the old system produced. The **sequence of test actions** and expected results should be presented to testers in a document – known as a **Test script**.

User acceptance testing

> **KEY TERM**
>
> **User acceptance testing** is carried out to determine whether or not a system meets previously defined acceptance criteria. The aim is for the customer to determine whether or not to accept the system.

2.21   Acceptance testing is usually performed by the **user department**.

2.22 The purposes of having trials conducted by the user department's managers are to:

(a) Find **software errors** which exist but have not yet been detected.
(b) Find out exactly what the **demands of the new system** are for users.
(c) Find out whether **operating procedures** are as anticipated.

2.23 Another aspect of the user department trials (or a subsequent stage of trials) might be to test the system with **large volumes of data,** and at the same time use the tests as an opportunity to **train staff** in the new system and the new procedures.

2.24 These tests involve a range of checks.

(a) **Error correction** procedures (ie user department routines).
(b) The inter-relationship between **clerical and computer procedures**.
(c) The **duration** of processing routines.
(d) The **capacity** of files, file handling, updating and amendment.
(e) System **controls**, including auditing requirements.
(f) Procedures for **data capture, preparation** and **input** and the distribution of **output**.

Automated testing tools

2.25 Software testing typically consumes 30 percent of software development effort and budget. The need for good testing to achieve a quality product often conflicts with the requirement to produce the system on time and within budget.

2.26 The need for more efficient testing has led to the development of automated software testing tools known as **Computer Aided Software Testing** (**CAST**) tools. Organisations that have implemented CAST tools have reduced their testing costs and effort by as much as 80 percent.

2.27 There are products available that can **automate a variety of testing tasks**, including repeating test executions, performance assessment, simulation of interfaces, checking of test results, logical and physical test case design, static and dynamic analysis and debugging.

2.28 Even with such a wide range of test automation targets, many organisations have found it **difficult to achieve the potential benefits** of CAST. There are several key reasons why:

- What is being tested and how to test are misunderstood
- There is no clear test process to automate
- Poor selection and implementation of test tools
- The poor quality of the CAST products

Decision tables

2.29 Decision tables (also known as **cause-effect charts**) are used as a method of demonstrating the effect of a process or action in a concise manner. Decision tables are useful in system testing, for example in developing a **test script**.

2.30 The basic format consists of four quadrants divided by intersecting double lines.

Condition stub	Condition entry
Action stub	Action entry

2.31 SIMPLE EXAMPLE: A DECISION TABLE

We start by considering a very simple decision that most of us face every day: whether to get up or stay in bed.

Suppose you have to get up at around 8 am during the week to enable you to get to work on time. You go to work on Monday to Friday only. If you woke up one Tuesday morning at 8.02 you would be faced with the following appalling dilemma. An X marks the action you should take.

Conditions	Entry
Is it 8 o' clock yet?	Yes
Is it the weekend?	No
Actions	Entry
Get up	X
Stay in bed	

2.32   We can expand this table so that it takes account of **all the possible combinations** of conditions and shows the action that would be taken in each case.

(a)   Because a condition can only apply or not apply (Yes or No), **the number of combinations (or 'rules') is 2^n, where n is the number of conditions.**

Here there are 2 conditions (n = 2) so the number of combinations is $2^2 = 4$. There are four columns.

	1	2	3	4
Is it 8 o' clock yet?				
Is it the weekend?				
Get up				
Stay in bed				

(b)   The conditions can either have a Yes or No answer (Y or N).

(i)   As there are **two** possible outcomes, fill **half** of each row with Ys and the other half with Ns. So, write in Y for the first half of the columns in row 1 (columns 1 and 2) and N for the other half (columns 3 and 4).

(ii)   For row 2, write in Ys and Ns for **half** the number of columns of each group in the previous row. In this example row 1 has Ys in groups of twos, so row 2 will have Ys in groups of 1.

(iii)   If there are more conditions continue **halving** for each row until you reach the final condition, which will always be consecutive Ys and Ns.

	1	2	3	4
Is it 8 o' clock yet?	Y	Y	N	N
Is it the weekend?	Y	N	Y	N
Get up				
Stay in bed				

(c) Now **consider what action** you would take if the condition(s) specified in each column applied. For column 1 it is 8 o'clock but it is the weekend so you can stay in bed. For column 2 it is 8 o' clock but it is not the weekend so you must get up. Explain the logic of columns 3 and 4 yourself.

	1	2	3	4
Is it 8 o' clock yet?	Y	Y	N	N
Is it the weekend?	Y	N	Y	N
Get up		X		
Stay in bed	X		X	X

(d) In more complicated problems you may find that there are some columns that do not have any Xs in the Action entry quadrant because **this combination of conditions is impossible**. We will show you how to deal with these columns later.

Question 1

Mr L Bones decided to draw up a decision table demonstrating the decision-making process he executed when he woke up each day.

He identified 3 conditions, mirroring his early-morning thought processes, and 2 possible actions.

Conditions   *Is it 8 o' clock yet? Is it a weekday? Is it the weekend?*

Actions   *Get up. Stay in bed.*

Draw up and complete the decision table.

Answer

There are 3 conditions so there will be 2^3 = 8 columns.

	1	2	3	4	5	6	7	8
Is it 8 o' clock yet?	Y	Y	Y	Y	N	N	N	N
Is it a weekday?	Y	Y	N	N	Y	Y	N	N
Is it the weekend?	Y	N	Y	N	Y	N	Y	N
Get up		X						
Stay in bed			X			X	X	

Columns 1, 4, 5 and 8 do not have any Xs because it cannot be both a weekday *and* a weekend. In more complex decision situations it may only become clear that certain combinations are impossible once the table has been drawn up.

In this example we could simplify the table by deleting columns 1, 4, 5 and 8. We then end up with the same decision table as the one we saw earlier (although with the columns in a different order.)

A more formal explanation

2.33 We can now explain this more formally and look at a business example.

- The purpose of the **condition stub** is to specify the values of the data that we wish to test for.

- The **condition entry** specifies what those values might be.

2.34 Between them, the condition stub and condition entry show what values an item of data might have that a computer program should test for. Establishing conditions will be done within a computer program by means of **comparison checks**.

2.35 The **action entry** quadrant shows the action or actions that will be performed for each rule. The columns are marked with an 'X' opposite the actions(s) to be taken. In the computer program, instructions specify the action to take, given the conditions established by comparison checks.

2.36 EXAMPLE: A DECISION TABLE

There are **three conditions** which might be encountered by a sales order processing clerk taking a telephone order.

- The caller may have an existing overdue balance their account
- The caller's account balance may already be in excess of their credit limit
- The caller may not have an account at all

2.37 The number of columns in the decision table is the number of options to the power of the number of conditions. In this example there are two options - 'Y' or 'N' and three conditions. The number of rules is therefore (2^3) - **eight rules.**

Rule	1	2	3	4	5	6	7	8
Account overdue?	Y	Y	Y	Y	N	N	N	N
Credit limit exceeded?	Y	Y	N	N	Y	Y	N	N
New customer (no account)?	Y	N	Y	N	Y	N	Y	N

2.38 The three conditions in this example are **not** totally **independent.** Therefore some rules can be eliminated as **impossible.** For example, a customer that does not currently have an account cannot have an overdue balance and therefore will not have a credit limit. In cases such as this you should **start with a complete table** like that shown above - and deal with the impossible combinations later.

2.39 Continuing the above example, suppose that the **actions** are as follows.

Orders from existing customers who do not have an overdue balance and have not exceeded their credit limit should **be processed**.

This organisation decides that customers requiring an account must **provide credit references** for checking before the account can be opened. If these customers attempt to place an order before an account is set up, the order is **placed on hold**.

The policy for orders from existing customers with a balance in **excess of their credit limit** is that these orders are **placed on hold** and **referred to the section head**.

The policy for existing customers who have overdue balances, but are within their credit limit, is to **process the order** but to **also generate a reminder** letter for overdue balances.

2.40 From this description we can isolate five actions.

- Process order
- Obtain reference
- Place order on hold
- Refer to head
- Send reminder

2.41 Consider the fourth rule in the following table. There is an overdue balance on the account, but the customer would remain within his credit limit. The action entry will therefore show an X against 'Process order' and 'Send reminder'.

Rule	1	2	3	4	5	6	7	8
Account overdue?	Y	Y	Y	Y	N	N	N	N
Credit limit exceeded?	Y	Y	N	N	Y	Y	N	N
New customer (no account)?	Y	N	Y	N	Y	N	Y	N
Process order				X				
Obtain reference								
Place order on hold								
Refer to head								
Send reminder				X				

2.42 By considering each rule in turn the table can be completed. The rules that are **logically not possible** are shaded in the lower half of the table – and crossed out in the top half of the table.

Rule	1	2	3	4	5	6	7	8
Account overdue?	Y	Y	Y	Y	N	N	N	N
Credit limit exceeded?	Y	Y	N	N	Y	Y	N	N
New customer (no account)?	Y	N	Y	N	Y	N	Y	N
Process order				X				X
Obtain reference							X	
Place order on hold		X				X	X	
Refer to head		X				X		
Send reminder				X				

Question 2

Sales orders are processed and approved by a computer. Management has laid down the following conditions. Construct a decision table to reflect these procedures.

(a) If an order is between £10 and £100 a 3% discount is given, if the credit rating is good. If the customer has been buying from the company for over 5 years, the discount is increased to 4%.

(b) If an order is more than £100 a 5% discount is given, if the credit rating is good. If the customer has been buying from the company for over 5 years, the discount is increased to 6%.

(c) If the credit rating is not good in either case the order is referred to the supervisor.

(d) For orders under £10 no discount is given.

Answer

There are five *conditions*.

(1) Is the order < £10?
(2) Is the order £10 - £100?
(3) Is the order > £100?
(4) Is the credit rating good?
(5) Has the customer been buying > 5 years?

Note that the 'cut-off' values must be precisely stated.

There are seven *actions:* approve, refer on, give one of 5 levels of discount.

32 rules are required (2^5). This results in the following table.

	1	2	3	4	5	6	7	8	9	10	11	12	13	14	15	16	17	18	19	20	21	22	23	24	25	26	27	28	29	30	31	32
Order < £10	Y	Y	Y	Y	Y	Y	Y	Y	Y	Y	Y	Y	Y	Y	Y	Y	N	N	N	N	N	N	N	N	N	N	N	N	N	N	N	N
Order £10 - £100	Y	Y	Y	Y	Y	Y	Y	Y	N	N	N	N	N	N	N	N	Y	Y	Y	Y	Y	Y	Y	Y	N	N	N	N	N	N	N	N
Order > £100	Y	Y	Y	Y	N	N	N	N	Y	Y	Y	Y	N	N	N	N	Y	Y	Y	Y	N	N	N	N	Y	Y	Y	Y	N	N	N	N
Rating good	Y	Y	N	N	Y	Y	N	N	Y	Y	N	N	Y	Y	N	N	Y	Y	N	N	Y	Y	N	N	Y	Y	N	N	Y	Y	N	N
5 years	Y	N	Y	N	Y	N	Y	N	Y	N	Y	N	Y	N	Y	N	Y	N	Y	N	Y	N	Y	N	Y	N	Y	N	Y	N	Y	N
Impossible	X	X	X	X	X	X	X	X	X	X	X	X					X	X	X	X									X	X	X	X
Approve													X	X	X	X																
0%													X	X	X	X																
3%																						X										
4%																					X											
5%																										X						
6%																									X							
Refer																							X	X			X	X				

This means unwieldy construction (particularly in an examination). Condition 3 can be removed from the decision table. For example, if the answers to conditions 1 and 2 are NO then the answer to condition 3 must be YES, (unless there is an error) and so it need not be tested. In this way the decision table will be reduced to 16 rules.

Order < £10?	Y	Y	Y	Y	Y	Y	Y	Y	N	N	N	N	N	N	N	N
Order £10 - £100	Y	Y	Y	Y	N	N	N	N	Y	Y	Y	Y	N	N	N	N
Rating good	Y	Y	N	N	Y	Y	N	N	Y	Y	N	N	Y	Y	N	N
5 years	Y	N	Y	N	Y	N	Y	N	Y	N	Y	N	Y	N	Y	N
Impossible	X	X	X	X												
Approve					X	X	X	X								
0%					X	X	X	X								
3%										X						
4%									X							
5%														X		
6%													X			
Refer											X	X			X	X

In addition, the over 5 year condition is only relevant to orders for £10 or more, and so we need not test this condition when the order is below £10. This cuts the number of rules to 10.

Original rule no	13	15	21	22	23	24	25	26	27	28
Order < £10	Y	Y	N	N	N	N	N	N	N	N
Order £10-£100	N	N	Y	Y	Y	Y	N	N	N	N
Rating good	Y	N	Y	Y	N	N	Y	Y	N	N
5 years	-	-	Y	N	Y	N	Y	N	Y	N
Approve	X	X								
0%	X	X								
3%				X						
4%			X							
5%								X		
6%							X			
Refer					X	X			X	X

Three points arise from the above exercise.

(a) Orders under £10 are processed whether the credit rating is good or not. Although this results in lack of control over small orders, management may feel that the risk is justified by the savings made in processing time.

(b) After the first construction (the draft) the decision table should be redrawn to take into account:

   (i) The impossible combinations - these rules can be removed.

   (ii) Take rules which result in identical actions. These indicate which conditions need not be tested by the computer program, and highlight the order in which the conditions should be examined (to save processing time). In the example, rules 13/15 and 23/24 can be combined and it then becomes apparent that credit rating is immaterial if the order is less than £10; but if the credit rating is bad, it is immaterial whether the order is between £10 and £100, or over £100.

(c) For the customer > 5 years check, customers are given an extra 1% discount if they have been with the company over 5 years. Instead of 2 action entries, discount 4% and discount 6%, we can have a single action entry - add 1% to discount. The decision table could be refined still further.

Exam focus point

You are most unlikely to get such a large decision table as the one in the question above in the exam. The logical nature of decision tables makes them an excellent way of defining the paths a process may pass through and predicting the outcome of these paths in advance. Examination questions are likely to test decision tables in the context of systems testing.

The two-table approach

2.43 Read through the following narrative. (CASE and 4GLs were explained in Chapter 6.)

'An organisation which has advertised for a systems analyst has received so many applications that it has devised a set of procedures for drawing up an interview shortlist.

All accredited systems analysts will be interviewed: those with CASE experience during the week commencing 27 June and those without during the following week. A reserve list will be drawn up of applicants with CASE experience but without systems analysis accreditation.

Applicants who are not accredited systems analysts but who have 4GL experience will have their application forms sent to an associated organisation which requires a 4GL expert. Those programmers with 4GL experience in a mainframe environment will be interviewed by this second organisation while others will be placed on a reserve list.

Any other applicants will receive a rejection letter.'

2.44 The standard single table approach to this problem would probably involve the identification of **four conditions**, as follows.

(a) Accredited systems analyst?
(b) CASE experience?
(c) 4GL experience?
(d) Mainframe experience?

2.45 This would give $2^4 = 16$ columns, and a total of **six actions**, as follows.

(a) Interview during w/c 27 June.
(b) Interview during w/c 4 July.
(c) Reserve list.
(d) Interview at associated organisation.
(e) Associated organisation's reserve list.
(f) Reject.

2.46 However, because condition (d) is relevant only to condition (c) and is not independent, and because condition (c) is not relevant if condition (a) applies, this approach is **inefficient**. For all the situations where the applicant is an accredited systems analyst, it simply does not matter whether he or she has 4GL experience, whether on mainframes or not.

2.47 The **recommended approach** is therefore to move **condition (d)** into a **separate table**, together with any **actions** which relate solely to that condition. A **cross-reference** from one table to the other must of course be added.

2.48 This amended approach produces the following tables.

Table A

Accredited systems analyst?	Y	Y	Y	Y	N	N	N	N
CASE Experience?	Y	Y	N	N	Y	Y	N	N
4GL experience?	Y	N	Y	N	Y	N	Y	N
Interview during w/c 27 June	X	X						
Interview during w/c 4 July			X	X				
Reserve list					X	X		
Do *Table B*					X		X	
Reject								X

Reduced Table A

Accredited systems analyst?	Y	Y	N	N	N	N
CASE Experience?	Y	N	Y	Y	N	N
4GL experience?	-	-	Y	N	Y	N
Interview during w/c 27 June	X					
Interview during w/c 4 July		X				
Reserve list			X	X		
Do *Table B*			X		X	
Reject						X

Table B

Mainframe experience?	Y	N
Interview at associated organisation	X	
Associated organisation's reserve list		X

Extended entry and mixed entry decision tables

2.49 Decision tables of the type we have just examined are called '**limited entry**' decision tables. In these, each condition is posed as a question requiring either a YES, NO or 'immaterial' answer and each action is either taken or not taken.

2.50 In an **extended entry decision table** the condition and the action stubs are more general, the exact condition or action being specified in the entry quadrants. A **mixed entry table** consists of both limited and extended entry lines within one table. An example will make this clear.

2.51 EXAMPLE: MIXED ENTRY DECISION TABLES

Reservation requests for the flights of the Caviar and Champagne Airline are dealt with according to the following rules. You are required to construct a mixed entry decision table of the procedure.

(a) All flights contain both first and second class cabins.

(b) If a seat is available on the flight of the requested class, allocate seat and output a ticket for that class.

(c) If not, where a first class passenger will accept a seat in the second class cabin and one is available, the seat is allocated and a second class ticket is output. Second class passengers are not offered a seat in the first class cabin.

(d) In cases where no seat is available to meet the request, output 'sorry, no seat' message.

2.52 SOLUTION

A mixed entry decision table is shown below.

Request is for:	1st	1st	1st	1st	2nd	2nd
1st class seat available?	Y	N	N	N		
2nd class acceptable?		Y	Y	N		
2nd class seat available?		Y	N		Y	N
Allocate seat	1st	2nd			2nd	
Issue ticket	1st	2nd			2nd	
Output 'sorry no seat'			X	X		X

2.53 Extended entry and mixed entry decision tables are **more compact** when constructed, and are useful as a **communication** method (eg to show the analysed problem to management).

2.54 However they are **more difficult** than limited entry decision tables to **prepare** and **check** for completeness.

The advantages and disadvantages of decision tables

2.55 The main **advantages** of using decision tables are as follows.

(a) It is possible to check that **all combinations** have been considered.
(b) They show a **cause and effect** relationship.
(c) It is easy to **trace from actions to conditions** (unlike in flowcharts).
(d) They are **easy to understand**.
(e) **Alternatives can be grouped** to facilitate analysis.

2.56 However, there are some **disadvantages**.

(a) They are not suited to problems with **unclear** conditions or actions.
(b) They do not show the process step-by-step.

3 TRAINING

3.1 Staff training in the use of information technology is as important as the technology itself as **without effective operation** at all levels computer systems can be an expensive **waste of resources** in any business.

3.2 The issue of training raises the wider matter of how to make personnel at all levels competent and willing to use IT. If organisations wish to encourage end-user computing then a training program should be part of a wider **information exercise**.

3.3 Training is not simply an issue that affects operational staff. As PCs are used more and more as management tools, training in information technology **affects all levels** in an organisation, from senior managers learning how to use an executive information system for example, to accounts clerks learning how to use an accounts management system.

The complete training requirement

3.4 A **systematic approach** to training can be illustrated in a flowchart as follows.

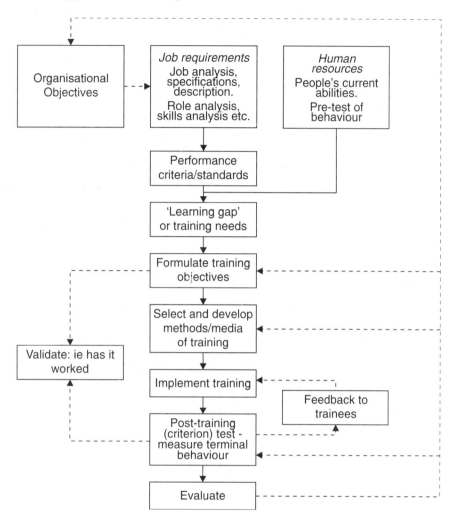

3.5 Note the following points in particular.

(a) Training is provided primarily to help the **organisation** achieve its **objectives,** not just for the benefit of staff.

(b) An individual's **training need** is generally defined as follows.

Required level of competence	X
Current level of competence	(Y)
Training need	Z

(c) Training should be **evaluated** to make sure that it has worked. If not the method may have been wrong. Whatever the cause, the training need still exists.

Senior management training

3.6 Senior management can be 'trained' in a number of ways of varying degrees of formality. The completely **informal** approach might include the provision of information from various sources.

- **Newspapers** (most of the quality press run regular articles on IT and computing).
- **Subordinates** (getting subordinate members of staff to demonstrate a system).
- **Individual demonstrations** of computer systems for senior executives.

3.7 **Semi-formal** training includes the following.

(a) Executive **briefings** (for example presentation before or after board meetings).

(b) Video **demonstrations** (for example during lunchtime).

(c) **Short seminars**, designed around an issue that is narrowly defined.

3.8 **Formal sessions** such as day **courses** are necessary if managers are to learn how to use a particular system, for example an Executive Information System or a spreadsheet package.

3.9 Some commentators have argued that senior managers who are knowledgeable about computers and related technologies **make wiser decisions** in the following areas.

(a) **Allocation of resources** to information systems (especially if the information system gives an organisation competitive advantage).

(b) **Planning** for information systems.

(c) Establishing an appropriate **corporate culture** for technological development.

(d) The establishment of an informed scepticism when dealing with IT professionals means that managers **won't be blinded by science**, and will be able to communicate their needs more effectively.

(e) Informed managers will have a **better understanding of their subordinates'** work.

Training middle management

3.10 The type of training middle management receives is likely to be **more structured** and **more tailored** to the particular applications within their remit.

3.11 Middle management are responsible for the **correct use of systems** in an age of distributed processing and end-user computing. Middle management are also responsible for implementing in detail the organisation's computer **security policy**.

3.12 The accent is also on the **business issues**. Managers do not necessarily need to know **how** computers work. They need to know **what** computing can do for them.

Training users

3.13 Users need a number of different types of computer and systems training.

(a) **Basic literacy** in computers such as the concept of a file, updating, maintenance and so forth, might be needed. This might help users relate the workings of a manual system to its computer replacement.

(b) Users need to get up and running with particular applications **quickly**, even if they do not go into the finer points of it. If the system is complex, such training gives users an **overall view** of the system, commands and procedures.

(c) Users might sometimes need a **refresher course**, especially if they do not use a particular application regularly.

(d) Users need training while operating the application (**on-the-job training**).

3.14 Some of these facilities are provided by the computer system itself. For example, many software packages have a **Help facility** which enables a user to learn facts about the system while they are using it.

3.15 **Computer based training** has the advantage of encouraging users to become acquainted with the technology they will be using, and to develop their skills at their own pace. **Multimedia training packages** exist for many widely-used software packages.

3.16 Training can also be provided by:

(a) Reading the **user manuals**

(b) Attending **courses** that the dealer or employer provides

(c) Attending **courses** on a leading software package provided by a third-party training establishment

3.17 With large computer systems, extensive training of large numbers of staff will probably be necessary, and so further training measures may include other media.

(a) **Lectures** on general or specific aspects of the system - possibly with the use of films, video, tape-recordings, slides, overhead projectors etc.

(b) **Discussion meetings**, possibly following on from lectures, which allow the staff to ask questions and sort out problems.

(c) **Internal company magazines**, to explain the new system in outline.

(d) **Handbooks**, detailing in precise terms the new documentation and procedures. Different handbooks for each function will often be prepared by different persons.

(e) Using **trials/tests** on the new system to give staff direct experience before the system goes live.

4 DOCUMENTATION

> **KEY TERM**
>
> **Documentation** includes a wide range of technical and non-technical books, manuals, descriptions and diagrams relating to the design, use and operation of a computer system. Examples include user manuals, hardware and operating software manuals, system specifications and program documentation.

The system specification

4.1 The system specification documents the structure and form of **the whole system.** As parts of the system are changed or added to, the specification should be updated.

4.2 Many of the problems in computer installations arise because of **inadequate** documentation. Controls must be set up to ensure that **updating procedures** are always carried out.

Program specifications

4.3 A program specification, or program documentation, is the complete description of a program, usually including **notes, flowcharts,** a listing of all the **codes,** and perhaps test data and expected results. There should be a program specification for every individual program in the system.

BPP PUBLISHING

4.4 **Initial specifications** are drawn up by the systems analyst and the programmer then uses the specification as the **basis of writing and testing the required program**.

4.5 When the program has been written and tested, one copy of the **final specification** will form part of the overall systems specification, and a second copy will be retained by the programmer to form part of the programmer's own documentation for the program.

Computer operations manual

4.6 This manual provides full documentation of the **operational procedures** necessary for the 'hands-on' running of the system. Amongst the matters to be covered by this documentation would be the following.

(a) **Systems set-up procedures**. Full details should be given for each application of the necessary file handling and stationery requirements etc.

(b) **Security procedures**. Particular stress should be placed on the need for checking that proper authorisation has been given for processing operations and the need to restrict use of machine(s) to authorised operators.

(c) **Reconstruction control procedures**. Precise instructions should be given in relation to matters such as file dumping and also the recovery procedures to be adopted in the event of a systems failure.

(d) **System messages**. A listing of all messages likely to appear on the operator's screen should be given together with an indication of the responses which they should evoke.

User manual

4.7 **Before staff training** takes place the system should be documented from the point-of-view of **users**. Matters to be dealt with include the following.

(a) **Input**. Responsibilities and procedures for preparation and conduct of input.

(b) **Error reports**. Full explanation of nature and form of error reports (eg exception reports for items rejected by data validation checks) and instructions as to the action to be taken.

(c) **Output**. What options are available and what should be done with it.

4.8 The user documentation is used to **explain** the system to the user and to help to train staff. It provides a **point of reference** should the user have problems with the system. Much of this information **may be available on-line** using context-sensitive help eg 'Push F1 for help'.

4.9 When a system is developed in-house, the user documentation might be written by a systems analyst. However, it might be considered preferable for the user documentation to have some input from **users**. As user-documentation is intended to help users, it must be written in a way that users are able to understand. The aim is to **ensure the smooth operation of the system** not to turn users into analysts.

System changes manual

4.10 Amendments to the original systems specification will almost inevitably occur. The objective of the system changes manual is to ensure that such changes are just as **strictly controlled** as was the case with the original systems development and introduction. Four matters to be covered in this respect are listed below.

(a) Recording of the request and **reason** for a change.
(b) Procedures for the **authorisation** of changes.
(c) Procedures for the **documentation** of changes.
(d) Procedures for the **testing** of changes.

4.11 Change procedures and control are covered in Chapter 11.

5 FILE CONVERSION

> **KEY TERM**
>
> **File conversion**, means converting **existing files** into a format suitable for the new system.

5.1 File conversion may be a **major part** of the systems implementation or it may be a simple process, if upgrading from version 1 of a standard package to version 2. If conversion requires the changing of existing manual file records into a medium used by the **computer** it may be very expensive.

5.3 Because of the volume of data that must be copied on to the new files, the problem of **input errors** is a serious one, whatever data validation checks may be operating.

5.4 Once the file has been created, **extensive checking** for accuracy is essential, otherwise considerable problems may arise when the system becomes operational.

5.5 Before starting to load live data about customers, suppliers or employees etc, management should check whether the system must be registered under the **Data Protection Act 1998**.

Existing computer files

5.6 If the system is already computerised on a system that the organisation now wishes to abandon, the difficulties of file conversion will usually (though not always) be reduced. When it comes to the actual transcription from the old files to the new computer files the use of a special **conversion program** or **translation program** will speed up the whole process.

5.7 The problem of conversion has reduced significantly as major **software manufacturers** have realised that it may be a barrier to people using their products. Thus an Excel spreadsheet can be saved in Lotus 1-2-3 format, if this is what the user wants.

Existing manual files

5.8 The stages in file conversion from manual files to computer files are normally as shown below.

(a) Ensuring that the **original** record files are **accurate, complete and up to date**.

(b) Recording the old file data on **specially designed input documents**.

This will usually be done by the user department personnel (with additional temporary staff if required) following detailed instructions laid down by the systems designer or software supplier.

The instructions will include the procedures for allocating **new code numbers** (a coding system, including check digits if necessary.

(c) **Transcribing** the completed input documents on to the **computer media**.

(d) Data entry programs would include **validation checks** on the input data. The contents of the file must then be printed out and **completely checked** back to the data input forms (or even the original file if possible).

(e) **Correcting any errors** that this checking reveals.

5.9 Other problems of file conversion which must be considered include the following.

(a) The possible provision of **additional staff,** or the use of a computer bureau, to cope with the file conversion and prevent bottlenecks.

(b) The establishment of **cut-off dates** where live files are being converted (should the conversion be during slack times, for example, during holidays, weekends?).

(c) The decision as to whether files should be converted **all at once,** or whether the conversion should be **file by file** or record group by record group (with subsequent amalgamation).

Question 3

You have been asked to transfer 400 Sales Ledger manual record cards to a PC based system. The program menu has a record create option. Explain how you would set about this process, and the steps you would take to ensure that the task was completed successfully.

Answer

The steps that should be taken are as follows.

(a) Check the manual records, and remove any dead accounts.

(b) Assign account codes to each record, ideally with codes that incorporate a check digit.

(c) If necessary transcribe the data from the card records on to documents which can be used for copying from, for data input.

(d) Add up the number of accounts and the total value of account balances as control totals (perhaps using a spreadsheet).

(e) Select the record create option from the program menu and key the standing data and current data onto the new computer file. This should ideally be done at a quiet time, perhaps over a weekend.

(f) Input that is rejected by a data validation check should be re-keyed correctly.

(g) A listing of the records put on to file should be printed out. This listing should be checked for errors, ideally by someone who did not do the keying in. Errors should be reported, and corrected data keyed in to amend the data on file.

(h) The program should produce control totals of the number of records put on to the file, and the total value of account balances. These control totals should be checked against the pre-prepared control totals. Discrepancies should be investigated, and any errors or omissions put right.

(i) A back-up copy of the new file should be made.

(j) The file and the new system should then be ready for use.

6 CHANGEOVER

6.1 Once the new system has been fully and satisfactorily tested the changeover can be made. This may be according to one of four approaches.

- Direct changeover
- Parallel running
- Pilot tests
- Phased or 'staged' implementation

Direct changeover

6.2 The old system is **completely replaced** by the new system **in one move**.

6.3 This may be unavoidable where the two systems are substantially different, or where extra staff to oversee parallel running are unobtainable.

6.4 While this method is comparatively **cheap** it is **risky** (system or program corrections are difficult while the system has to remain operational). Management must have complete confidence that the new system will work.

6.5 The new system should be introduced during **slack periods,** for example over a bank holiday weekend or during an office closure such as a factory's summer shutdown or in the period between Christmas and the New Year.

Parallel running

6.6 The **old and new** systems are **run in parallel** for a period of time, both processing current data and enabling cross checking to be made.

6.7 This method provides a **degree of safety** should there be problems with the new system. However, if there are differences between the two systems cross-checking may be difficult or impossible.

6.8 There is a **delay** in the actual implementation of the new system, a possible indication of **lack of confidence,** and a need for **more staff** to cope with both systems running in parallel.

6.9 This cautious approach, if adopted, should be properly planned, and the plan should include.

  (a) A firm **time limit** on parallel running.

  (b) Details of **which data** should be **cross-checked** - all of it? - some of it on a sample basis?

  (c) Instructions on how **errors** are to be dealt with - they could be errors in the old system.

  (d) Instructions on how to cope with **major problems** in the new system.

Pilot operation

6.10 This is **cheaper** and **easier to control** than parallel running, and provides a **greater degree of safety** than does a direct changeover. There are two types of pilot operation.

  (a) **Retrospective parallel running**

    The new system operates on **data already processed** by the old system. Existing results are available for cross-checking and the system can be tested without the problems of staffing and disruption caused by parallel running.

(b) **Restricted data running**

This involves a **complete logical part** of the whole system being chosen and run as a unit on the new system. If that is shown to be working well the remaining parts are then transferred. Gradually the whole system can be transferred in this piecemeal fashion.

For example, one group of customer accounts from the sales ledger might be run on the new system. Planning should involve the setting of strict time limits for each phase and instructions on how problems are to be dealt with. It must be remembered that two systems have to be controlled and additional staff, as well as a longer period for implementation, may be required.

Phased implementation

6.11 Phased implementation takes two possible forms.

(a) It can on the one hand resemble **parallel running**, the difference being that only a portion of the data is run in parallel, for example for **one branch** only.

(b) Alternatively, phased implementation may consist of a number of **separate direct changeovers**, for example where a large system is to be replaced and the criteria for direct changeover apply.

6.12 The use of this method of implementation is best suited to very **large projects** and/or those where distinct parts of the system are **geographically dispersed**.

6.13 Where this approach is adopted care must be taken to control any **systems amendments** incorporated in the later phases in order to ensure that the overall system remains totally compatible.

7 QUALITY ASSURANCE (QA)

7.1 Quality is concerned with 'fitness for purpose'.

> **KEY TERMS**
>
> In the context of software and information systems **Quality** may be defined as conformance to customer needs.
>
> **Quality management** is concerned with controlling activities with the aim of ensuring that products or services are fit for their purpose, and meet specifications. Quality management encompasses quality assurance and quality control.
>
> **Quality assurance** focuses on the way a system is produced. Procedures and standards are devised with the aim of ensuring defects are eliminated (or at least minimised) during the development process.
>
> **Quality control** is concerned with checking and reviewing work that has been done. Quality control therefore has a narrower focus than quality assurance.

7.2 **Quality management** is a type of control system involving the activities outlined below.

Step 1. **Plan**. Establish:

(i) **Standards** of quality for a product (eg a software package) or service (eg performance and volume requirements).

> (ii) **Procedures** or production methods that ought to ensure that these required standards of quality are met (eg a systems development methodology).

Step 2. Devise suitable instruments and techniques to **monitor** actual quality.

Step 3. **Compare** actual quality with planned quality using **feedback**.

Step 4. Take control action when actual quality falls below standard.

Step 5. Review the plan and standards to ensure **continuous improvement**.

7.3 A goal for quality management in systems development should be the **prevention** of system defects. Examples of defects include 'bugs' that prevent the system operating correctly or a badly designed system that does not meet user needs.

The Quality Plan and the role of standards

7.4 We covered the role and contents of the Quality Plan in Chapter 5. The Quality Plan should be produced early in the project lifecycle - by the project manager together with the project team.

The quality plan may be based on a specific Quality Management System such as ISO 9000.

7.5 ISO 9000 is the International Standards Organisation's (ISO) generic Quality Management System (QMS). In the UK the Department of Trade and Industry established the relevance of these standards to the production of software under the BS EN ISO 9001/TickIT scheme. Software vendors can apply for accreditation under this scheme.

7.6 The ISO itself has developed a more specific quality standard for software development – the SPICE standard.

7.7 The SPICE standard resulted from the **S**oftware **P**rocess **I**mprovement **C**apability d**E**termination project that aimed to develop an international standard for software process assessment.

7.8 SPICE is a document based standard that addresses three issues:
- How to identify key processes
- How to assess the efficiency of the processes
- How to undertake work improving the processes

7.9 The SPICE standard resulted from the **S**oftware **P**rocess **I**mprovement **C**apability d**E**termination project that aimed to develop an international standard for software process assessment.

The 'V' model

7.10 The 'V' model shows the relationship between system development, testing and quality assurance throughout the project lifecycle. The model is a variation of the waterfall model we covered in Chapter 6.

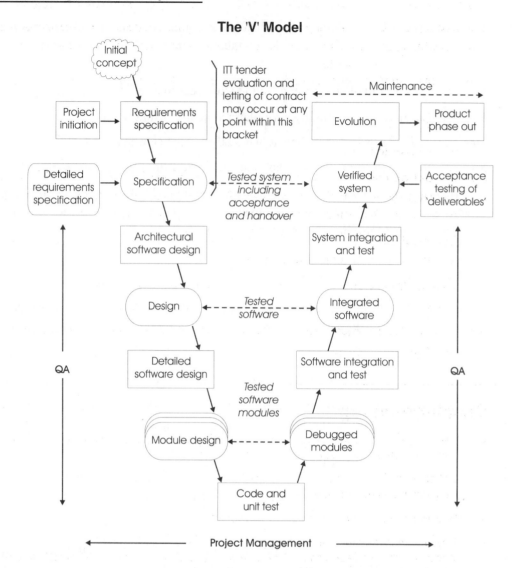

The 'V' Model

7.11 The left leg of the V shows the system development stages of analysis and design - including programming. The upward leg covers the assembly and testing phases and product delivery.

7.12 The V shape enables the model to demonstrate the relationship between the stages of system development and the testing and quality assurance process. It shows that individual programs are tested against individual module designs, the integrated software tested against the system design and the final complete system is user accepted tested against the requirements specification.

Unit testing and unit integration testing

7.13 The lowest point of the V is where individual units of the program are tested.

KEY TERMS

Unit testing means testing one function or part of a program to ensure it operates as intended.

Unit integration testing involves testing two or more software units to ensure they work together as intended. The output from unit integration testing is a debugged module.

7.14   The developer uses test cases (in terms of inputs, expected results, and evaluation criteria), test procedures, and test data for conducting unit testing and integration testing.

7.15   The test cases should cover all aspects of the part of the program concerned.

The cost of quality

7.16   Quality involves four types of cost.

(a)   **Prevention costs** are costs incurred to ensure the work is done correctly – for example ensuring the system design is correct before beginning production. Prevention costs are the cost of avoiding poor quality.

(b)   **Appraisal costs** are the costs of inspection and testing – for example design reviews, structured walkthroughs and program testing.

(c)   **Internal failure costs** are the costs of correcting defects discovered before the system is delivered.

(d)   **External failure costs**. These are costs arising to fix defects discovered after the system has been delivered.

Chapter roundup

- The main stages in the systems **implementation** process are installation of hardware and software, staff training, testing, file creation and changeover.

- **Installation** of equipment requires careful planning. Considerations include site selection, site preparation and delivery itself.

- **Training** is vital if a new system is to be used efficiently and effectively.

- A system must be thoroughly **tested** to ensure it operates as intended. The nature and scope of testing will vary depending on the size and type of the system. After **systems testing** is completed, the user department will carry out **acceptance testing**.

- **Decision tables** show the effect of a process, decision or action. They are often used in the context of system testing.

- **Software testing** accounts for a significant amount of development costs and effort.

- The need for more efficient testing has led to the development of **CAST tools**.

- **Documentation** includes a wide range of manuals, diagrams and descriptions relating to the design, use and operation of the system.

- File creation involves the creation or **conversion** of files for use with the new system. This process must be **controlled** to ensure accuracy.

- There are four approaches to **changeover**: direct changeover, parallel running, pilot tests and phased implementation. These vary in terms of time required, cost and risk.

- In the context of information systems **quality** may be defined as conformance to customer needs.

- The '**V model**' shows the relationship between system development, testing and quality.

Quick quiz

1   Define 'dynamic testing'.

2   Why is usability testing important?

3   What does CAST stand for?

4   Decision tables consist of four quadrants. Label the four quadrants below.

5   What does the file conversion process achieve?

6   Distinguish quality assurance from quality control.

7   Define 'unit testing'.

Answers to quick quiz

1   Dynamic testing is testing that is performed by executing a program.

2   Because a system may look fine on paper and perform well when tested, but prove inefficient when used in the context it will operate in.

3   Computer Assisted Software Testing.

4

Condition stub	Condition entry
Action stub	Action entry

5   The file conversion process ensures existing files are in a format the new system is able to use.

6   See the Key Terms under paragraph 7.1.

7   Unit testing means testing one function or part of a program to ensure it operates as intended.

The material covered in this Chapter is tested in Question 3 in the Exam Question Bank.

Chapter 10

SECURITY AND LEGAL COMPLIANCE

Topic list	Syllabus reference
1 Security	3(c)
2 Physical threats	3(c)
3 Physical access control	3(c)
4 Building controls into an information system	1(a),3(c)
5 Privacy and data protection	3(b)
6 Internet security issues	3(c)
7 Information systems and the accountant	3(i)

Introduction

Organisations are becoming increasingly **reliant on computerised information systems**. It is vital therefore to ensure these systems are secure – to protect the information held on them, to ensure operations run smoothly, to prevent theft and to ensure compliance with legislation.

Study guide

Part 1.4 – Organising information systems – structural issues

- Discuss the meaning and need for a disaster recovery plan

Part 3.19 – Technical information system requirements

- Discuss the need for archiving, backup and restore and other housekeeping functions
- Explain the need for a software audit trail and define the content of such a trail

Part 3.20 – Legal compliance in information systems

- Describe the principles, terms and coverage typified by the UK Data Protection Act
- Describe the principles, terms and coverage typified by the UK Computer Misuse Act

Part 3.21 – Implementing security and legal requirements

- Describe methods to ensure the physical security of IT systems

- Discuss the role, implementation and maintenance of a password system

- Explain representative clerical and software controls that should assist in maintaining the integrity of a system

- Describe the principles and application of encryption techniques

- Discuss the implications of software viruses and malpractice

- Discuss how the requirements of the UK Data Protection and UK Computer misuse legislation may be implemented

Part 3.27 – Relationship of management, development process and quality

- Explain the role of the accountant in information systems management, delivery and quality assurance

BPP
PUBLISHING

> # Exam guide
>
> Data protection and privacy are extremely topical at the moment, as is Internet Security.

1 SECURITY

The responsibilities of ownership

1.1 If you own **something that you value** – you **look after it.** You keep it somewhere safe, you regularly check to see that it is in good condition and you **don't allow it to upset others.**

1.2 **Information** is a valuable possession and it deserves similar care.

> **KEY TERM**
>
> **Security**, in information management terms, means the **protection of data** from accidental or deliberate threats which might cause unauthorised modification, disclosure or destruction of data, and the **protection of the information system** from the degradation or non-availability of services.

1.3 Security refers to **technical** issues related to the computer system, psychological and **behavioural** factors in the organisation and its employees, and protection against the unpredictable occurrences of the **natural world.**

1.4 Security can be subdivided into a number of aspects.

   (a) **Prevention.** It is in practice impossible to prevent all threats cost-effectively.

   (b) **Detection.** Detection techniques are often combined with prevention techniques: a log can be maintained of unauthorised attempts to gain access to a computer system.

   (c) **Deterrence.** As an example, computer misuse by personnel can be made grounds for dismissal.

   (d) **Recovery procedures.** If the threat occurs, its consequences can be contained (for example checkpoint programs).

   (e) **Correction procedures.** These ensure the vulnerability is dealt with (for example, by instituting stricter controls).

   (f) **Threat avoidance.** This might mean changing the design of the system.

2 PHYSICAL THREATS

2.1 The **physical environment** quite obviously has a major effect on information system security, and so planning it properly is an important precondition of an adequate security plan.

Fire

2.2 Fire is the **most serious hazard** to computer systems. Destruction of data can be even more costly than the destruction of hardware.

2.3 A proper fire safety plan is an essential feature of security procedures, in order to prevent fire, detect fire and put out the fire. Fire safety includes:

(a) **Site preparation** (for example, appropriate building **materials,** fire doors).

(b) **Detection** (for example, smoke detectors).

(c) **Extinguishing** (for example, CO^2 systems).

(d) Training for staff in observing **fire safety procedures** (for example, no smoking in computer room).

Water

2.4 Water is a serious hazard. Flooding and water damage are often encountered following firefighting activities elsewhere in a building.

2.5 This problem can be countered by the use of waterproof ceilings and floors together with the provision of adequate drainage.

2.6 In some areas flooding is a natural risk, for example in parts of central London and many other towns and cities near rivers or coasts. Basements are therefore generally not regarded as appropriate sites for large computer installations.

Weather

2.7 Wind, rain and storms can all cause substantial **damage to buildings**. In certain areas the risks are greater, for example the risk of typhoons in parts of the Far East. Many organisations make heavy use of prefabricated and portable offices, which are particularly vulnerable.

2.8 Cutbacks in maintenance expenditure may lead to leaking roofs or dripping pipes, which can invite problems of this type, and maintenance should be kept up if at all possible.

Lightning

2.9 Lightning and electrical storms can play havoc with power supplies, causing power failures coupled with power surges as services are restored. Minute adjustments in power supplies may be enough to affect computer processing operations (characterised by lights which dim as the country's population turns on electric kettles following a popular television program).

2.10 One way of combating this is by the use of **uninterrupted (protected) power supplies.** This will protect equipment from fluctuations in the supply. Power failure can be protected against by the use of a **separate generator**.

Terrorist activity

2.11 **Political terrorism** is the main risk, but there are also threats from individuals with **grudges.**

2.12 In some cases there is very little that an organisation can do: its buildings may just happen to be in the wrong place and bear the brunt of an attack aimed at another organisation or intended to cause general disruption.

2.13 There are some avoidance measures that should be taken, however.

(a) **Physical access** to buildings should be controlled (see the next section).

(b) Organisations involved in controversial activities may consider moving into other lines of business.

BPP PUBLISHING

(c) The organisation should consult with police and fire authorities about potential risks, and co-operate with their efforts to avoid them.

Accidental damage

2.14 **People** are a physical threat to computer installations: there can be few of us who have not at some time spilt a cup of coffee over a desk covered with papers, or tripped and fallen doing some damage to ourselves or to an item of office equipment.

2.15 Combating accidental damage is a matter of:

(a) Sensible **attitudes** to office behaviour.
(b) Good office **layout**.

Question 1

You are the financial controller of your organisation. The company is in the process of installing a mainframe computer, and because your department will be the primary user, you have been co-opted onto the project team with responsibility for systems installation. You have a meeting at which the office services manager will be present, and you realise that no-one has yet mentioned the risks of fire or flooding in the discussions about site selection. Make a note of the issues which you would like to raise under these headings.

Answer

(a) **Fire**. Fire security measures can usefully be categorised as preventative, detective and corrective. Preventative measures include siting of the computer in a building constructed of suitable materials and the use of a site which is not affected by the storage of inflammable materials (eg stationery, chemicals). Detective measures involve the use of smoke detectors. Corrective measures may include installation of a sprinkler system (water-based or possibly gas-based to avoid electrical problems), training of fire officers and good siting of exit signs and fire extinguishers.

(b) **Flooding**. Water damage may result from flooding or from fire recovery procedures. If possible, large installations should not be situated in basements.

3 PHYSICAL ACCESS CONTROL

3.1 Access control aims to prevent intruders getting near the computer equipment or storage media. Methods of controlling human access range from:

(a) **Personnel** (security guards).
(b) **Mechanical devices** (eg keys, whose issue is recorded).
(c) **Electronic identification devices** (eg card-swipe systems).

3.2 Obviously, the best form of access control would be one which **recognised** individuals immediately, without the need for personnel, who can be assaulted, or cards, which can be stolen. However, machines which can identify a person's fingerprints or scan the pattern of a retina are too **expensive** for many organisations.

3.3 It may not be cost effective or convenient to have the same type of access controls around the whole building all of the time. Instead, the various **security requirements of different departments** should be estimated, and appropriate boundaries drawn. Some areas will be very restricted, whereas others will be relatively open.

3.4 Guidelines for security against physical threats which should be applied **within the office** are.

(a) **Fireproof cabinets** should be used to store files, or **lockable metal boxes** for floppy disks. If files contain confidential data, they should be kept in a safe.

(b) Computers with **lockable keyboards** are sometimes used. Computer terminals should be **sited carefully**, to minimise the risk of unauthorised use or observation.

(c) If computer printout is likely to include confidential data, it should be **shredded** before it is eventually thrown away after use.

(d) **Disks** should not be left lying around an office. They can get lost or stolen. More likely still, they can get damaged, by spilling **tea or coffee** over them, or allowing the disks to gather **dust**, which can make them unreadable.

(e) The computer's **environment** (humidity, temperature, dust) should be properly controlled. This is not so important with PC systems as for mainframes. Even so, the computer's environment, and the environment of the files, should **not be excessively hot**.

3.5 Measures that can be **designed** into programs will be discussed later in this chapter.

PINs

3.6 In some systems, the user might have an individual **personal identification number**, or PIN, which identifies him or her to the system. Based on the security privileges allocated, the user will be **allowed** access and editing rights to certain parts of the system, but **forbidden** access or editing rights to other parts.

Door locks

3.7 Conventional door locks are of value in certain circumstances, particularly where users are only required to pass through the door a **couple of times a day**. If the number of people using the door increases and the frequency of use is high, it will be difficult to persuade staff to lock a door every time they pass through it.

3.8 A 'good' lock must be accompanied by a **strong door**. Similarly, other points of entry into the room/complex must be as well protected, otherwise the intruder will simply use a **window** to gain access.

3.9 One difficulty with conventional locks is the matter of **key control**. Each person authorised to use the door will need a key. Cleaners and other contractors might also be issued with keys. Practices such as lending out keys or taking duplicate keys may be difficult to prevent.

3.10 One approach to this is the installation of **combination locks,** where a numbered keypad is located outside the door and access allowed only after the correct 'code', or sequence of digits has been entered. This will only be fully effective if users ensure the combination is kept confidential, and the combination is **changed** frequently.

Card entry systems

3.11 Card entry systems are a more sophisticated means of control than the use of locks, as **cards can be programmed** to allow access to certain parts of a building only, between certain times.

3.12 Cars allow a high degree of monitoring of staff movements; they can for example be used instead of clock cards to record details of time spent on site. Such cards can be incorporated into **identity cards**, which also carry the photograph and signature of the user and which must be 'displayed' at all times.

Computer theft

3.13 A problem which is related to the problem of physical access control is that of equipment theft. As computer equipment becomes **smaller** and **more portable,** it can be 'smuggled' out of buildings with greater ease. Indeed much equipment is specifically **designed for use off-site**.

3.14 A **log of all equipment** should be maintained. This may already exist in basic form as a part of the fixed asset register. The log should include the **make, model** and **serial number** of each item, together with some other organisation-generated code which identifies the **department** which owns the item, the **individual** responsible for the item and its **location**. Anyone taking any equipment off-site should book it out and book it back in.

3.15 Computer theft may be carried out by persons who have official access to equipment. It may equally be carried out by those who do not. **Burglar alarms** should be installed.

3.16 **Smaller items** of equipment, such as laptop computers and floppy disks, should always be **locked securely away**. Larger items cannot be moved with ease and one approach adopted is the use of **bolts** to secure them to desks. This discourages 'opportunity' thieves. Larger organisations may also employ site security guards and install closed circuit camera systems.

Question 2

You are the chief accountant at your company. Your department, located in an open-plan office, has five networked desktop PCs, a laser printer and a dot matrix printer.

You have just read an article suggesting that the best form of security is to lock hardware away in fireproof cabinets, but you feel that this is impracticable. Make a note of any alternative security measures which you could adopt to protect the hardware.

Answer

(a) 'Postcode' all pieces of hardware. Invisible ink postcoding is popular, but visible marking is a better deterrent. Soldering irons are ideal for writing on plastic casing.

(b) Mark the equipment in other ways. Some organisations spray their hardware with permanent paint, perhaps in a particular colour (bright red is popular) or using stencilled shapes.

(c) Hardware can be bolted to desks. If bolts are passed through the desk and through the bottom of the hardware casing, the equipment can be rendered immobile.

(d) Ensure that the organisation's standard security procedures (magnetic passes, keypad access to offices, signing in of visitors etc) are followed.

4 BUILDING CONTROLS INTO AN INFORMATION SYSTEM

4.1 We studied systems development models in Chapter 6 of this text. The following exercise will give you an idea of whether you have retained this knowledge.

Question 3

(a) Outline the main phases of a 'typical' systems development lifecycle model.

(b) At what stages of the SDLC should controls be considered?

Answer

(a) The SDLC models a disciplined approach to system development intended to reduce the possibility of ending up with a system that does not meet the needs of the organisation.

There are six stages, although in practice some stages may overlap.

SYSTEMS DEVELOPMENT LIFE CYCLE	
Feasibility study	Briefly review the existing system Identify possible alternative solutions
Systems investigation	Obtain details of current requirements and user needs such as data volumes, processing cycles and timescales Identify current problems and restrictions
Systems analysis	Consider why current methods are used and identify better alternatives
Systems design	Determine what inputs, processing and storage facilities are necessary to produce the outputs required Consider matters such as program design, file design and security Prepare a detailed specification of the new system.
Systems implementation	Write or acquire software, test it, convert files, install hardware and start running the new system
Review and maintenance	Ensure that the new system meets current objectives, and that it continues to do so

The cycle begins again when a review suggests that it is becoming difficult for an installed system to continue to meet current objectives through routine maintenance.

(b) Controls should be considered at *each* stage: ensuring that *all* alternatives are properly considered, highlighting control problems that the new system might rectify, drawing attention to controls in existing systems that should not be abandoned, reviewing specifications, checking that purchases are controlled and suppliers are vetted.

4.2 It is possible to **build controls** into computerised processing. A balance must be struck between the degree of control and the requirement for a user friendly system.

4.3 Controls can be classified into:

- Security controls
- Integrity controls
- Contingency controls

Security controls

> **KEY TERM**
>
> **Security** can be defined as 'The protection of data from accidental or deliberate threats which might cause unauthorised modification, disclosure or destruction of data, and the protection of the information system from the degradation or non-availability of services'.
>
> (Lane: *Security of computer based information systems*)

BPP PUBLISHING

4.4 **Risks to data**

- Human error
    - ◦ Entering incorrect transactions
    - ◦ Failing to correct errors
    - ◦ Processing the wrong files

- Technical error such as malfunctioning hardware or software
- Natural disasters such as fire, flooding, explosion, impact, lightning
- Deliberate actions such as fraud
- Commercial espionage
- Malicious damage
- Industrial action

4.5 Security can be subdivided into a number of aspects.

(a) **Prevention**. It is in practice impossible to prevent all threats cost-effectively.

(b) **Detection**. Detection techniques are often combined with prevention techniques: a log can be maintained of unauthorised attempts to gain access to a computer system.

(c) **Deterrence**. As an example, computer misuse by personnel can be made grounds for dismissal.

(d) **Recovery procedures**. If the threat occurs, its consequences can be contained (for example checkpoint programs).

(e) **Correction procedures**. These ensure the vulnerability is dealt with (for example, by instituting stricter controls).

(f) **Threat avoidance**. This might mean changing the design of the system.

Physical security

4.6 A system needs to be protected against **natural and man-made disasters**. Protective measures include the following.

- Site preparation, eg fireproof materials
- Detection equipment, eg smoke detectors
- Extinguishing equipment, eg sprinklers
- Use of uninterruptable power supplies (UPS)

4.7 Physical access controls are designed to prevent intruders getting near to computer equipment and/or storage media.

(a) Personnel, including receptionists and, outside working hours, security guards, can help control human access.

(b) Door locks can be used where frequency of use is low.

(c) This is not practicable if the door is in frequent use.

(d) Locks can be combined with:

(i) A keypad system, requiring a code to be entered.

(ii) A card entry system, requiring a card to be 'swiped'.

(e) Intruder alarms are vital.

4.8 Much computer equipment is easily portable and therefore susceptible to theft. Laptops and small printers are designed for portability; even desktops and laser printers can be easily carried by one person. Several protective measures can be taken.

- An equipment log, including booking out procedures
- Postcoding of equipment
- Bolts and/or locks to secure equipment to desks
- Secure storage of disks and CDs

Integrity controls

> ### KEY TERMS
>
> **Data integrity** in the context of security is preserved when data is the same as in source documents and has not been accidentally or intentionally altered, destroyed or disclosed.
>
> **Systems integrity** refers to system operation conforming to the design specification despite attempts (deliberate or accidental) to make it behave incorrectly.

4.9 Data will maintain its **integrity** if it is **complete** and **not corrupted**. This means that:

(a) The original **input** of the data must be controlled in such a way as to ensure that the results are complete and correct.

(b) Any **processing and storage** of data must maintain the completeness and correctness of the data captured.

(c) That reports or other **output** should be set up so that they, too, are complete and correct.

4.10 **Input controls** should ensure the **accuracy, completeness and validity** of input.

(a) **Data verification** involves ensuring data entered matches source documents.

(b) **Data validation** involves ensuring that data entered is not incomplete or unreasonable. Various checks can be used, depending on the data type.

    (i) **Check digits**. A digit calculated by the program and added to the code being checked to validate it eg modulus 11 method.

    (ii) **Control totals**. For example, a batch total totalling the entries in the batch.

    (iii) **Hash totals**. A system generated total used to check the reasonableness of numeric codes entered.

    (iv) **Range checks**. Used to check the value entered against a sensible range, eg balance sheet account number must be between 5,000 and 9,999.

    (v) **Limit checks**. Similar to a range check, but usually based on a upper limit eg must be less than 999,999.99.

4.11 Data may be **valid** (for example in the **correct format**) but still **not match source documents**.

4.12 **Processing controls** should ensure the **accuracy and completeness of processing**. Programs should be subject to development controls and to rigorous testing. Periodic running of test data is also recommended.

4.13 **Output controls** should ensure the accuracy, completeness and security of output. The following measures are possible.

- Investigation and follow-up of error reports and exception reports

227

- Batch controls to ensure all items processed and returned
- Controls over distribution/copying of output
- Labelling of disks/tapes

4.14 **Back-up controls** aim to maintain system and data integrity. We have classified back-up controls as an integrity control rather than a contingency control (see later this section) because back-ups should part of the day-to-day procedures of all computerised systems.

> ### KEY TERM
>
> **Back-up** means to make a copy in anticipation of future failure or corruption. A back-up copy of a file is a duplicate copy kept separately from the main system and only used if the original fails.

4.15 The **purpose of backing up data** is to ensure that the most recent usable copy of the data can be recovered and restored in the event of loss or corruption on the primary storage media.

4.16 A related concept is that of **archiving.** Archiving data is the process of moving (by copying) data from primary storage, such as a hard disk, to tape or other portable media for long-term storage.

4.17 Archiving provides a legally acceptable **business history**, while freeing up **hard disk space**. If archived data is needed, it can be restored from the archived tape to a hard disk. Archived data can be used to recover from site-wide disasters, such as fires or floods, where data on primary storage devices is destroyed.

4.18 How long data should be retained will be influenced by:

- Legal obligations
- Other business needs

4.19 Data stored for a long time should be tested periodically to ensure it is **still restorable** – it may be subject to **damage** from environmental conditions or mishandling.

4.20 In a well-planned data back-up scheme, a copy of backed up data is delivered (preferably daily) to a secure **off-site** storage facility.

4.21 A tape **rotation scheme** can provide a restorable history from one day to several years, depending on the needs of the business.

4.22 A well-planned **back-up and archive strategy** should include:

(a) A plan and schedule for the **regular back-up of critical data**.
(b) **Archive plans**.
(c) A **disaster recovery plan** that includes off-site storage.

4.23 As with archiving, regular tests should be undertaken to **verify that data backed up can be successfully restored**.

4.24 The **intervals** at which back-ups are performed must be decided. Most organisations back up their data daily, but back-ups may need to be performed more frequently, depending on the nature of the data and of the organisation.

4.25 A **rotation scheme** that provides an appropriate data history must be selected. The **Grandfather, Father, Son** scheme uses twelve tapes or other portable media - allowing recovery of three months data.

Grandfather, Father, Son back-up rotation scheme

Tape No.	Tape name	When written to	Overwritten
Tape 1	Son 1	Every Monday	Weekly
Tape 2	Son 2	Every Tuesday	Weekly
Tape 3	Son 3	Every Wednesday	Weekly
Tape 4	Son 4	Every Thursday	Weekly
Tape 5	**Father** week 1	**First** Friday	**Monthly**
Tape 6	Father week 2	Second Friday	Monthly
Tape 7	Father week 3	Third Friday	Monthly
Tape 8	Father week 4	Fourth Friday	Monthly
Tape 9	Father week 5 (if needed)	Fifth Friday	Monthly
Tape 10	**Grandfather** month 1	**Last business day** month 1	**Quarterly**
Tape 11	Grandfather month 2	Last business day month 2	Quarterly
Tape 12	Grandfather month 3	Last business day month 3	Quarterly

4.26 Even with a well planned back-up strategy some re-inputting may be required. For example, if after three hours work on a Wednesday a file becomes corrupt, the Tuesday version can be restored – but Wednesday's work will need to be re-input.

Passwords and logical access systems

KEY TERM

Passwords are a set of characters which may be allocated to a person, a terminal or a facility which are required to be keyed into the system before further access is permitted.

4.27 Unauthorised persons may circumvent physical access controls. A **logical access system** can prevent access to data and program files, by measures such as the following.

- Identification of the user
- Authentication of user identity
- Checks on user authority

4.28 Virtually all computer installations use passwords. Failed access attempts may be logged. Passwords are not foolproof.

- Standard system passwords must be changed

- Passwords must never be divulged to others and must never be written down

- Passwords must be changed regularly – and changed immediately if it is suspected that the password is known by others

- Obvious passwords must not be used

BPP
PUBLISHING

Administrative controls

4.29 **Personnel selection** is important. Some employees are always in a position of trust.

- Computer security officer
- Senior systems analyst
- Database administrator

4.30 Measures to control personnel include the following.

- Careful recruitment
- Job rotation and enforced vacations
- Systems logs
- Review and supervision

4.31 For other staff, **segregation of duties** remains a core security requirement. This involves division of responsibilities into separate roles.

- Data capture and data entry
- Computer operations
- Systems analysis and programming

Audit trail

4.32 The original concept of an audit trail is to enable a manager or auditor to follow transactions stage-by-stage through a system to ensure that they had been processed correctly. The intention is to:

- **Identify errors**
- **Detect fraud**

4.33 Modern integrated computer systems have cut out much of the time-consuming stage-by-stage working of older systems, but there should still be some **means of identifying individual records** and the **input and output documents** associated with the processing of any individual transaction.

> **KEY TERM**
>
> An **audit trail** is a record showing who has accessed a computer system and what operations he or she has performed. Audit trails are useful both for maintaining security and for recovering lost transactions. Accounting systems include an audit trail component that is able to be output as a report.
>
> In addition, there are separate audit trail software products that enable network administrators to monitor use of network resources.

4.34 An audit trail should be provided so that every transaction on a file contains a **unique reference** (eg a sales system transaction record should hold a reference to the customer order, delivery note and invoice).

4.35 Typical contents of an accounting software package audit trail include the following items.

(a) A system generated **transaction number.**
(b) A meaningful reference number eg invoice number.
(c) Transaction type eg reversing journal, credit note, cashbook entry etc.
(d) Who input the transaction (user ID).

(e)   Full **transaction details** eg net and gross amount, customer ID and so on.

(f)   The **PC or terminal** used to enter the transaction.

(g)   The **date** and **time** of the entry.

(h)   Any additional reference or **narration** entered by the user.

Systems integrity in a small company

4.36   By 'small' we envisage a company with, say, three **stand-alone PCs**. Possible controls are as follows.

(a)   Installation of a **password** routine which is activated whenever the computer is booted up, and activated after periods of inactivity.

(b)   The use of additional passwords on 'sensitive' files eg employee salaries spreadsheet.

(c)   Any data stored on floppy disk, Zip-disk or CD-R should be locked away.

(d)   **Physical access controls**, for example door locks activated by swipe cards or PIN numbers, to prevent access into the room(s) where the computers are kept. This is probably not feasible in an open plan office.

Systems integrity with a LAN

4.37   In this scenario there might be, say, **ten to twenty PCs** linked on a **Local Area Network**. Each PC would have its own processing ability, but would be linked via the LAN to central printers and a file server.

4.38   The main risk on a system of this type is the risk of a fault or breakdown in one area **spreading across the system**. This is particularly true of **viruses**. A virus introduced onto one machine could replicate itself throughout the network. All files coming in to the organisation should be scanned using **anti-virus software** and all machines should have anti-virus software running constantly.

4.39   A second risk is that an **unauthorised user** could gain access to the **system**. This would require implementation of the controls described for the small company. A further risk, depending on the type of network configuration, is that an extra PC could be 'plugged in' to the network to gain access to it. The **network management software** should detect and prevent breaches of this type.

Systems integrity with a WAN

4.40   Here there might be **four processing locations** connected by a **Wide Area Network**. Each location would have its own LAN, although there might also be a dedicated land line to the other three offices. Each file server is updated with data from the other three locations at regular intervals.

4.41   Additional issues over and above those already described relate to the wide area network. Dedicated land lines are more secure from hacking, but encryption software may need to be considered. If Internet access is possible **firewall security** should be implemented.

4.42   If **commercially sensitive data** is being transferred it would be necessary to specify high quality communications equipment and to use sophisticated network software to prevent and detect any security breaches. The security issues surrounding the Internet are covered later in this chapter.

Contingency controls

> ### KEY TERM
>
> A **contingency** is an unscheduled interruption of computing services that requires measures outside the day-to-day routine operating procedures.

4.43 The preparation of a contingency plan (also known as a disaster recovery plan) is one of the stages in the development of an organisation-wide security policy. A contingency plan is necessary in case of a major **disaster,** or if some of the **security measures** discussed elsewhere **fail**.

4.44 A **disaster** occurs where the system for some reason breaks down, leading to potential **losses** of equipment, data or funds. The system **must recover as soon as possible** so that further losses are not incurred, and current losses can be rectified.

Question 4

What actions or events might lead to a system breakdown?

Answer

System breakdowns can occur in a variety of circumstances, for example:

(a) Fire destroying data files and equipment.
(b) Flooding.
(c) A computer virus completely destroying a data or program file or damaging hardware.
(d) A technical fault in the equipment.
(e) Accidental destruction of telecommunications links (eg builders severing a cable).
(f) Terrorist attack.
(g) System failure caused by software bugs which were not discovered at the design stage.
(h) Internal sabotage (eg logic bombs built into the software).

4.45 Any disaster recovery plan must therefore provide for:

(a) **Standby procedures** so that some operations can be performed while normal services are disrupted.

(b) **Recovery procedures** once the cause of the breakdown has been discovered or corrected.

(c) **Personnel management** policies to ensure that (a) and (b) above are implemented properly.

Contents of a disaster recovery plan

4.46   The contents of a disaster recovery (or contingency plan) will include the following.

Section	Comment
Definition of responsibilities	It is important that somebody (a manager or co-ordinator) is designated to take control in a crisis. This individual can then delegate specific tasks or responsibilities to other designated personnel.
Priorities	Limited resources may be available for processing. Some tasks are more important than others. These must be established in advance. Similarly, the recovery program may indicate that certain areas must be tackled first.
Backup and standby arrangements	These may be with other installations, with a company that provides such services (eg maybe the hardware vendor); or reverting to manual procedures.
Communication with staff	The problems of a disaster can be compounded by poor communication between members of staff.
Public relations	If the disaster has a public impact, the recovery team may come under pressure from the public or from the media.
Risk assessment	Some way must be found of assessing the requirements of the problem, if it is contained, with the continued operation of the organisation as a whole.

5   PRIVACY AND DATA PROTECTION

KEY TERM

Privacy is the right of the individual to control the use of information about him or her, including information on financial status, health and lifestyle (ie prevent unauthorised disclosure).

Why is privacy an important issue?

5.1   In recent years, there has been a growing fear that the ever-increasing amount of **information** about individuals held by organisations could be misused.

5.2   In particular, it was felt that an individual could easily be harmed by the existence of computerised data about him or her which was inaccurate or misleading and which could be **transferred to unauthorised third parties** at high speed and little cost.

5.3   In the UK the current legislation covering this area is the **Data Protection Act 1998**.

The Data Protection Act 1998

5.4   The Data Protection Act 1998 is an attempt to protect the **individual**. The terms of the Act cover data about individuals - **not data about corporate bodies**.

Definitions of terms used in the Act

5.5 In order to understand the Act it is necessary to know some of the technical terms used in it.

> **KEY TERMS**
>
> **Personal data** is information about a living individual, including expressions of opinion about him or her. Data about organisations is not personal data.
>
> **Data users** are organisations or individuals who control personal data and the use of personal data.
>
> A **data subject** is an individual who is the subject of personal data.

The data protection principles

5.6 There are certain Data Protection Principles which registered data users must comply with.

> **DATA PROTECTION PRINCIPLES**
> Schedule 1 of the Act contains the data protection principles.
>
> 1 Personal data shall be processed fairly and lawfully and, in particular, shall not be processed unless:
>
>   (a) At least one of the conditions in Schedule 2 is met (see paragraph 5.11 (c) on the following page).
>
>   (b) In the case of sensitive personal data, at least one of the conditions in Schedule 3 is also met (see 5.11 (d)).
>
> 2 Personal data shall be obtained only for one or more specified and lawful purposes, and shall not be further processed in any manner incompatible with that purpose or those purposes.
>
> 3 Personal data shall be adequate, relevant and not excessive in relation to the purpose or purposes for which they are processed.
>
> 4 Personal data shall be accurate and, where necessary, kept up to date.
>
> 5 Personal data processed for any purpose or purposes shall not be kept for longer than is necessary for that purpose or those purposes.
>
> 6 Personal data shall be processed in accordance with the rights of data subjects under this Act.
>
> 7 Appropriate technical and organisational measures shall be taken against unauthorised or unlawful processing of personal data and against accidental loss or destruction of, or damage to, personal data.
>
> 8 Personal data shall not be transferred to a country or territory outside the European Economic Area unless that country or territory ensures an adequate level of protection for the rights and freedoms of data subjects in relation to the processing of personal data.

5.7 The Act has two main aims:

   (a) To protect **individual privacy**. Previous UK law only applied to **computer-based** information. The 1998 Act applies to **all personal data, in any form.**

   (b) To **harmonise data protection legislation** so that, in the interests of improving the operation of the single European market, there can be a **free flow of personal data** between the member states of the EU.

The coverage of the Act

5.8 Key points of the Act can be summarised as follows.

    (a) **Data users** have to **register** under the Act with the **Data Protection Registrar**.

    (b) **Individuals** (data subjects) are awarded certain **legal rights**.

    (c) **Data holders** must adhere to the **data protection principles**.

Registration under the Act

5.9 The Data Protection Registrar keeps a Register of all data users. Only registered data users are permitted to hold personal data. The data user must only hold data and use data for the registered **purposes**.

The rights of data subjects

5.10 The Act establishes the following rights for data subjects.

    (a) A data subject may seek **compensation** through the courts for damage and any associated distress caused by the **loss, destruction** or **unauthorised disclosure** of data about himself or herself or by **inaccurate data** about himself or herself.

    (b) A data subject may apply to the courts for **inaccurate data** to be **put right** or even **wiped off** the data user's files altogether. Such applications may also be made to the Registrar.

    (c) A data subject may obtain **access** to personal data of which he or she is the subject. (This is known as the 'subject access' provision.) In other words, a data subject can ask to see his or her personal data that the data user is holding.

    (d) A data subject can **sue** a data user for any **damage or distress** caused to him by personal data about him which is **incorrect** or **misleading** as to matter of **fact** (rather than opinion).

5.11 **Other features of the legislation**

    (a) Everyone has the right to go to court to seek redress for **any breach** of data protection law.

    (b) Filing systems that are structured so as to facilitate access to information about a particular person now fall within the legislation. This includes systems that are **paper-based** or on **microfilm** or **microfiche**. Personnel records meet this classification.

    (c) Processing of personal data is **forbidden** except in the following circumstances.

        (i) With the **consent** of the subject. Consent cannot be implied: it must be by freely given, specific and informed agreement.

        (ii) As a result of a **contractual arrangement**.

        (iii) Because of a **legal obligation**.

        (iv) To **protect the vital interests** of the subject.

        (v) Where processing is in the **public interest**.

        (vi) Where processing is required to exercise **official authority**.

    (d) The processing of 'sensitive data' is forbidden, unless express consent has been obtained or there are conflicting obligations under employment law. Sensitive data includes data relating to **racial origin, political opinions, religious beliefs,** physical or mental **health, sexual proclivities** and **trade union** membership.

(e) If data about a data subject is **obtained from a third party** the data subject must be given.

    (i)   The identity of the **controller** of the data.

    (ii)   The **purposes** for which the data are being processed.

    (iii)   **What data** will be disclosed and **to whom.**

    (iv)   The existence of a right of subject **access** to the data.

(f) Data subjects have a right not only to have a **copy of data** held about them but also the right to know **why** the data is required.

5.12 The 1998 Act replaced the 1984 Act. The updated legislation provided for a transitional period to bring existing systems into line with the new law. The Act finally came into force on March 1 2000, and all data controllers will have to comply fully with the Act by October 2001.

Question 5

(a) Your MD has asked you to recommend measures that your company, which is based in the UK, could take to ensure compliance with data protection legislation. Suggest what measures should be taken.

(b) Watch the newspapers and the *ACCA Student Accountant* for details of developments in legislation.

Answer

(a) Measures could include the following.

- Obtain consent from individuals to hold any sensitive personal data you need.
- Supply individuals with a copy of any personal data you hold about them if so requested.
- Consider if you may need to obtain consent to process personal data.
- Ensure you do not pass on personal data to unauthorised parties.

6   INTERNET SECURITY ISSUES

6.1 Establishing organisational links to the Internet brings numerous security dangers.

(a) Corruptions such as **viruses** on a single computer can spread through the network to all of the organisation's computers. (Viruses are described at greater length later in this section.)

(b) Disaffected employees have much greater potential to do **deliberate damage** to valuable corporate data or systems because the network could give them access to parts of the system that they are not really authorised to use.

(c) If the organisation is linked to an external network, persons outside the company (**hackers**) may be able to get into the company's internal network, either to steal data or to damage the system.

(d) Employees may **download inaccurate information** or imperfect or **virus-ridden software** from an external network. For example 'beta' (free trial) versions of forthcoming new editions of many major packages are often available on the Internet, but the whole point about a beta version is that it is not fully tested and may contain bugs that could disrupt an entire system.

(e) Information transmitted from one part of an organisation to another may be **intercepted**. Data can be 'encrypted' (scrambled) in an attempt to make it unintelligible to eavesdroppers, this is covered later in this section.

(f) The **communications link itself may break down or distort data**. The worldwide telecommunications infrastructure is improving thanks to the use of new technologies, and there are communications 'protocols' governing the format of data and signals transferred.

Hacking

6.2 A **hacker** is a **person who attempts to invade the privacy of a system**.

6.3 Hackers require only limited programming knowledge to cause large amounts of damage. The fact that billions of bits of information can be transmitted in bulk over the public telephone network has made it **hard to trace** individual hackers, who can therefore make repeated attempts to invade systems. Hackers, in the past, have mainly been concerned to **copy** information, but a recent trend has been their desire to **corrupt it**.

6.4 Phone numbers and passwords can be guessed by hackers using **electronic phone directories** or number generators and by software which enables **rapid guessing** using hundreds of permutations per minute.

6.5 **Default passwords** are also available on some electronic bulletin boards and sophisticated hackers could even try to 'tap' messages being transmitted along phone wires (the number actually dialled will not be scrambled).

Viruses

KEY TERM

A **virus** is a piece of software which infects programs and data and possibly damages them, and which replicates itself.

6.6 Viruses need an **opportunity to spread**. The programmers of viruses therefore place viruses in the kind of software which is most likely to be copied. This includes:

(a) **Free software** (for example from the Internet).
(b) **Pirated software** (cheaper than original versions).
(c) **Games software** (wide appeal).
(d) **E-mail attachments** (often with instructions to send the message on to others).

6.7 The problem has been exacerbated by the portability of computers and disks and the increased availability and use of e-mail.

6.8 Whilst it is possible to disable floppy disk drives to prevent files entering the organisation via floppy disk, this can severely disrupt work processes. At the very least, organisations should ensure all files received via floppy disk and e-mail are virus checked.

6.9 Very new viruses may go undetected by anti-virus software (until the anti-virus software vendor updates their package - and the organisation installs the update). Two destructive viruses of recent times are:

- **Melissa** - which corrupts Microsoft Office documents

- **Love bug** – which attacks the operating system

6.10 Viruses can spread via floppy disk, but the most destructive viruses utilise e-mail links – **travelling as attachments to e-mail messages**. When the file attachment is opened or executed, the virus infects that system. Recent viruses have been programmed to send themselves to all addresses in the user's electronic address book.

Type of virus	Explanation/Example
File viruses	File viruses infect program files. When you run an infected program the virus runs first, then passes control to the original program. While it has control, the virus code copies itself to another file or to another disk, replicating itself.
Boot sector viruses	The boot sector is the part of every hard disk and diskette which is read by the computer when it starts up. If the boot sector is infected, the virus runs when the machine starts.
Overwriting viruses	An overwriting virus overwrites each file it infects with itself, so the program no longer functions. Since this is very easy to spot these viruses do not spread very well.
Worms	A worm is a program which spreads (usually) over network connections. It does not attach itself to a host program.
Dropper	A dropper is a program, not a virus itself, that installs a virus on the PC while performing another function.
Macro viruses	A macro virus is a piece of self-replicating code written in an application's 'macro' language. Many applications have macro capabilities including all the programs in **Microsoft Office**. The distinguishing factor which makes it possible to create a virus with a macro is the existence of **auto-execute events**. Auto-execute events are opening a file, closing a file, and starting an application. Once a macro is running, it can copy itself to other documents, delete files, and create general havoc. Melissa was a well publicised macro virus.

Case example

Love bug virus creates worldwide chaos

A computer virus which exploits office workers' yearnings for love shut down computer systems from Hong Kong to the Houses of Parliament yesterday and caused untold millions of pounds worth of delays and damage to stored files across the world.

The virus, nicknamed 'the love bug' and 'the killer from Manila' after its apparent Philippine origins, is carried in an email with the heading 'ILOVEYOU'.

The text of the message reads: 'Kindly check the attached love letter from me!' A click on the attached file launches the virus, which promptly spreads by sending itself to everyone in the recipient's email address book, overloading email systems.

Once embedded in a host computer, the virus can download more dangerous software from a remote website, rename files and redirect Internet browsers. 'It's a very effective virus. It's one of the most aggressive and nastiest I've ever seen,' said Kieran Fitzsimmons of MessageLabs, which screens millions of company emails for viruses. 'It manifests itself almost everywhere in the computer.'

One tenth of the world's mail servers were down as a result of the love bug, he said. Estimates suggested that between 10% and 30% of UK businesses were hit. Among the firms and organisations affected in the UK yesterday were Microsoft, News International - publishers of the Times and the Sun - the BBC, a number of FTSE-100 companies and parliament.

In an announcement to the Commons, Margaret Beckett, leader of the House, said that the parliamentary email system had crashed. 'I have to tell you that, sadly, this affectionate greeting contains a virus which has immobilised the house's internal communication system,' she said.

At the UK arm of Reed International, publisher of trade magazines, IT engineers alerted staff with Tannoy announcements after the bug had already crippled their computer system. 'It completely wipes out your network,' said Sarah Perkins of PC Pro magazine. 'Ours is down and we're going to lose a day's business.'

The virus spread west from Asia as offices opened and workers checked their emails. The only clue to its origins lies in the first few lines of the code which makes it work. They are headed: 'I hate go to school.' The next line identifies the author as 'spyder' and the next refers to 'Manila, Philippines'.

Daphne Ghesquiere, a Dow Jones spokesman in Hong Kong, said: 'It crashed all the computers. You get the message and the topic says ILOVEYOU, and I was among the stupid ones to open it. I got about five at one time and I was suspicious, but one was from Dow Jones Newswires, so I opened it.' Later Germany, France, Switzerland and the Low Countries were seriously affected.

IT specialists described the love bug as **'a visual basic worm'** far **more dangerous** and fast-spreading than the similar **Melissa virus, which also replicated itself by email**. Melissa infected about a million computers and caused £50m of damage.

ILOVEYOU is eight times bigger, sends itself to everyone in a recipient's address book instead of just the first 50 (and then deletes the address book), and, unlike Melissa, **tampers with operating systems**.

By yesterday afternoon MessageLabs had picked up 10,000 infected emails. The highest number in one day until now has been 700. Last night another virus tracker, TrendMicro, was reporting more than 800,000 infected files around the world, the bulk of them in the US. One expert said the love bug spread 'like wild-fire' in Britain after 11.30am. 'It's taking out computers right, left and centre,' he said.

The Guardian May 5, 2000

The Computer Misuse Act

6.11 The (UK) Computer Misuse Act 1990 was enacted to respond to the growing threat of hacking to computer systems and data. Hacking means obtaining unauthorised access, usually through telecommunications links. The Act defines three levels of hacking.

Crime	Explanation
Unauthorised access	This means that a hacker, who, knowing he or she is unauthorised, tries to gain access to another computer system. It is the **attempt** which is the crime: the hacker's success or failure is irrelevant.
Unauthorised access with the **intention** of committing another offence	This results in **stricter penalties** than unauthorised access alone.
Unauthorised **modification** of data or programs	In effect this makes the deliberate introduction of computer **viruses** into a system a **criminal offence**. Guilt is based on the **intention to impair** the operation of a computer or program, or prevent or **hinder access** to data.

Encryption and other safety measures

6.12 **Encryption** is the only secure way to prevent eavesdropping (since eavesdroppers can get round password controls, by tapping the line or by experimenting with various likely passwords).

KEY TERM

Encryption involves scrambling the data at one end of the line, transmitting the scrambled data, and unscrambling it at the receiver's end of the line.

6.13 **Authentication** is a technique of making sure that a message has come from an authorised sender. Authentication involves adding an extra field to a record, with the contents of this field derived from the remainder of the record by applying an algorithm that has previously been agreed between the senders and recipients of data.

6.14 Systems can have **firewalls** (which disable part of the telecoms technology) to prevent unwelcome intrusions into company systems, but a determined hacker may well be able to bypass even these.

6.15 **Dial-back security** operates by requiring the person wanting access to the network to dial into it and identify themselves first. The system then dials the person back on their authorised number before allowing them access.

6.16 All attempted **violations of security** should be automatically **logged** and the log checked regularly. In a multi-user system, the terminal attempting the violation may be automatically disconnected.

Jokes and hoaxes

6.17 Some programs claim to be doing something destructive to your computer, but are actually 'harmless' jokes. For example, a message may appear suggesting that your hard disk is about to be reformatted. Unfortunately, it is **easy to over-react** to the joke and cause more damage by trying to eradicate something that is not a virus.

6.18 There are a number of common hoaxes, which are widely believed. The most common of these is **Good Times**. This hoax has been around for a couple of years, and usually takes the form of a virus warning about viruses contained in e-mail. People pass along the warning because they are trying to be helpful, but they are wasting the time of all concerned.

7 INFORMATION SYSTEMS AND THE ACCOUNTANT

7.1 Depending on the size and structure of the organisation, the responsibility for ensuring an organisation's information systems operate efficiently and comply with relevant legislation may fall to the accountant. In other organisations these responsibilities may rest with the Company Secretary or the Information Systems Manager.

7.2 Historically, accountants have played an important role in information systems installations. The accounting function was often the first area of an organisation to be computerised and many organisations lacked specialist IS/IT staff.

7.3 As the importance of IS/IT has increased large and medium sized organisations have created specialist IS/IT departments. In many smaller organisations the accountant still has responsibility for information systems.

7.4 Even in larger organisations, the accountant still has an important role to play in the information systems function. Key areas include:

- Investment appraisal

- Cost-benefit analysis
- Internal audit requirements
- Performance measurement eg metrics
- Presenting user concerns (eg accounts department staff)
- Assessing usability

Chapter roundup

- **Security** is the protection of data from accidental or deliberate threats and the protection of an information system from such threats.

- **Physical threats** to security may be natural or man made. They include fire, flooding, weather, lightning, terrorist activity and accidental damage.

- **Physical access control** attempts to stop **intruders** or other unauthorised persons getting near to computer equipment or storage media.

- Important aspects of physical access of control are **door locks** and **card entry systems**. Computer theft is becoming more prevalent as equipment becomes smaller and more portable.

- It is possible to **build controls into computerised processing**. A **balance** must be struck between the degree of control and the requirement for a user friendly system.

- Controls can be classified into:
  - **Security** controls
  - **Integrity** controls
  - **Contingency** controls

- A **back-up** and **archive** strategy should include:
  - Regular back-up of data (at least daily)
  - Archive plans
  - A **disaster recovery** plan including off-site storage

- An **audit trail shows who has accessed a system and the operations performed.**

- **Privacy** is the right of the individual not to suffer unauthorised disclosure of information.

- The (UK) **Data Protection Act 1998** protects individuals about whom data is held. Both manual and computerised information must comply with the Act.

  - Data users must **register** with the Data Protection Registrar and announce the uses to which the data will be put.

  - The Act contains eight **data protection principles**, to which all data users must adhere.

- Establishing organisational **links to the Internet** brings numerous **security dangers**.

- The (UK) **Computer Misuse Act 1990** was enacted to respond to the growing threat of **hacking** to computer systems and data

- A **virus** is a piece of software which infects programs and data and possibly damages them, and which replicates itself.

- In many organisations the accountant plays an important role in the IS/IT function.

Quick quiz

1 List three physical access control methods.

2 List four risks to data.

3 What is the purpose of taking a back-up?

4 Why should certain duties be segregated between staff members?

5   List six possible items shown on an accounting package audit trail report.

6   What is 'personal data' under the (UK) Data Protection Act (1998)?

7   Does the (UK) Data Protection Act 1998 cover data held on manual system, on computerised systems or on both manual and computerised systems?

8   Briefly describe the process of encryption.

9   List the three levels of hacking referred to in the (UK) Computer Misuse Act 1990.

10   What is the most common method of spreading a virus?

Answers to quick quiz

1   Personnel (security guards), mechanical devices (eg keys), electronic devices (eg card-swipe systems, PIN keypads).

2   Human error
        Hardware error
        Software error
        Deliberate actions

        You may have come up with others.

3   To enable valid files to be restored in case of a future corruption or failure.

4   To reduce the opportunity for fraud and/or malicious damage.

5   [Six of]

        Transaction number
        Transaction date and time
        User ID
        Transaction type
        Amount
        Terminal/PC used to input
        User entered description or narration

6   Information about a living individual.

7   Both.

8   Encryption involves scrambling data at one end of the communications link, transmitting the scrambled data, then receiving and unscrambling the data at the other end of the link.

9   Unauthorised access, unauthorised access with the intention of modification and finally unauthorised modification.

10   E-mail.

The material covered in this Chapter is tested in Questions 13 and 16 in the Exam Question Bank.

Chapter 11

POST IMPLEMENTATION ISSUES

Topic list	Syllabus reference
1 Post-implementation review	3(g)
2 Systems maintenance	3(h)
3 End-user development and user groups	3(h)
4 Information centres and help desks	3(g)
5 Evaluation	3(g), 3(i)
6 Computer-based monitoring	3(g)
7 System performance	3(g)

Introduction

In this final chapter we explore the issues surrounding the running of an Information System. Throughout its life, a system should operate effectively and efficiently. To do this, the system needs to be **maintained** and its users need to be **supported**. The first half of this chapter looks at how this may be done.

We then look at the **evaluation process.** This aims to ensure the system continues to meet requirements.

Study guide

Part 3.25 – Post implementation issues

- Describe the metrics required to measure the success of the system

- Discuss the procedures that have to be implemented to effectively collect the agreed metrics

- Identify what procedures and personnel should be put in place to support the users of the system

- Explain the possible role of software monitors in measuring the success of the system

- Describe the purpose and conduct of an end-project review and a post-implementation review

- Describe the structure and content of a report from an end-project review and a post-implementation review

Part 3.26 – Change control in systems development and maintenance

- Describe the different types of maintenance that a system may require

- Explain the need for a change control process for dealing with these changes

- Describe a maintenance lifecycle

- Explain the meaning and problems of regression testing

- Discuss the role of user groups and their influence on system requirements

---

Study guide (continued)

Part 3.27 – Relationship of management, development process and quality

- Discuss the need for automation to improve the efficiency and effectiveness of information systems management, delivery and quality assurance

Part 1.4 – Organising information systems – structural issues

- Discuss the relationship of information systems with end-users and the implications of the expectations and skills of end users

Exam guide

The purpose and conduct of the post-implementation review proved a popular examination topic under the previous syllabus – and is likely to remain so under this syllabus.

---

1 POST-IMPLEMENTATION REVIEW

1.1 **Post-implementation review** should establish whether the objectives and targeted performance criteria have been met, and if not, why not, and what should be done about it.

1.2 In appraising the operation of the new system immediately after the changeover, comparison should be made between **actual and predicted performance**. This will include:

(a) Consideration of **throughput speed** (time between input and output).
(b) Use of computer **storage** (both internal and external).
(c) The number and type of **errors/queries**.
(d) The **cost** of processing (data capture, preparation, storage and output media, etc).

1.3 A special **steering committee** may be set up to ensure that post-implementation reviews are carried out, although the **internal audit** department may be required to do the work of carrying out the reviews.

1.4 The post-implementation measurements should **not be made too soon** after the system goes live, or else results will be abnormally affected by 'teething' problems, lack of user familiarity and resistance to change.

The post-implementation review report

1.5 The findings of a post-implementation review team should be formalised in a **report**.

(a) A **summary** of their findings should be provided, emphasising any areas where the system has been found to be **unsatisfactory**.

(b) A review of **system performance** should be provided. This will address the matters outlined above, such as run times and error rates.

(c) A **cost-benefit review** should be included, comparing the forecast costs and benefits identified at the time of the feasibility study with actual costs and benefits.

(d) **Recommendations** should be made as to any **further action** or steps which should be taken to improve performance.

2   SYSTEMS MAINTENANCE

Types of maintenance

2.1   There are three types of maintenance activity.

- Corrective
- Perfective
- Adaptive

> **KEY TERMS**
>
> **Corrective maintenance** is carried out when there is a systems failure of some kind, for example in processing or in an implementation procedure. Its objective is to ensure that systems remain operational.
>
> **Perfective maintenance** is carried out in order to perfect the software, or to improve software so that the processing inefficiencies are eliminated and performance is enhanced.
>
> **Adaptive maintenance** is carried out to take account of anticipated changes in the processing environment. For example new taxation legislation might require change to be made to payroll software.

2.2   **Corrective** maintenance usually consists of action in response to a **problem**. Much **perfective** maintenance consists of making enhancements requested by **users** to improve or extend the facilities available. The user interface may be amended to make software more user friendly.

2.3   The key features of system maintenance ought to be **flexibility** and **adaptability**.

(a)   The system, perhaps with minor modifications, should cope with changes in the computer user's procedures or volume of business.

(b)   The computer user should benefit from advances in computer hardware technology without having to switch to another system altogether.

The causes of systems maintenance

2.4   Besides environmental changes, three factors contribute to the need for maintenance.

Factor	Comment
Errors	However carefully and diligently the systems development staff carry out systems testing and program testing, it is likely that **bugs** will exist in a newly implemented system. Most should be identified during the first few runs of a system. The effect of errors can obviously vary enormously.

Factor	Comment
Changes in requirements	Although users should be consulted at all stages of systems development, problems may arise after a system is implemented because users may have found it difficult to express their requirements, or may have been concerned about the future of their jobs and not participated fully in development.
	Cost constraints may have meant that certain requested features were not incorporated. Time constraints may have meant that requirements suggested during development were ignored in the interest of prompt completion.
Poor documentation	If old systems are accompanied by poor documentation, or even a complete lack of documentation, it may be very difficult to understand their programs. It will be hard to update or maintain such programs. Programmers may opt instead to patch up the system with new applications using newer technology.

The systems maintenance lifecycle

2.5 Corrective and adaptive maintenance should be carried out **as and when** problems occur, but perfective maintenance may be carried out on a more scheduled system-by-system basis.

2.6 Business growth may lead to increased transaction volumes that requires hardware maintenance. It may be possible to enhance the existing system by:

- Installing **disks** of **greater capacity**
- Installing a **more powerful processor**
- Installing **additional terminals** or **network facilities**

2.7 Systems should have a certain amount of flexibility built-in, so that the system can **adapt** to change.

2.8 However, there will come a point at which **redevelopment** is necessary, for example where hardware upgrades or the availability of new software make radical change necessary, or following a company restructuring.

In-house maintenance

2.9 With **large computer systems**, developed by the organisation itself, **in-house** systems analysts and programmers might be given the responsibility for **software** maintenance.

2.10 To ensure that maintenance is carried out efficiently, the principles of **good programming practice** should be applied.

(a) Any change must be **properly authorised** by a manager in the user department (or someone even more senior, if necessary).

(b) The new program requirements must be **specified in full and in writing**. These specifications will be prepared by a systems analyst. A programmer should use these specifications to produce an amended version of the program.

(c) In developing a new program version, a programmer should keep **working papers**. He or she can refer back to these papers later to check in the event that there is an error in the new program or the user of the program asks for a further change in the program.

(d) The new program version should be **tested** when it has been written. A programmer should prepare test data and establish whether the program will process the data according to the specifications given by the systems analyst.

(e) **Provisions** should be made for **further program amendments** in the future. One way of doing this is to leave space in the program instruction numbering sequence for new instructions to be inserted later. For example, instructions might be numbered 10,20,30,40 etc instead of 1,2,3,4.

(f) A **record** should be kept of **all program errors** that are found during 'live' processing and of the corrections that are made to the program.

(g) Each **version** of a program (versions that are produced with processing modifications or corrections to errors) should be **separately identified**, to avoid a mix-up about what version of a program should be used for 'live' operating.

2.11 A problem with systems development and maintenance is that it is **hard to predict all the effects of a change** to the system.

2.12 A 'simple' software change in one area of the system may have unpredicted effects elsewhere. It is important therefore to carry out **regression testing**.

> **KEY TERM**
>
> **Regression testing** involves the retesting of software that has been modified to fix 'bugs'. It aims to ensure that the bugs have been fixed **and** that no other previously working functions have failed as a result of the changes.

2.13 Regression testing involves **repeating system tests** that had been executed correctly before the recent changes were made.

2.14 Only the changes expected as a result of the system maintenance should occur under the regression test – other changes could be due to errors caused by the recent change.

2.15 Problems with regression testing include:

- Deciding on the extent of testing required
- Envisaging all areas possibly effected
- Convincing users and programmers that the tests are necessary

Purchased software maintenance

2.16 With **purchased software** (whether off-the-shelf or bespoke), the **software house** or **supplier** is likely to provide details of any new versions of the software as they are produced, simply for marketing purposes.

Maintenance contracts

2.17 There is also likely to be an **agreement** between the supplier of software and the customer for the provision of a **software support service**. A maintenance contract typically includes the following services.

(a) **Help**

When a customer runs into difficulties operating the system help will initially be given by a **telephone 'hot line'**. If a telephone call does not resolve the problem, the software

BPP
PUBLISHING

expert may arrange to visit the customer's premises (within a period of time agreed in the contract), although this would be rare for standard packages.

(b) **Information**

Extra information about using the package may be provided through factsheets or a magazine sent free to subscribers. This may include **case studies** showing how other users have benefited from using the package in a particular way and **technical tips** for common user problems

(c) **Updates**

Free updates are provided to **correct errors** in part of a package, or if there is something **inevitable** that will mean that some aspect of a package **has to be changed**. For example payroll software has to reflect the latest Finance Act.

(d) **Upgrades**

When the **whole package** is revised the contract often provides for subscribers to get the new version at a heavily **discounted price**. Upgrades usually include **new features** not found in the previous versions or updates.

(e) **Legal conditions**

There will be provisions about the **duration** of the contract and in what circumstances it terminates, about the **customer's obligations** to use the software in the way it was intended to be used, on the right sort of hardware, and not to make illegal copies. The **liability of the supplier** will also be set out, especially regarding consequential loss.

Hardware maintenance

2.18 Computer **hardware** should be kept serviced and maintained too. Maintenance services are provided by:

- The computer **manufacturers**
- **Third-party** maintenance companies

2.19 Maintenance of hardware can be obtained:

- On a **contract** basis
- On an **ad hoc** basis

3 END-USER DEVELOPMENT AND USER GROUPS

End-user development

3.1 End-user computing has been fuelled by the introduction of **PCs** to user departments, by **user-friendly software**, and by **greater awareness** of computers and what they can do.

KEY TERM

End-user development is the direct, hands-on development of computer systems by users.

3.2 Accounts staff designing and using complex **spreadsheet models** is an example of end-user computing.

3.3 Many users who develop their own applications have **little or no formal training** in programming, consequently their programs might be extremely crude and virtually incomprehensible.

3.4 While these programs may work they will be very **difficult to modify** and they will very often be the personal property of the individual who developed the system, with **no wider use**. This is undesirable from the organisation's viewpoint: a great deal of time and energy is going into producing inefficient programs which are unusable by anyone other than their developer.

3.5 Other disadvantages are as follows:

(a) The risk from the elimination of the **separation of the functions of user and analyst**.

(b) The risk from **limits on user ability** to identify correct and complete requirements for an application.

(c) The risk from **lack of user knowledge and acceptance of application quality assurance procedures** for development and operation.

(d) The risk from **unstable user systems**.

(e) The risk from encouraging **private information systems**.

(f) The risk from permitting **unstructured information systems development**.

User groups

3.6 The concept of user groups has existed in the computer industry for some time.

> **KEY TERM**
>
> A **user group** is a forum for users of particular hardware or, more usually, software, so that they can **share ideas and experience**.

3.7 User groups are usually set up either by the software manufacturers themselves (who use them to **maintain contact** with customers and as a source of **new product ideas**) or by groups of users. The term is used most commonly with users of packaged software.

3.8 Users of a particular package can meet, or perhaps exchange views over the **Internet** to discuss solutions, ideas or 'short cuts' to improve productivity. An (electronic) newsletter service might be appropriate, based on views exchanged by members, but also incorporating ideas culled from the wider environment by IT specialists.

3.9 Sometimes user groups are set up **within** individual organisations. Where an organisation has written its own application software, or is using tailor-made software, there will be a very **small knowledge base** initially, and there will obviously not be a national user group, because the application is unique.

3.10 'Interested parties', including, as a minimum, representatives from the **IT department** and **users** who are familiar with different parts of the system can attend monthly or quarterly **meetings** to discuss the **operation** of the system, make **suggestions for improvements** (such as the production of new reports or time-tabling of processing) and raise any **queries**.

BPP PUBLISHING

Question 1

Trends in IT such as distributed processing, increased use of PCs and wide availability of sophisticated general purpose packages have resulted in more responsibility for information systems being transferred to end-users. What problems may this result in for organisations?

Answer

Here are some suggestions.

(a) Lack of formal training could result in inefficient or even 'faulty' systems.

(b) User requests for assistance that overwhelm the IS/IT department.

(c) Lack of user knowledge or concern may lead to inadequate controls being built into the system.

(d) Lack of integration across the organisation with many users developing systems to suit themselves.

(e) Poor maintainability of user-developed systems as only the person that developed it understands it

(f) Lack of centralised management of resources.

(g) A lack of understanding of the organisations use of IS/IT may develop – it becomes difficult to see the 'big picture'.

---

4   INFORMATION CENTRES AND HELP DESKS

> ### KEY TERM
>
> An **Information Centre (IC)** is a small unit of staff with a good technical awareness of computer systems, whose task is to provide a support function to computer users within the organisation.

4.1   Information centres are particularly useful in organisations which use **distributed** processing systems or **PCs** quite heavily, and so have many 'non-technical' people in charge of hardware, files and software scattered throughout the organisation.

Help

4.2   An IC usually offers a **Help Desk** to solve IT problems. Help may be via the **telephone** or in person. Networks allow help to be provided using an **e-mail** system, and the posting of common problems and their solutions on a **bulletin board**.

4.3   **Remote diagnostic software** is available which enables staff in the IC to 'take control' of a computer and sort out the problem without leaving their desk.

4.4   The help desk needs sufficient **staff and technical expertise** to respond quickly to problems. This means that it must also maintain good contacts and relationships with **suppliers** to ensure that they fulfil their maintenance obligations and their maintenance staff are quickly on site when needed.

Problem solving

4.5   The IC will maintain a **record of problems** and identify those that occur most often. If the problem is that users do not know how to use the system, **training** is provided.

4.6   Training applications often contain **analysis software**, drawing attention to trainee progress and **common problems** (the Software Toolworks *Mavis Beacon* typing tutor is a well-known example), and the availability of such information will enable the IC to identify and address specific **training needs** more closely.

4.7   If the problem is with the system itself, a solution is found, either by **modifying the system** or by investment in **new hardware or software**.

Improvements

4.8   The IC can also consider the viability of **suggestions for improvements** to the system and bring these into effect, where possible, for all users who stand to benefit.

Standards

4.9   The IC is also likely to be responsible for setting, and encouraging users to conform to, common **standards**.

(a)   **Hardware standards** ensure that all of the equipment used in the organisation is **compatible** and can be put into use in different departments as needed.

(b)   **Software standards** ensure that information generated by one department can easily be **shared** with and worked upon by other departments.

(c)   **Programming standards** ensure that applications developed by individuals end-users (for example complex spreadsheet macros) follow **best practice** and are **easy to modify.**

(d)   **Data processing standards** ensure that certain conventions such as the format of **file names** are followed throughout the organisation. This facilitates **sharing, storage and retrieval** of information.

Security

4.10   The IC may help to preserve the **security** of data in various ways.

(a)   It may develop **utility programs** and **procedures** to ensure that **back-ups** are made at regular intervals.

(b)   The IC may help to preserve the company's systems from attack by computer **viruses**, for instance by ensuring that the latest versions of **anti-virus software** are available to all users, by reminding users regularly about the **dangers** of viruses, and by setting up and maintaining '**firewalls**', which deny access to sensitive parts of the company's systems.

Applications development

4.11   An IC can help applications development by providing **technical guidance** to end-user developers and to encourage comprehensible and well documented programs. **Understandable** programs can be maintained or modified more easily. **Documentation** provides a means of teaching others how the programs work. These efforts can greatly extend the usefulness and life of the programs that are developed.

5 EVALUATION

5.1 In most systems there is a constant need to maintain and improve applications and to keep up to date with technological advances and changing user requirements. A system should therefore be **reviewed** after implementation, and periodically, so that any unforeseen problems may be solved and to confirm that it is achieving the desired results.

5.2 The system should have been designed with clear, specified **objectives**, and justification in terms of **cost-benefit analysis** or other **performance criteria**.

5.3 Just as the feasibility of a project is assessed by reference to **technical, operational, social and economic factors**, so the same criteria can be used for evaluation. We need not repeat material that you have covered earlier, but here are a few pointers.

Cost-benefit review

5.4 A cost-benefit review is similar to a cost-benefit analysis, except that **actual** data can be used.

5.5 For instance when a large project is completed, techniques such as **DCF appraisal** can be performed **again**, with actual figures being available for much of the expenditure.

Question 2

A cost-benefit review might categorise items under the five headings of direct benefits, indirect benefits, development costs, implementation costs and running costs.

Give two examples of items which could fall to be evaluated under each heading.

Answer

Direct benefits might include reduced operating costs, for example lower overtime payments.

Indirect benefits might include better decision-making and the freeing of human 'brainpower' from routine tasks so that it can be used for more creative work.

Development costs include systems analysts' costs and the cost of time spent by users in assisting with fact-finding.

Implementation costs would include costs of site preparation and costs of training.

Running costs include maintenance costs, software leasing costs and on-going user support.

Efficiency and effectiveness

5.6 In any evaluation of a system, two terms recur. Two key reasons for the introduction of information systems into an organisation are to improve the **efficiency** or the **effectiveness** of the organisation.

KEY TERM

Efficiency can be measured by considering the resource **inputs** into, and the **outputs** from, a process or an activity.

5.7 An activity uses **resources** such as staff, money and materials. If the same activity can be performed using **fewer resources**, for example fewer staff or less money, or if it can be completed **more quickly**, the efficiency of the activity is improved. An improvement in efficiency represents an improvement in **productivity**.

5.8 Automation of an organisation's activities is usually expected to lead to greater efficiency in a number of areas.

(a) The **cost** of a computer system is lower than that of the manual system it replaces, principally because jobs previously performed by human operators are now carried out by computer.

(b) The **accuracy** of data information and processing is improved, because a computer does not make mistakes.

(c) The **speed** of processing is improved. Response times, for example in satisfying customer orders, are improved.

KEY TERM

Effectiveness is a measurement of how well the organisation is achieving its **objectives**.

5.9 Effectiveness is a **more subjective** concept than efficiency, as it is concerned with factors which are less easy to measure. It focuses primarily on the relationship of the organisation with its environment. For example, automation might be pursued because it is expected that the company will be more effective at **increasing market share** or at satisfying **customer needs**.

5.10 Computing was originally concerned with the automation of '**back office**' functions, usually aspects of data processing. Development was concerned with improving **efficiency**.

5.11 Recent trends are more towards the development of '**front office**' systems, for example to improve an organisation's decision-making capability or to seek competitive advantage. This approach seeks to improve the **effectiveness** of the organisation.

Metrics

KEY TERM

Metrics are quantified measurements used to measure system performance.

5.12 The use of **metrics** enables **system quality** to be **measured** and the early identification of problems.

5.13 **Examples** of metrics include system response time, the number of transactions that can be processed per minute, the number of bugs per hundred lines of code and the number of system crashes per week.

5.14 Metrics should be devised that **suit the system in question** – those given above are simply typical examples.

5.15 Many facets of system quality are **not easy to measure** statistically (eg user-friendliness). Indirect measurements such as the number of calls to the help-desk per month can be use as an indication of overall quality/performance.

5.16 Metrics should be carefully thought out, objective and stated **clearly**. They must measure **significant aspects** of the system, be used consistently and **agreed with users.**

6 COMPUTER-BASED MONITORING

6.1 Computers themselves can be used in systems evaluation. Three methods used are hardware monitors, software monitors and systems logs.

Hardware monitors

6.2 Hardware monitors are devices which measure the presence or absence of electrical signals in selected circuits in the computer hardware.

6.3 They might measure **idle time** or **levels of activity** in the CPU, or peripheral activity. Data is sent from the sensors to counters, which periodically write it to disk or tape.

6.4 A program will then **analyse** the data and produce an analysis of findings as output. It might identify for example **inefficient co-ordination** of processors and peripherals, or **excessive delays** in writing data to backing storage.

Software monitors

6.5 Software monitors are computer programs which **interrupt the application in use** and record data about it. They might identify, for example, **excessive waiting** time during program execution. Unlike hardware monitors, they may slow down the operation of the program being monitored.

Systems logs

6.6 Many computer systems provide automatic log details, for example **job start and finish** times or which employee has used which program and for how long. The systems log can therefore provide useful data for analysis.

 (a) Unexplained **variations in job running** times might be recorded.
 (b) Excessive machine **down-time** is sometimes a problem.
 (c) **Mixed workloads** of large and small jobs might be scheduled inefficiently.

7 SYSTEMS PERFORMANCE

Performance measurement

7.1 It is not possible to identify and isolate every consequence of a project and the impact of each on organisational effectiveness. To achieve some approximation to a complete evaluation, therefore, certain **indirect measures** must be used.

 (a) **Significant task relevance** attempts to observe the results of system use.

  For example, document turnround times might have improved following the acquisition of a document image processing system, or minutes of meetings might be made available and distributed faster following the addition of a company secretarial function to a local area network.

 (b) The **willingness** of users **to pay** might give an indication of value.

Charge-out mechanisms may provide an indication of how much users would be prepared to pay in order to gain the benefit of a certain upgrade, for example the availability of a particular report.

(c) **Systems logs** may give an indication of the value of the system if it is a 'voluntary use' system, such as an external database.

(d) **User information satisfaction** is a concept which attempts to find out, by asking users, how they rate their satisfaction with a system. They may be asked for their views on timeliness, quality of output, response times, processing and their overall confidence in the system.

(e) The adequacy of system **documentation** may be measurable in terms of how often manuals are actually used and the number of errors found or amendments made. However, low usage of a user manual, for instance, may mean either that the manual is unclear or that the system is easy to operate.

Question 3

Operational evaluation should consider, among other issues, whether input data is properly provided and output is useful. Output documents are often produced simply because 'we always print it'.

How might you identify whether a report is being used?

Answer

You could simply ask recipients if they would object to the report being withdrawn.

A questionnaire could be circulated asking what each recipient of the report does with it and assess its importance.

A charge-out system could be implemented - this would be a strong incentive to cancel requests for unnecessary output.

7.2 **Performance reviews** will vary in content from organisation to organisation, but the matters which will probably be looked at are as follows.

(a) The **growth** rates in file sizes and the number of transactions processed by the system. Trends should be analysed and projected to assess whether there are likely to be problems with lengthy processing time or an inefficient file structure due to the volume of processing.

(b) The clerical **manpower** needs for the system, and deciding whether they are more or less than estimated.

(c) The identification of any **delays** in processing and an assessment of the consequences of any such delays.

(d) An assessment of the efficiency of **security** procedures, in terms of number of breaches, number of viruses encountered.

(e) A check of the **error rates** for input data. High error rates may indicate inefficient preparation of input documents, an inappropriate method of data capture or poor design of input media.

(f) An examination of whether **output** from the computer is being used to good purpose. (Is it used? Is it timely? Does it go to the right people?)

(g) Operational **running costs**, examined to discover any inefficient programs or processes. This examination may reveal excessive costs for certain items although in total, costs may be acceptable.

Improving performance

7.3 **Computer systems efficiency audits** are concerned with improving **outputs** from the system and their use and/or reducing the costs of system **inputs**. With falling costs of computer hardware and software, and continual technological advances, there should often be **scope for improvements** in computer systems.

Outputs from a computer system

7.4 With regard to outputs, the efficiency of a computer system would be enhanced in any of the following ways.

(a) **More outputs** of some value could be produced by the **same input** resources.

For example:

(i) If the system could process **more transactions** per minute.

(ii) If the system could produce **better quality management information** (eg sensitivity analysis).

(iii) If the system could make information **available to more people**.

(b) **Outputs of little value** could be **eliminated** from the system, thus making savings in the cost of inputs, processing and handling.

For example:

(i) If reports are produced **too frequently**, should they be produced less often?
(ii) If reports are **distributed too widely**, should the distribution list be shortened?
(iii) If reports are **too bulky**, can they be reduced in size?

(c) The **timing** of outputs could be better.

Information should be available in good time for the information-user to be able to make good use of it. Reports that are issued late might lose their value. Computer systems could give managers **immediate** access to the information they require, by means of file enquiry or special software (such as databases or spreadsheet modelling packages).

(d) It might be found that outputs are not as satisfactory as they should be, perhaps because:

(i) **Access** to information from the system is limited, and could be improved by the use of a **database** and a **network** system.

(ii) Available outputs are **restricted** because of the **method of data processing** used (eg batch processing instead of real-time processing) or the **type of equipment** used (eg stand-alone PCs compared with client/server systems).

Question 4

What elements of hardware and software might restrict the capabilities of a system?

Answer

A system's capabilities might be limited by the following restrictions.

(a) The size of the computer's memory.
(b) The power of the processor.
(c) The capacity of the computer's backing storage.
(d) The number of printers available.
(e) The number of terminals.
(f) The software's capabilities.

Inputs to a computer system

7.5 The efficiency of a computer system could be improved if the same volume (and frequency) of output could be achieved with **fewer input** resources, and at **less cost**. Here's how.

(a) **Multi-user or network systems might be more efficient than stand-alone systems.** Multi-user systems allow several input operators to work on the same files at the same time, so that if one person has a heavy workload and another is currently short of work, the person who has some free time can help his or her busy colleague - thus improving operator efficiency.

(b) **Real-time** systems might be more efficient than batch processing.

(c) Using computers and external storage media with **bigger storage** capacity. A frequent complaint is that 'waiting time' for the operator can be very long and tedious. Computer systems with better backing storage facilities can reduce this operator waiting time, and so be more efficient.

(d) Using more **up-to-date software**.

7.6 Management might also wish to consider whether time spent **checking and correcting** input data can be eliminated. An **alternative method of input** might be chosen. For example bar codes and scanners should eliminate the need to check for input errors.

Chapter roundup

- During a **post-implementation review**, an evaluation of the system is carried out to see whether the targeted performance criteria have been met and to carry out a review of costs and benefits. The review should culminate in the production of a report and recommendations.

- There are three types of systems maintenance. **Corrective** maintenance is carried out following a systems failure, **perfective** maintenance aims to make enhancements to systems and **adaptive** maintenance takes account of anticipated changes in the processing environment.

- **User groups** enable personnel who come into contact with a particular system (not just users) to meet and share their views on the system in question. User groups are a useful forum for generating ideas, suggesting improvements and resolving problems.

- Some organisations have an **information centre** to support and streamline end-user computing. An information centre is a small unit manned by staff with a good technical knowledge. Their task is to provide a link between users and computer operations.

- The criteria for **systems evaluation** mirror those used in the feasibility study. A system can be evaluated by reference to technical, operational, social and economic factors. Similarly, the techniques used are similar to those already employed. A cost-benefit review can be performed and compared with the original cost-benefit analysis, and investment appraisal techniques are still applicable.

- **Efficiency** is a measure of how well **resources** have been utilised irrespective of the purpose for which they are employed. **Effectiveness** is a measure of whether the organisation has achieved its **objectives**.

- Systems evaluation may use **computer-based monitoring**. Methods include the use of hardware monitors, software monitors and systems logs.

- **Performance reviews** can be carried out to look at a wide range of systems functions and characteristics. Technological change often gives scope to **improve** the quality of outputs or reduce the extent or cost of inputs.

- Possible **problem areas** that may hinder the development of an information system that is produced on time, within budget and to specification, are shown on the mind-map following the quick quiz.

Quick quiz

1   What should the post-implementation review establish?

2   Adaptive maintenance is carried out to fix 'bugs'. TRUE or FALSE?

3   What is the purpose of regression testing?

4   Define 'end-user development'.

5   What is an information centre?

6   How does a cost-benefit review differ from a cost-benefit analysis?

7   What are metrics used for?

8   What does a systems efficiency audit measure?

Answers to quick quiz

1   Whether the system objectives and targeted performance criteria have been met.

2   FALSE. See paragraph 2.1.

3   To ensure a change to a program has not resulted in unforeseen changes elsewhere in the system.

4   The direct, hands-on development of computer systems without the involvement of systems professionals.

5   A unit of staff with good awareness of computer systems who provide support to users.

6   The review uses actual data. The analysis relies on estimates.

7   To measure system quality.

8   The efficiency of the system. The audit focuses on inputs and outputs.

The material covered in this Chapter is tested in Questions 6 and 17 in the Exam Question Bank.

INFORMATION SYSTEMS: POSSIBLE PROBLEM AREAS

MANAGEMENT

- Feasibility study
- Project management
- Risk analysis
- Quality standards
- Methodology
- Implementation
- Control

• • • • • • •

USER ACCEPTANCE

- User involvement
- Communication
- Realistic testing
- Training
- User-friendly

• • • • •

INFORMATION SYSTEM

- ON-TIME
- TO SPECIFICATION
- WITHIN BUDGET

• • •

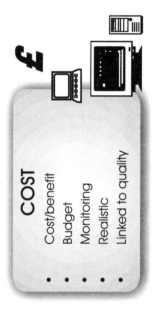

COST

- Cost/benefit
- Budget
- Monitoring
- Realistic
- Linked to quality

• • • • •

DESIGN

- User requirements
- Modelling
- Analysts/programmers/testers/users
- User-friendly
- Package/bespoke

• • • • •

BPP PUBLISHING

Exam question bank

Questions 1 - 6 of this Exam question bank are from the **Pilot Paper**.

QUESTIONS 1 - 3 ARE BASED ON THE FOLLOWING SCENARIO

CAET Insurance offers motor, home, property and personal insurance. It has recently developed a holiday insurance product that it provides to the public. A potential customer is able to telephone a specially trained adviser who asks a number of pertinent questions. The answers to these questions are entered directly into a computer system that calculates and displays the premium. The adviser communicates the premium to the potential customer who may either accept or reject it. Accepted quotations are paid for by credit card and printed off and sent to the customer, along with the payment details.

The software to support the on-line holiday insurance quotation was developed in-house by the Information Systems (IS) department. It was developed in a GUI-based programming language and was the first system to be produced by the Information Systems department using this language. The project was delivered late and it exceeded its budget. The software has suffered many problems since it was installed. Some of these have been solved. However, there are still significant problems in the actual function that the advisers use to record the details of potential customers and produce the quotation.

In a recent meeting with the IS department, the advisers identified four main problems.

Illogical data entry

The advisers claim that the sequence is illogical. The questions jump from personal details, to holiday location, to travel details, back to personal details, to holiday location etc. There seems to have been little thought about logically grouping the questions and as a result potential customers become 'confused'.

Unclear field entry

Some of the information we ask for is mandatory and some is optional. Furthermore, the relevance of some questions depends on the answer to a previous question. For example, travel method is only relevant if the potential customer is travelling abroad. Unfortunately, the system does not show if a field is mandatory or optional and it shows all fields, whether they are relevant or not to a particular quotation.

Inconsistent cursor control

The information has to be entered very quickly. Many fields are filled completely during data entry. On some screens, the cursor jumps to the next field immediately after filing the previous field. In other screens, the cursor only moves after pressing the TAB key even when the field is filled. This inconsistency is very irritating, we often find ourselves over-typing completed fields and it is particular confusing for new advisers who are not used to the software.

Performance problems

One of the primary requirements of the system was the ability to process enquiries on-line and to produce instant quotations. However, at peak times the system is too slow to produce the quotation. Consequently, we have to promise to telephone the potential customer back and this destroys the immediate impact of the system. Hence the system is not fulfilling one of its primary requirements.

CAET Insurance has brought in a consultant to review the on-line holiday insurance system. The consultant has made a number of observations regarding the project and the developed software. Two summary paragraphs are repeated below.

Extract from the management summary

Project

The IS department failed to recognise that this was a very risky project. Three issues made it particularly risky.

- The users of the system had no experience in the holiday insurance industry hence they found it difficult to specify their requirements in advance.

- The decision to use a programming language that the department had not used before.

- The system had exacting performance requirements.

All projects at CAET Insurance are supposed to undergo a risk assessment as part of producing the Project Quality Plan (PQP). This risk assessment was omitted from this project for reasons that are still unclear. This was a serious omissioin.

The software

There is considerable evidence that the product is unstable and suffers from significant performance problems. My recommendation is that the bespoke system is abandoned and a suitable application software package is selected and installed. My research suggests that there are a number of possible solutions in the marketplace and these packages offer 'tried, tested, and error-free solutions'. It will be more cost-effective, in the long run, to adopt one of these packages rather than maintain the bespoke in-house software.

---

1   **CAET INSURANCE: PROJECT MANAGEMENT**   *36 mins*

The consultant has pointed out that the project did not undergo the required risk assessment. This risk assessment would have required the project team to identify ways to avoid or reduce the chance of each risk occurring.

Required

(a) **In retrospect what could have been suggested at the start of the project to avoid or reduce each of the following three risks identified in the consultant's report?**

    (i)   **The users of the system had no experience in the holiday insurance industry hence they found it difficult to specify their requirements in advance.**

    (ii)   **The decision to use a programming language that the department had not used before.**

    (iii)   **The system had exacting performance requirements.**   **(12 marks)**

(b) **The risk assessment is an important part of the Project Quality Plant (PQP). Two other terms used in the CAET Insurance PQP are:**

    (i)   **Project Sponsor.**
    (ii)   **Project Plan.**

Explain the meaning and significance of each of these items.   **(8 marks)**

---

2   **CAET INSURANCE: SOFTWARE DESIGN**   *36 mins*

One of the key requirements of the holiday insurance system was the need to speedily process requests for an insurance quotation over the telephone. The users have identified four specific problems with the on-line insurance quotation function.

(i)   Illogical data entry.
(ii)   Unclear field entry.
(iii)   Inconsistent cursor control.
(iv)   Performance problems.

The IS department still believes that these four problems can be solved and that there is no need to abandon the development of the bespoke system and use an application package solution.

Required

(a) **Suggest how each of the following four problems could be solved, now that the system is live, and comment on the difficulty of implementing your solutions.**

    (i)   **Illogical data entry.**   **(2 marks)**
    (ii)   **Unclear field entry.**   **(3 marks)**
    (iii)   **Inconsistent cursor control.**   **(2 marks)**
    (iv)   **Performance problems.**   **(4 marks)**

(b) **Suggest how each of the following four problems could have been prevented or detected before the system went live.**

    (i)   **Illogical data entry.**   **(2 marks)**
    (ii)   **Unclear field entry.**   **(2 marks)**
    (iii)   **Inconsistent cursor control.**   **(2 marks)**
    (iv)   **Performance problems.**   **(3 marks)**

3   CAET INSURANCE: QUALITY ASSURANCE AND TESTING   *36 mins*

The consultant has suggested that one of the main advantages of the application software package approach is that the software is tried and tested.

Required

(a)   Bespoke application systems developed in the IS department has to pass through the following three stages

   (i)   Requirements analysis.
   (ii)   Systems design.
   (iii)   Programming.

   Describe the quality assurance and testing associated with each of these three stages of the IS development process.   **(12 marks)**

(b)   Explain where quality assurance and testing should still be applied by the IS department when using an application software package approach and hence comment on the consultant's assertion that the software is 'tried, tested and error-free'.   **(8 marks)**

4   OUTSOURCING, LEGACY SYSTEMS AND PM SOFTWARE   *36 mins*

Managing information systems

A recently appointed financial director has reviewed how information systems are developed in a public sector authority. She has suggested that the information systems (IS) staff should concentrate on developing new systems, rather than maintaining the existing ones. She suggests that 'the maintenance of legacy systems should be outsourced to an external software house'.

Required

(a)   Briefly explain what is meant by the term 'outsourced'.   **(3 marks)**

(b)   Briefly explain what is meant by the term 'legacy systems'.   **(3 marks)**

(c)   Describe two likely benefits of the financial director's recommendation to outsource the maintenance of legacy systems.   **(4 marks)**

She has also suggested that all systems development projects should use a project management software package to help plan, control, monitor and report progress in the proposed new development projects.

(d)   Explain what is meant by a project management software package.   **(4 marks)**

(e)   Briefly describe two advantages of using a project management software package.
                                                                              (6 marks)

5   EVENT MODEL   *36 mins*

A business analyst is preparing to interview a user about how insurance claims are handled by the business.

Required

(a)   Briefly describe four specific activities the business analyst should undertake in preparation for the meeting.   **(8 marks)**

During the meeting, the user specifies the following requirements.

Insurance claims are received into the department. These are defined as Pending Claims until a Claims Inspector can review them. The result of the review is either an Accepted Claim or a Rejected Claim. Only Accepted Claims can be paid. After six months all Paid Claims are archived.

(b)   Construct an appropriate event model for this business requirement.   **(8 marks)**

(c)   Provide an explanatory key to this model so that the user can understand it.   **(4 marks)**

6   POST-IMPLEMENTATION AND CHANGE ISSUES   *36 mins*

Required

(a)   **Describe the meaning and purpose of a post-implementation review.**   **(4 marks)**

The Human Resources Directors of a large company wants to measure the success of the application software he has commissioned and implemented for a personnel system.

(b)   **Briefly describe three measures he could use to quantify the success of the application software and state what each of these three measures is attempting to assess.**   **(9 marks)**

It is expected that the user will define new requirements (and change old ones) throughout the life of the system.

(c)   **List the components of a procedure for recording, prioritising and implementing these changes.**   **(7 marks)**

QUESTIONS 7 - 9 ARE BASED ON THE FOLLOWING SCENARIO

The Accounting Academy (AA) is a specialist ACCA training company offering Study Schools in Foundation, Certificate and Professional Stage examination papers. It was formed eight years ago by the charismatic lecturer and author Jon Lowe to offer courses that helped students prepare for the examinations. The courses are essentially pre-revision courses intended to concentrate students' minds for the final revision phase. The company currently organises 15 courses in 7 different countries for each examination sitting. These courses are residential and are held in universities or conference centres. The Foundation Stage is covered in a five day course and the Certificate and Professional Stages combined in a nine day course. The average attendance is 30 on a Foundation course, 25 on a Certificate and 50 at the Professional level.

Jon Lowe is currently Course Director of the Accounting Academy and the only full-time lecturer. All other lecturers are employed on a freelance basis. Courses are advertised in accounting publications throughout the world. The Study Schools achieve pass rates well above the national average.

The company's headquarters are in London where three administrative assistants handle enquiries, take course bookings, send out joining instructions, photocopy lecture notes and book conference facilities and lecturers. A further administrative assistant maintains the accounting records on a single user personal computer (PC). The office suite occupied by AA is divided into the Admin. Office, a small Accounts Office, a meeting room and Jon Lowe's office. The total space occupied is about 1200 sq. feet.

A year ago Jon Lowe decided to seek new investment in the company. Initial meetings with an investment group were successful and the investors commissioned a business review to identify the company's strengths and weaknesses. The review summarised these as follows:

Strengths
Consistent achievement of high pass rates
International reputation of Jon Lowe
High quality residential conference centre provision
Focus on ACCA examinations
Pre-payment for courses leads to strong cashflow position

Weaknesses
Inconsistency in the quality of course material produced by individual freelance lecturers
Strong seasonal variation in cash flow
Over-reliance on the lecturing of Jon Lowe
Time-consuming administrative procedures
Inadequate and untimely financial information

As a result of their review the new investors in the company have suggested that the company should begin to employ full-time lecturers and offer an all-year-round course programme covering full-time courses, Study Schools and Revision Courses. Their plan also suggests that ways should be found to exploit related markets. The plan has been accepted by Jon Lowe and the company's bankers.

However, it is envisaged that there will be a six-fold increase in student numbers in the next three years and hence a thorough review of the company's administrative procedures has been recommended because it is recognised that these are unlikely to be adequate to meet the requirements of the newly expanded company. A preliminary interview has been held with administrative staff. The summarised results of this meeting follow:

Administrative arrangements

The three staff in the Admin. Office all undertake the following tasks:

They take telephone and written enquiries from students about the Study Schools. Each enquiry is logged on a standard form giving the enquirer's name, address, details of the enquiry itself, action taken and the source of the enquiry. The last piece of information is particularly important as it allows the Academy to target its advertising more carefully. Consequently, the assistant must look at a standard Source List while processing the enquiry and code it accordingly. Typical codes are:

0001 The Accounting Professional
0002 Accountants Training Update
0003 Accountancy Today... etc
0020 Personal recommendation

The enquiry forms are stored in order of receipt until the end of the week. On the following Monday one of the administrative assistants goes through each enquiry form to create an Enquiry Summary List which is sent to Jon Lowe. This is a list of each source code, the source description and the number of enquiries logged the previous week for each source. This information is taken into consideration by Jon Lowe when he is reviewing his advertising strategy.

Completed application forms from students are also handled in this office. The application form is checked against the Course list to make sure that valid dates and courses have been booked. It is a rule of the company that the application form must be accompanied with a cheque or bankers draft for the full Study School fee. If a payment is not enclosed or invalid dates or courses have been booked then the application form is returned to the student with an explanatory note about the error or omission. However, if the course details are correct and a payment has been enclosed then the application form is copied and the copy sent with the payment to Edith Donaldson who handles accounting and financial matters. She will also deal with any over or under-payment of the course fee. The original copy of the application form is filed in the appropriate section of a ring binder and a booking confirmation letter is sent to the student. This is produced on an electronic typewriter.

Four weeks before the course, joining instructions are sent to each student due to attend the Study School. These are currently prepared on an electronic typewriter. The assistant checks the venue (from the Course List) and calls in a set of standard paragraphs concerning administrative and travel arrangements for that venue. The student's name and address is found on the application form in the binder and is individually typed in. A Delegate List is also typed up and sent to the Lecturer showing delegate name, company and any special dietary requirements. A copy of this is also sent to the conference centre where the course is being held.

Once the course is completed the lecturer collects post-course questionnaires from the students and sends them to the Admin. Office. Theses are stored until time allows one of the assistants to type up a one-page summary report to send to Jon Lowe. This report is essentially a statistical summary of the questionnaires together with positive and negative comments entered by the delegate. Particularly adverse statements will be followed up by Jon Lowe.

7   **THE ACCOUNTING ACADEMY: FEASIBILITY STUDY**   *36 mins*

The company intends to undertake a feasibility study to identify the costs and benefits of computerisation.

Required

(a) **Identify and briefly describe four areas of the current or proposed business that you recommend should be included within the scope of such a study.**   **(10 marks)**

(b) **Justify your selection of the business areas by discussing the business benefits that should result from their computerisation.**   **(10 marks)**

8   **THE ACCOUNTING ACADEMY: 'OFF THE SHELF' V BESPOKE SOFTWARE; SECURITY ISSUES**
                                                                                    36 mins

The head of the investment group is keen for the rapid computerisation of the company. He has indicated that he wishes to fulfil system requirements using 'off-the-shelf' application software packages rather than commissioning a bespoke software solution.

Required

(a) Discuss four potential disadvantages or problems of adopting this approach at the Accounting Academy. **(10 marks)**

(b) It is likely that the system will be implemented with a PC network linked to a central file server. What are the security and audit issues raised by this type of implementation and what steps and precautions might be taken to address these? **(10 marks)**

---

9 **THE ACCOUNTING ACADEMY: PROCESS MODEL** *36 mins*

Required

(a) Draw either a Data Flow Diagram or a Flowchart of the administrative arrangements described in the notes summarising the preliminary meeting with staff of the Accounting Academy. **(15 marks)**

(c) Provide an explanatory key to this model. **(5 marks)**

---

10 **COST-BENEFIT ANALYSIS; CRITICAL PATH** *36 mins*

You are the project manager responsible for a proposed new computer-based application for a medium sized retail chain.

Required

(a) Identify and briefly describe the techniques you would make use of to demonstrate the costs and benefits of the proposed new system. **(10 marks)**

You have drawn up an outline timetable for the introduction of the new system. The first draft of this is shown below.

Task	Description	Planned duration (weeks)	Preceding activities
A	Communication – inform staff at each shop of the proposal and indicate how it will affect them	1	-
B	Carry out systems audit at each shop	2	A
C	Agree detailed implementation plan with board of directors	1	B
D	Order and receive hardware requirements	4	C
E	Install hardware at all shops	4	D
F	Install software at all shops	2	D
G	Arrange training	3	D
H	Test systems at all shops	4	E and F
I	Implement changeover at all shops	10	G and H

(b) Produce a critical path analysis of the draft implementation plan. (This should identify the critical path and the total elapsed time.) **(10 marks)**

QUESTIONS 11 - 13 ARE BASED ON THE FOLLOWING SCENARIO

Bay Town Health Centre is a non-profit-making medical practice serving a small town. It employs four doctors, one nurse, one receptionist and a clerk. All managerial decisions are taken by the four doctors.

There are approximately seven thousand patients registered with the practice. The state pays a fee to the practice for each registered patient. The income from the state is sufficient to fund the operating costs of the practice and the salaries of the doctors and support staff. The doctors can supplement their income by treating a small number of private patients and by performing minor operations. In such cases the doctor will pay a charge to the practice to cover the use of the facilities in the medical centre.

Approximately seven years ago the doctors purchased a computerised database to record patient details, medical history and treatment given. All accounting functions are paper-based. Recent changes in legislation require the practice to submit monthly reports that provide accurate figures for:

- The number of registered patients
- The number of patients treated in the preceding month
- The cost of the treatment
- The administrative costs for the preceding month
- Any income received from private patients

The doctors believe that there is no alternative other than to replace the existing information system with a new, integrated system if they are to meet the demands of the new legislation. In addition, the doctors would like the new system to provide electronic diaries for work-scheduling and making appointments for patients, on-line searching of medical literature and the automatic generation of repeat prescriptions for patients who have long-term treatment.

11   BAY TOWN HEALTH CENTRE: COSTS AND BENEFITS   *36 mins*

Required

Identify, with your reasons, the costs and benefits of purchasing a new information system for the practice. **(20 marks)**

12   BAY TOWN HEALTH CENTRE: DECISION MAKING   *36 mins*

Required

'*A new information system always aids decision making*'. Discuss the validity of this statement both in general terms and with respect to the practice. **(20 marks)**

13   BAY TOWN HEALTH CENTRE: ENSURING ACCURACY   *36 mins*

Required

Outline the steps that you would take to ensure that information held on the new system would be secure, accurate and coherent. **(20 marks)**

14   GANTT CHART   *36 mins*

The Drugs Advisory Service is a charitable organisation which provides advice and counselling to clients from three offices in residential areas approximately twenty miles apart. The service was established three years ago and funded by the government. New funding arrangements have recently been agreed with the Health Authority under a contract which obliges the service to measure all aspects of its performance and provide information which indicates that it is giving 'value for money'. Many of the counsellors feel that completing statistical records is inappropriate to the work they do, especially in dealing with very distressed clients.

Required

Prepare a Gantt chart to show the principal project management stages in preparing to meet the new information requirements of the funders. **(20 marks)**

QUESTIONS 15 - 17 ARE BASED ON THE FOLLOWING SCENARIO

SWM Ltd is a manufacturing company with three divisions, all of which operate from the same site. The company's main finished goods warehouse is located about one mile away. The main manufacturing site is the location for all other functions, including the IT department.

The company runs a corporate database on a mainframe computer with networked terminals. The terminals do not at present have any independent processing capacity. Departmental managers have become concerned at the speed of processing when several applications or users require computer time at the same time. The chief executive has also expressed concern about the high cost of software maintenance.

The warehouse stock records are maintained on a minicomputer in the warehouse. Each morning, details of the previous day's sales orders taken are sent by courier to the warehouse. The data, which is stored on a floppy disk, is downloaded to the warehouse system, which generates despatch documentation, including invoices, and picking lists. The warehouse's 'free' and 'allocated' stock records are updated.

At the end of each day, details of stock movements are sent to the main site and the mainframe's stock records are updated. These are referred to by sales order processing staff to ensure goods are in stock when booking orders. Copy invoices are also sent to the accounts department for posting to customer ledgers.

A recent review of software maintenance costs by the chief accountant has revealed the following.

(a)   The mainframe has limited reporting capabilities. Recent requests for the provision of reports of sales by region and by product group have resulted in substantial reprogramming effort in order to add the required fields and routines.

(b)   It is not possible to produce reports containing summary level information at the same time as routine reports are generated. This has meant that senior managers either content themselves with working with the long transactions listings used by operational staff in the relevant department or ask subordinates to prepare summaries 'manually', which the latter usually do with spreadsheet packages.

15   **SWM LTD: SYSTEM DEFICIENCIES**   *36 mins*

    Required

    Write a report to Departmental Managers identifying any information deficiencies in the current system and recommending ways in which the processing of data could be speeded up.

    (20 marks)

16   **SWM LTD: SYSTEM CONTROLS**   *36 mins*

    Required

    What controls should be adopted to retain the integrity and the security of the data in the system.   **(20 marks)**

17   **SWM LTD: SOFTWARE MAINTENANCE**   *36 mins*

    Required

    Draft a report to the chief executive describing the types of software maintenance encountered in computer systems.   **(20 marks)**

Exam
answer bank

1   **CAET INSURANCE: PROJECT MANAGEMENT**

(a) (i)   **Risk: Lack of user experience in the holiday industry**

Avoiding risk

Experience in the holiday industry could be obtained by either recruiting new staff with the appropriate experience, or by helping existing staff obtain that experience, through their work and possibly by attendance on some appropriate training courses. However, using the latter option will almost certainly have delayed the systems project.

Reducing risk

Involving users throughout the design process could reduce the risk of implementing an incorrect or partly functional system. Specifically, system prototypes and pilot testing could be carried out to check the appropriateness of any system design.

Reviewing similar systems that may already be available on the market or at third parties may also reduce risk. The latter will be difficult to achieve where third parties do not want to share their knowledge although a review of propriety software will at least indicate the functionality that can be included in any new system.

(ii) **Decision to use a programming language with no experience of that language in-house**

Avoiding risk

This risk can be avoided, either gaining the appropriate experience in-house, or by using a different programming language that in-house already have experience in. The choice will depend on how important it is to use the functionality in the chosen language.

Reducing risk

If the unfamiliar language has to be used, then risk of failure can be reduced firstly, by allowing more time in the project plan for training or hiring of staff. Another alternative is to put back the project delivery time to recognise that problems may occur in writing and testing the software. These alternatives may be more appropriate than implementing software that fails or causes errors shortly after implementation.

(iii) **Exacting performance problems**

Avoiding risk

Performance problems can be avoided by decreasing the use of the computer system at busy times. This may mean storing customer telephone calls in a queue and only taking the number of calls that the system will process or promising to call customers back at a less busy time. As a last resort, CAET could stop giving quotes on-line, although this may not an acceptable option, given CAET's commitment to using the system.

Reducing risk

Checking that high specification hardware is installed to provide adequate processing power can reduce the risk of poor performance. Faster hardware will decrease the waiting time for response from the system.

Alternatively, prototypes can be produced during the design and build phase to test the system response times. If performance cannot be improved, then at least expectations of users and customers regarding performance can be managed.

(b) (i)   **Project sponsor**

The project sponsor is the customer for the system. This person is not necessarily the finance director, but the manager of the business unit or department where the new system will be implemented. The sponsor will have made the business case for any new or revised system, and will seek to ensure that those benefits are delivered in the final system.

As the project sponsor is responsible for delivering the benefits of the project, that person will also be promoting the project prior to implementation. Promotion in this case will mean ensuring that appropriate resources are allocated to the project as well as ensuring potential users are aware of the project and are briefed on the benefits of that project. Lack of a project sponsor will increase the risk of project failure, due to lack of co-ordination of the activities of the project and possible lack of priority for the project within the organisation.

273 **BPP**

(ii)   **Project plan**

The project plan provides an overall picture of the project showing the activities to be carried out, the time of those activities and how the different activities are related to each other. Most project plans are presented as some form of chart (eg GANTT chart) or network so that interconnections between the activities can be seen clearly.

The project plan is used to estimate the total time to complete the project and identify those activities, which must be completed on time to avoid the whole project being finished late. The effect on total project duration from changes in activities can also be estimated by entering revised times for activities into the plan. If no plan is produced, then the overall project time and critical activities will be difficult to predict. There will also be an increased risk of late completion due to overall lack of control.

2   CAET INSURANCE: SOFTWARE DESIGN

(a)   (i)   **Illogical data entry**

The logical order to input data into the system needs to be ascertained from the users of the system. This error could have been identified in a prototype and the screen design amended at this time. However, given that the correct fields appear to be available, rather than some fields actually missing, the screen should be fairly easy to amend. Within the GUI interface, each field will have its own placeholder (similar to those in Microsoft Access), so these can be dragged to a new location and the order of using the fields amended to reflect the user requirement.

(ii)   **Unclear field entry**

Mandatory fields should be easy to identify, possibly by using a different colour to shade the field or providing a darker boarder around the input box. Similarly, displaying some fields should be made dependent on entries actually made in previous fields. Again, using the GUI interface tools, amendments to field properties should be fairly easy to accomplish.

(iii)   **Inconsistent cursor control**

Inconsistent cursor control is difficult for the user as the action of the cursor is difficult to predict, as the case study shows. A survey of users will help to identify which action on the completion of each field is actually appropriate. Pressing the tab key may be the easiest option because the software may not always identify when a field is complete (eg when does an address end?). However, as long as the action is consistent and logical, then the actual alternative chosen is irrelevant.

The change should again be easy to implement by ensuring that the properties for completion of input in each field are the same.

(iv)   **Performance problems**

Performance problems are more difficult to remedy as they may require amendments to hardware or software, which are simply not possible post-implementation. However, it may be possible to:

Add additional disk space, RAM memory or upgrade network cards to a higher specification or install a more recent processor to try and improve overall system performance. All of these alternatives should help to reduce the response time.

Alternatively, the actual use of system resources in terms of which programs are being run at specific times can also be reviewed. If resource-intensive programs, such as file re-organisation, are being run during the day, then these can be deferred to a less busy time. This will free up system resources for more important programs such as the on-line insurance system.

(b)   (i)   **Illogical data entry**

Ensuring that the screen correctly reflects the method of work would normally be checked during the design stage of a system, specifically by using a prototype of the screen layout. At this time, amendments to the screen design could be made prior to the final system being built, avoiding these errors at the user acceptance test. However, given that this is a new system, even a prototype may have been of limited use because users could still have been uncertain about how they wanted to input data.

(ii)   **Unclear field entry**

The issue of some fields being optional could again have been detected at the build stage using a prototype to check which fields actually needed to be completed for each data record. Alternatively, data collection during the building of a logical model during system design may also have detected that some fields were optional.

However, in the current situation, some design standard is required to distinguish optional from mandatory fields. This will ensure that optional fields will only be shown when they are required.

(iii)   **Inconsistent cursor control**

The lack of consist use of the cursor again implies a lack of standards during the design phase of the software. Stating the action to take on completion of a field in a style manual would help to ensure this error did not occur, or if it did, the manual would show which style should be applied.

Design errors would be detected during systems testing, as this is now a systems standard.

(iv)   **Performance problems**

The performance of the system should be checked during system testing; specifically when the response times to processing increasing large amounts of data were checked. It is possible that this load testing was not carried out, or that the system was inadequately tested at this time, with only a small number of transactions being processed. If the problem had been detected during testing, then the software could have been amended to try and enhance performance prior to going live.

3   CAET INSURANCE: QUALITY ASSURANCE AND TESTING

(a)   The three areas of application development mentioned in the question relate to the three stages of testing outlined in the 'V' model of system development. In this model, analysis and testing are linked at three specific points:

1.   Requirements analysis and user acceptance testing
2.   Systems design and systems testing
3.   Program design and unit or module testing.

This format is followed in the answer.

(i)   **Requirements analysis**

In the requirements analysis stage, documentation is produced to show what the system is required to do in terms of input, output and processing. The documentation will be produced in text or graphical form, and then checked to ensure that it is complete and adheres to appropriate design standards.

In user acceptance testing, the requirements analysis is re-visited and checked against the new system. The new system should fulfil the requirements previously defined in the requirements analysis; if it does not, then further amendments may be required before the users sign-off the system.

(ii)   **Systems design**

During system design, the architectural software design is produced from the business requirements and technical specification for the software. Documentation is produced to specific design standards so it can be checked using formal walkthroughs.

In systems testing, all of the individual programs are tested together as one integrated suite of software. The integrated software is compared back to the original design specification to check that the programs work as outlined in this design. If the design is not met then the systems testing fails and amendments to the overall design of the software may still be required. When the systems testing is complete, the integrated software is forwarded for user acceptance testing.

(iii)   **Programming**

At this stage, the individual programs or modules of the software are designed. The actual designs will again be produced in accordance with specific design standards and tested prior to the program itself being written.

After the program is written, it is checked back to the program specification to ensure that this has been met. This testing is normally called unit testing. Any errors in the program modules are corrected or debugged before the individual programs are sent for systems testing.

(b) Using an application software package approach means that software is purchased from a third party supplier ready for use within the organisation. This means that systems design and program design and their associated testing phases are not required because the software house will have already performed this testing.

However, a specification of requirements will still be required, and therefore user acceptance testing will also be required. The specification of requirements is necessary because the software must still meet the business needs of the organisation. The requirements must therefore be listed and compared to the specification for the program. It will be very difficult to amend the application software after it has been implemented, so checking requirements is essential.

User acceptance testing is also necessary to ensure that the requirement specification is met, and that the software adequately supports the business needs of the users as well as the volume of transactions.

The comment concerning 'tried, tested and error free' may be incorrect.

Firstly, the software has not been tested in the organisation, so it may not meet the specific requirements of users. The testing to date has been against the requirements of designers in the software house, not the organisation where the software is being implemented.

Secondly, the software is unlikely to be 100% error free. The software house may not have been able to test all combinations of the different software modules or with the specific transactions that will be used in the organisation in a live situation. Errors may still occur.

4 OUTSOURCING, LEGACY SYSTEMS AND PM SOFTWARE

(a) Outsourcing means that the part of all of or the IT systems within an organisation are provided or maintained by a third party supplier. In this situation, it is the legacy systems that are to be outsourced.

The terms of the outsourcing contract will include number of years and cost of the service, as well as precise details of the service such as changes to be made to the systems or any new reports that will be generated.

(b) The term legacy systems in an organisation relates to the old systems, implemented some time ago, which are no longer updated. Legacy systems are likely to have been written in older languages such as COBOL or FORTRAN, which are rarely used. So it is possible that the software cannot communicate with more recent systems, and the data is only accessible from within the legacy system.

However, the systems are generally reliable, and the users see very little need to amend or upgrade. Similarly, it may be difficult to present a business case to replace the systems.

(c) Outsourcing of the legacy systems may provide the following benefits to the organisation. [Only two required – three are provided here for study purposes]

(i) Access to programming expertise

Most new software systems are written in more modern computer languages, so it is not necessary to maintain expertise in relatively old languages in-house. It may even be difficult to find programmers with appropriate experience to maintain the programmes, as the computer language is old.

However, an outsourcing company may still employ COBOL programmers, because the costs can be shared across a wider client base. The company can continue to obtain access to this expertise as required.

(ii) Cost savings

Outsourcing may provide a cheaper alternative to employing staff to maintain the legacy systems. Very few changes are likely to be required to the systems, so it is unlikely that in-house staff would be fully employed maintaining them. Purchasing the expertise as and when required is likely to be a cheaper option.

Cost may also be saved because all changes to the legacy systems will need a business case to justify the expenditure. As this is now an external cost, very good business cases will be required to justify the amendments.

(iii)   Morale

If a third party provides maintenance of the legacy systems, then programming staff can concentrate on new in-house projects. This is likely to enhance employee morale, as producing new systems is normally more enjoyable than maintaining old systems.

(d)   Project management software is a specific program which is design to help plan and control a project. Popular examples include Microsoft Project and Project Manager Workbench.

These packages allow managers to plan projects by constructing network diagrams or GANTT charts along with budgets when costs are allocated to individual activities within each project. Network diagrams will also allow the critical path of the project to be highlighted. The cost effect of amendments to a project may also be determined.

Inputting completed activities can help monitor the progress of a project, and a variety of reports are normally available to help monitor the progress of the project.

(e)   Advantages of using project management software

(i)   Allocation of resources across projects

Project management software will identify the critical path for a project. This will help to ensure that appropriate resources are allocated to the activities on the critical path to ensure that they are not delayed. The software can also be used to allocate resources over several projects running at the same time. Updating several manual project plans and keeping these concurrent with each other will be quite difficult; however, this activity will be relatively simple using project management software.

(ii)   Changes to projects

Amendments to projects can be input into project management software to quickly identify the effects on the timescale and resources needed for the project. The effect of making different amendments could also be compared so that amendments causing the smallest change to the project can be selected. The effect of amending resource allocation over all projects can easily be seen by reviewing outputs from the software.

5   EVENT MODEL

> **Tutorial note**: In part (b) we have produced a simple flowchart type model as this suits the circumstances outlined. Other types of model could have been used. The Key should enable an 'outsider' to understand the conventions used in the model.

(a)   To prepare for the meeting with the user, the analyst will need to carry out the activities below.

Confirm the time and location of the meeting. All attendees will need to know where the meeting is held, and the analyst may need to ensure sufficient chairs tables etc. are available and book refreshments.

Confirm the objectives of the meeting. The user will need to know why the meeting is being held; a list of objectives should be circulated to all attendees prior to the meeting.

Prepare for the meeting – background information. The analyst will need to research the history of the company, check current procedure manuals and clarify any technical terms that may be used. This will help the analyst identify the situation of the user and 'talk the user's language'.

Prepare for the meeting – questions to ask. The analyst will need to plan and write out the questions to be asked during the meeting. A checklist of points to be covered may also be required to ensure that all the information required is actually obtained.

(b) **Event model for Insurance claim**

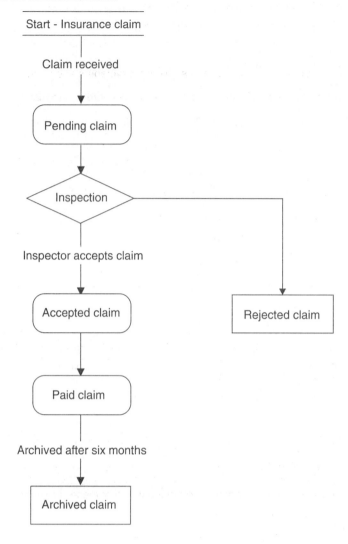

Start - Insurance claim

Claim received

Pending claim

Inspection

Inspector accepts claim

Accepted claim

Rejected claim

Paid claim

Archived after six months

Archived claim

(c) **Key for event model**

Symbol	Explanation
_____	The start of the model stating the event being modelled.
↓	Possible transitions between different states of an object.
◇	An activity, the outcome of which decides the next transition.
▢ (rounded)	A state of an object awaiting further transition.
▭	The final state of an object.

6   POST-IMPLEMENTATION AND CHANGE ISSUES

(a)   A post-implementation review takes place a few months after system implementation is complete. The review is to receive feedback from users on how well the system is working and to check that the objectives of the project have been met. The review normally takes the form of a meeting between the project sponsor, systems analyst, developers and users.

The review will investigate both the procedures used throughout the project and the systems that have been produced. The purpose of doing this is to identify what features of the project went well, and what went wrong or badly, so that future projects will avoid these problems.

In reviewing the objectives of the project, the review will also check whether or not the business benefits expected from the project have been achieved. Where benefits have not been achieved, or other objectives of the project have not been met, the review may also recommend remedial action to ensure that the required benefits are obtained.

(b)   **Measures of success for application software**

(i)   Number of calls to the help desk

Ascertaining the number of help desk calls per 100 employees (or some other useful number) will help to determine how useable and user-friendly the system is. The number of calls may also give an indication of the effectiveness of the training provided.

(ii)   Number of errors reported

A log can be maintained, either by individual users or the help desk, of the number and type of errors found in the system. The actual error rate provides an indication of the quality of programming and the effectiveness of the different stages of testing (user acceptance, system and module).

(iii)   Number of transactions processed

The original software specification will indicate how many transactions should be processed. Comparing the specification with the actual number processed will provide information on the usefulness of the system (if the system is not useful then presumably it will be used less than expected). A small number of transactions being processed could also be indicative of poor programming or inadequate hardware specifications, so further analysis may be needed to determine which of these is relevant.

(iv)   Number of change requests

Users may request changes to the system, either where that system did not meet their original requirements, or where the system as implemented does not meet their expectations in some way. Changes requested due to initial specifications not being met provides some measure on the quality of the design and testing processes. Changes requested because the software is not meeting expectations may indicate weaknesses in this method of obtaining data for the initial specification.

(c)   A procedure for recording, prioritising and implementing change requested for a live system are outlined below.

- A means for the user to record and request a change to the system
- A method of collating these change requests
- A means of providing a impact analysis and business case for each change
- A process for reviewing each request with agreed criteria for accepting or rejecting a request
- A method of prioritising requests that have been accepted
- Provision of appropriate documentation to record each change request with analysis and design implications for the existing system
- A method of allocating amendments to programmers
- A process for reviewing the work of programmers and ensuring that the change meets the initial specification
- A process for testing the change within the whole program suite
- Procedures for informing users date and nature of the change
- Procedures for updating system and user documentation prior to the release of the change
- A process for releasing that change into the live software

7   **THE ACCOUNTING ACADEMY: FEASIBILITY STUDY**

(a)   The areas of the business recommended for inclusion within the scope of the feasibility study are as follows.

(i)   *Production of course material.* Inconsistencies in quality have been identified. Greater control is required over individual freelance lecturers. A 'house style' could be imposed and a central databank of material maintained to enable use of material in appropriate modules.

(ii)   *Finance.* Since there are strong seasonal variations in cashflow, a cashflow forecasting model should be a key part of this. The opportunity should also be taken to review accountancy procedures, including invoicing and cash handling. 'Inadequate and untimely financial information' is a key area to address.

(iii) *Marketing.* There is potentially useful data available in the organisation in the form of the source data about the origin of student enquiries. This data is not really being used to its full potential. The Academy should also consider mailshots, an obvious target for computerisation.

(iv)   *Administration.* Administrative arrangements are fairly complex. A review of this area of the business would be extremely useful. WP in particular is needed, as various pieces of mail are sent to each student.

(b)   Areas where business benefits could be identified are as follows.

(i)   *Increased income (and profitability).* If marketing activities are improved to make them more focused, attendances could rise further than anticipated. The six-fold increase referred to is presumably 'across-the-board'. Good marketing could help attract students who might otherwise select rival courses.

(ii)   *Cost savings.* An area often identified as being justification for computerisation of business activities is cost-cutting. There is certainly scope for this here. The small size of personnel in administrative operation makes redundancies unlikely, but it is likely that the same staff, once trained, will be able to take on *more* work, so that when student numbers increase, fewer new staff will be required than would be the case under the current system.

(iii) *Improved control of financial position.* Computerisation will overcome the problem of inadequate and untimely financial information, allowing better planning in the light of available and forecast cash resources. Reliance on such factors as short-term overdrafts may be eliminated if these are a feature.

(iv)   *Improved quality.* Improvements in the quality of material (as identified in (a) above) may help to enhance the image of the Academy, as will word processed (as opposed to typewritten) documents/letters.

8   **THE ACCOUNTING ACADEMY: 'OFF-THE-SHELF' V BESPOKE SOFTWARE; SECURITY ISSUES**

(a)   Disadvantages of off-the-shelf packages are as follows.

(i)   The *requirements* of the Accounting Academy are extremely *varied.* It may be difficult to identify suitable packages for all these requirements. WP is probably the least problematic as modern packages will provide facilities such as mailmerge and address labelling. A spreadsheet *could* be used for cashflow forecasting, but a dedicated package would probably be preferable. As for finance, given the status of the Academy and the nature of its operation it might be difficult to identify a suitable package. Some tailoring of packages might be necessary; alternatively some amendments to the company's operations could be necessitated if the package solution is inadequate.

(ii)   Given that one package will not satisfy all the Academy's requirements, the issue of *compatibility* arises. The company will have to consider whether different packages might produce incompatible data. A further problem, whether or not data is compatible is the issue of interface. If data needs to be transferred between packages, they will need to be able to recognise each other's file formats. The requirement for different packages might result in *duplication* of data, for example student and lecturer names and addresses might be held in more than one package. This would make file maintenance difficult.

(iii) Use of a package (or packages) involves reliance on the supplier of the package. Not all suppliers have the reputation and stability of, say, Microsoft, Lotus or Borland. Suppliers can go out of business or change their strategic direction (eg from products into services)

and this can leave a package without support. This results in it not being upgraded while rival packages improve and possibly in the loss of technical support. If an organisation buys a bespoke package, the organisation becomes the 'owner' and, provided that the package is of a certain standard, the owner can commission upgrades and enhancements. In addition, some packages are supplied with poor *documentation* and without tutorial facilities. These, while not affecting the package's functionality, can impede users wishing to use the package effectively.

(iv)   The decision to purchase a package can be made without adequate *recognition* of the organisation's *requirements*. The Academy is going through a period of change and it might be difficult to identify the organisation's requirements clearly (let alone meet them, as described in (i)). If the requirements analysis is poor or non-existent, the package might be purchased for the wrong reasons, for example, it is a good offer or it has a 'nice' interface! This could lead to a package which is inappropriate for actual business requirements being acquired.

(b)   Physical security comprises two sorts of controls, protection against natural and man-made disasters, such as fire, flood and sabotage, and protection against intruders gaining physical access to the system. These threats can be grouped alternatively as accidental and deliberate. The physical environment has a major effect on information system security, and so planning it properly is an important precondition of an adequate security plan.

Fire is the most serious hazard to computer systems. Destruction of data can be even more costly than the destruction of hardware. A proper fire safety plan is an essential feature of security procedures, in order to prevent fire, detect fire and put out the fire.

The other main area of physical security is *access control*, to prevent intruders getting anywhere near the computer equipment or storage media. Methods of controlling human access include:

(i)   Personnel (security guards).

(ii)   Mechanical devices (eg keys, whose issue is recorded).

(iii)   Electronic identification devices (eg card-swipe systems, where a card is passed through a reader).

Theft is also a problem, particularly where so much computer equipment is easily portable. A PC need not be larger than a briefcase and even a laser printer can be carried by one person. To some extent this can be guarded against by means similar to those described above, but with much equipment located in ordinary offices and no longer kept in a single secure location other measures must be taken. Regular 'stock controls' or physical inspections may be necessary, and a strictly imposed form of bookings used when staff take PCs off-site, either to customers or home.

Hacking has received newspaper coverage in recent years. The use of telecommunications links across, and between, large organisations, whether multinational companies or national defence departments, makes them vulnerable to determined hackers. Again the risk varies from 'nuisance value' to potential loss of material either through destruction or to competitors. Certain companies in London now advertise a service by which, for a fee, they can obtain bank account details and financial information about any named individual for customers: this kind of illegal activity is made easier by the use of IT.

Another risk is from *viruses*. These may be carried on games software or pirated software; they can be also spread on computer networks and via e-mail. At best, they are a nuisance; at worst tremendously harmful to data to the extent of wiping hard disks clean. All disks coming into an organisation and, periodically, all computers, should be checked using proprietary anti-virus software.

In smaller companies the security officer is normally responsible for the whole computer function and is often the finance manager or equivalent. System security may be less formal especially where the officer knows all the users personally. Nevertheless it is advisable that at least a basic password structure is applied to the system.

Data integrity can be corrupted by system faults and user error as well as unauthorised access. The regular back up of data should be a disciplined procedure for all computer systems. This may happen daily and the copies are often kept off premises. Security copies of the system programs may be kept at a bank or with solicitors (possibly at the request of insurers). Proper shut-down procedures should also be carried out only by authorised personnel and the network should not be left on and unattended.

Data integrity will also be maintained by keeping information on the system to a realistic minimum. This will involve deleting or archiving redundant data. This has the additional benefits of improving response times and reducing the time taken for back-up procedures. Random checks and reconciliations of data from audit trails or system enquiry will also highlight, by exception, problems which have occurred.

9 THE ACCOUNTING ACADEMY: PROCESS MODEL

(a)

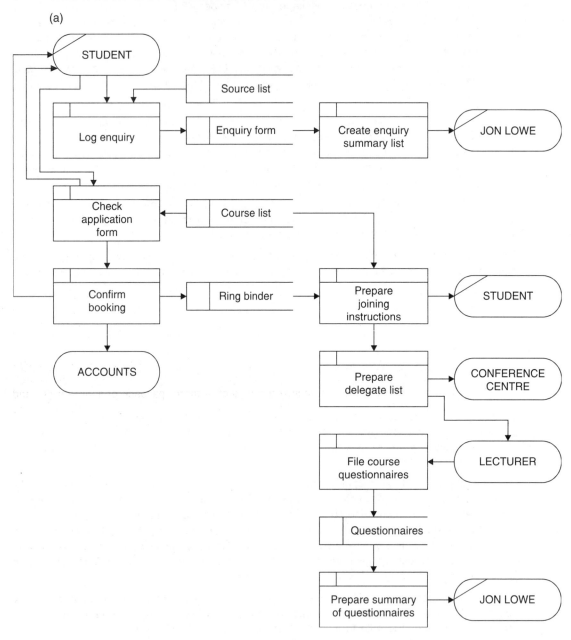

(b) Explanatory Key.

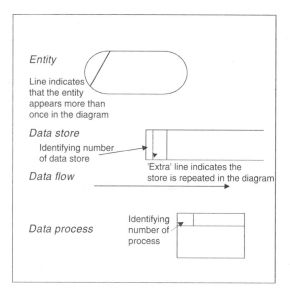

10   COST-BENEFIT ANALYSIS; CRITICAL PATH

(a) Techniques which might be used to evaluate the costs and benefits of a new system include the following.

(i) *Cash flow analysis.* At the end of the project the result should be that the project produces a positive balance. The problem with this is that although many costs will be tangible, many benefits will be intangible, and might need to be estimated in order to establish any kind of sensible figure.

(ii) *Payback period.* Assuming that the result of implementing the system is positive then after some period of time the benefits outweigh the costs. This is the payback period. The shorter the payback period the more attractive the project. If target payback periods are set and capital project approval only given to projects meeting the target, it will be necessary to apply different periods to different scales of investment. Differences in payback patterns must also be taken into account.

(iii) *Return on investment.* This is the method of quantifying the benefit in terms of the rate per year expressed as a percentage of the costs. Normally all costs and benefits are totalled and the result spread over the anticipated life of the project, giving the ROI figure. No attempt is made to account for the value of holding the investment in the project.

(iv) *Discounted cash flow.* The discounted cash flow takes into account the timing of both payments and benefits, and returns a figure which more meaningfully estimates the value of the project taking into account both the sums involved and their timings. Flows are discounted so that their present values are obtained.

The results from the analysis methods above might be compared to results which could be obtained from using the same funds elsewhere, to establish whether there were compelling financial reasons to proceed with the project.

Each of the sets of figures from the accounting mechanisms listed above could be perhaps better presented graphically rather than in tabular form. This would visually emphasise that the project was going to make a 'profit', and over what period (which is what in essence the figures illustrate).

(b) **Critical path analysis**

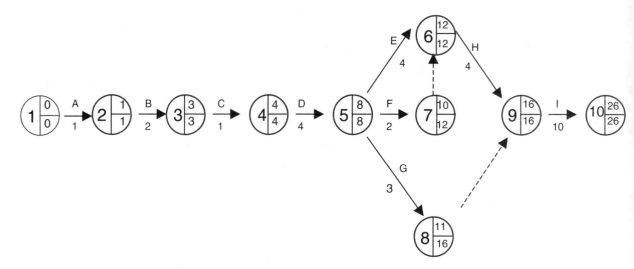

The critical path is A, B, C, D, E, H, I. The total elapsed time is 26 weeks.

11 BAY TOWN HEALTH CENTRE: COSTS AND BENEFITS

Costs

Most of the costs of the new information system are tangible, that is they can be quantified and relate to specific items of computer hardware or software. There may be an intangible cost to the practice in that if an upgrade is not carried out, then patient service, as compared to other practices, may decline. In the medium- to long-term, the practice may lose income as patients switch to other practices providing better information and service.

New software

It is unlikely that the current software will meet the requirements of either the government legislation, or the requirements of doctors. While the old software would appear to provide information on number of registered patients and number of patients treated, it does not give information on cost of treatments or diary features etc. New software will therefore be required to:

(i) Meet the new legislation requirements including computerising the accounting function
(ii) Provide electronic diaries
(iii) Provide access to on-line medical information
(iv) Enable the tracking of repeat prescriptions

If possible, the doctors should try to purchase software that is specifically written for medical practices. This will make it easier to use and provide an easy upgrade route when the software requires amendment due to further changes in legislation.

Cost of software must include an appropriate number of user licences; effectively one for each computer.

New hardware

It is not clear from the question what computer hardware the practice currently owns. However, given that the hardware was purchased seven years ago, it is unlikely that this will be suitable for running more recent programs. Computer programs today require a lot more RAM and hard disk space than seven years ago, so existing hardware will have to be replaced.

Given that doctors want to share information on diaries and access online information on medical literature, then some form of networking solution will be required. The final hardware specification will include the following.

(i) A PC for each user, capable of running the network software and all other applications required.

(ii) A central file store to store central files, possibly the medical information on CD, e-mail, and diary software

(iii) A backup solution (such as a tape backup system)

(iv) Printers

(v) Either a CD-ROM drive on the central file server or a secure server for Internet access, depending on whether the medical database is available on CD or from the Internet

Data conversion

Some of the data on the existing system, particularly the medical history files, will be needed on the new database. The doctors will need to ensure that the data files from the old software can be transferred onto the new software. Depending on the compatibility of the systems, there will be cost involved in transferring the data. Quotes will be necessary from the software house supplying the new system to determine the cost of conversion.

Internet access

Internet access may be necessary either for the medical database information or to allow for e-mail (possibly for advising patients of appointments in the future). Future use of e-mail will confirm the requirement for a secure server.

Benefits

Many of the benefits will be intangible and therefore difficult to quantify.

Meet government legislation

The main benefit of the new system is that the medical practice will meet the requirements of the new government legislation.

Better information for doctors

The doctors have indicated that they require additional information to run the practice. The hardware and software specification above will help to provide this information. Having access to this information will be a motivational factor for the doctors, as well as helping them to provide more accurate diagnosis because they will have on-line access to appropriate medical information and patients' medical histories.

Better information for administration staff

The administration person will also have access to improved information; in particular the patient booking systems and databases will provide a better and more accurate information on patients.

Better information for patients

Patients will receive a better service from the medical practice, both in terms of booking appointments and service from doctors.

Repeat prescriptions

The repeat prescription part of the software will also enable the practice to provide a better service as well as saving some time for the administrator.

Competitive advantage for practice

Finally, by providing a better service to patients (that is the customers), the practice may obtain some competitive advantage over similar practices. It is therefore possible that the practice income will increase as more patients are attracted to the practice.

12 BAY TOWN HEALTH CENTRE: DECISION MAKING

Problems with the information system

Accuracy of systems specification

To provide accurate information to the users, any new system will need to be based on an accurate systems specification. This means that user requirements will be collected during the planning phase of the systems change, and these requirements incorporated into the systems specification and final systems design. If user requirements are omitted from the specification, or the final design is not based on the specification, then user requirements will not be met.

In the case of the Bay Town Health Centre, the doctors have suggested some requirements for a new system, such as the electronic diaries. However, it is not clear whether these requirements have been included in any specification. Similarly, the requirements from the doctors appear to be quite vague which may result in the delivered system not meeting the expectations of the doctors. Prior to the purchase of any system, detailed user requirements will be needed to ensure that the system does meet doctors' needs.

Type of system used

The type of system that is being used will limit provision of information by computer systems. Many systems, which are written to provide current or historical information, are unlikely to be able to give indications concerning future trends or events. Care is therefore required in implementing a system that is appropriate for the tasks being undertaken.

In the case of the medical practice, all the systems being implemented appear to produce historical or similar factual information. However, implementing some form of Expert System may provide additional information for doctors, either during diagnosis or by identifying future illness from past data.

Provision of information

Information provided by the system may not aid decision making because it does not comply with the characteristics of good information.

Timeliness of information

The timing of provision of information from a system will have a major effect on its usefulness. Information that is provided late may not be particularly useful.

If doctors at the Bay Town Medical Centre only received electronic diary updates every day, rather than in real-time, they may not know which patient they are seeing next. Incorrect medical histories will be accessed possibly resulting in inaccurate or poor decisions.

Accessibility to information system

To aid decision making, information from the system must be accessible. There is little point in information being available if it cannot be used.

It is not clear from the information about the Bay Town Medical Centre, whether on-line terminals will be available for each doctor. These will be needed to access the medical databases and patient treatment information.

Accuracy of information

If information is not accurate, then incorrect decisions may be taken. Provision of inaccurate information may not be a fault of the information system, but rather an error caused by the human operator.

If medical history information is updated incorrectly, either the wrong patient files are amended or incorrect illness details are entered into the correct patient file, then the medical information will be inaccurate and incorrect decisions may be made. Appropriate training will be required for the administrator at the Centre, although this will not guard against the occasional human error.

Other factors preventing the information system from aiding decision-making

Lack of training

Many new information systems are implemented into organisations where the staff are very busy. This means that sufficient time will not always be made available for training and familiarisation with the system. Although the system provides the information needed for decision making, lack of knowledge of that system by users precludes them from using that information and therefore making accurate decisions.

Staff at the Bay Town Health Centre appear to be very busy, and this may impact on the amount of training time. In particular, doctors must provide an appropriate service to their patients; if they are conscientious then they may be unwilling to take time away from patient consultation for training. However, given the diverse nature of the new systems being implemented, sufficient time must be found for training. If this is not done then customer service will suffer in the medium-term because doctors will not be able to find the information to carry out their jobs correctly.

Hardware specification causing delays

The hardware being used by the information system may be inadequate. This may result in delays in processing and displaying information on-screen, or even loss of information where processing memory or hard disk space is inadequate.

There does not appear to be a formal systems specification for the medical centre. It is important to produce this to ensure that the software will run without any degradation in performance caused by the issues noted above.

In conclusion, a properly planned and implemented information system will always be able to aid decision-making. However, problems with the development process or other factors outside the control of the system will normally mean that there will be limits to the effectiveness of the system.

13   BAY TOWN HEALTH CENTRE: ENSURING ACCURACY

Security

Information on the medical centre's computer system must be kept secure. Under the Data Protection Act, access to medical information must be restricted to authorised individuals, and access by data subjects is also restricted. Therefore, additional security will be required to ensure that data subjects cannot review their records.

It is recommended that the main steps taken to ensure the security of data include the following:

(i)   Restricting PC access to authorised users by implementing the following measures.

   (1)   Locking rooms where the PCs are located when not in use.
   (2)   Having screen-savers with passwords which are activated after a few minutes idle time.

(ii)   The following steps should be taken to restrict access to sensitive data held on the system.

   (1)   Keeping the data on a server that is not attached to the Internet. This will remove the threat of hacking from outside the medical centre.

   (2)   Password protecting the individual data files so that they cannot be opened without the appropriate password being used.

   (3)   If necessary, encrypting the data files so if they are stolen they cannot be read without the decryption software and key.

   (4)   The system backup should be maintained in a secure location.

Accuracy

Data on the PCs needs to be accurate partly as a result of the Data Protection Act requirements, but also because inaccurate data may either breach the new government reporting requirements or even cause an incorrect diagnosis to be made.

The method of ensuring accuracy of data depends on the data being discussed.

Medical history files

Accuracy of personal information can normally be checked by printing out that information and asking the data subject to verify that the information is correct. This approach cannot be taken with medical information due to the restrictions of the Data Protection Act, as already noted. There is the additional complication that errors may have occurred in transferring the information from the old to the new system. Steps that can be taken to ensure accuracy will include the following.

(i)   Performing a manual comparison (by medical centre staff) of data from the old and new systems with any differences being corrected.

(ii)   Doctors checking information on-screen during consultations with patients.

(iii)   A review of patient's medical history by doctors with an investigation into any unusual entries.

(iv)   Having input controls built into the software to try and detect inaccurate information. This control will be effectively limited to factual information such as names and addresses, due to the diverse nature of the medical information being input.

Accounting information and statistics on patients

Verifying the accuracy of this information is likely to be easier because there are fewer security issues regarding the Data Protection Act.

(i)   Any items of expenditure can be agreed to supporting purchase invoices.

(ii)   Individual patients can be matched to the electoral roll to ensure that they exist (frauds have been uncovered in some medical practices where patients have remained on the records of a medical practice, even though they have either moved to a new location or died).

(iii)   A list of all patients can be obtained and signed as correct by one or more of the doctors.

(iv)   The new computer program can be reviewed to ensure that there are appropriate controls over the input of data, such as range and completeness checks on names, addresses and telephone numbers.

Coherent

Coherent normally means sticking together or consistent or orderly. This answer assumes that the examiner requires comment on whether the information is consistent and essentially easy to access and use (orderly).

Medical history files

These files will need to present information in the same manner on-screen so doctors are not confused by different screen layouts and possibly miss important information. The main method of checking this objective will be to review the software prior to implementation to ensure that it meets the needs of the doctors and that the screen designs are understandable and logical. In particular, information on the screen should follow the order that it is required by the doctor, such as name, address, details of last visit etc.

The software program itself will also need reviewing to ensure that information is filed appropriately, with access being quick and effective. The doctor and patient will not want to have to wait for more than say 10 seconds for the required medical information to be displayed on-screen.

Accounting information and statistics on patients

Checking that the information is in a common format and easy to access will again be a function of the software itself. A review of any new software will need to be undertaken to ensure that these objectives are met.

14 GANTT CHART

A Gantt chart showing the principal management stages for this project is shown below.

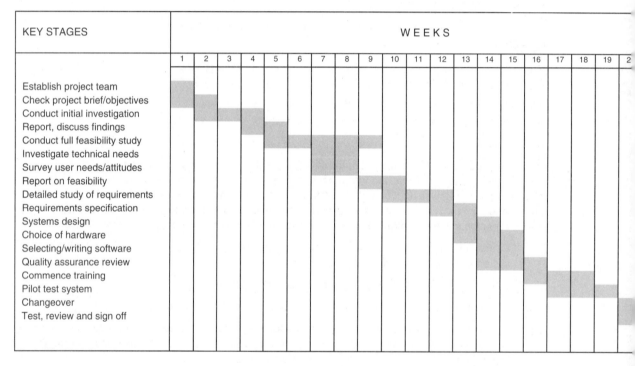

Note

Preparation for a number of the stages may begin earlier, the time must be regarded as the 'core time' during which intensive attention will be given.

15 SWM LTD: SYSTEM DEFICIENCIES

REPORT

To: Departmental Managers
From: Systems Accountant
Date: 4 May 200X
Subject: **Recommendations for speeding up data processing**

In response to the chief executive's memo of 21 April 200X, I have pleasure in enclosing a report on SWM's information system. The report covers the topic listed above. Please contact me with feedback and/or queries by 11th May.

Information deficiencies

The following information deficiencies are apparent in the system.

(i) The stock records held on the mainframe and used by the sales order team will inevitably show different positions from the warehouse's own stock control system on the warehouse minicomputer. Duplication of stock records in this way should be eliminated if possible.

(ii) The listings sent to the warehouse must sometimes include orders for out-of-stock items, as the records used for sales order booking are a day out-of-date at all times. Customers might be unhappy not to be notified that there is a problem when ordering.

(iii) It is not clear whether there is a procedure for same day despatch of urgent orders.

(iv) Keying in of customer invoices in the accounts department is inefficient and provides a likely source of errors during input. Such re-keying of data should be eliminated.

(v) Provision of management information is, as noted in the company's own review, poor.

The first major issue is therefore for the company to ensure that the new database should hold a single set of stock records, available to all departments on both sites. Telecommunications links will eliminate the physical risks inherent in the use of couriers and will also allow all records to be updated at the same time. Similarly, billing details should be posted to ledgers without re-keying.

The second issue concerns management information. A system with a much more flexible reporting framework is required. A good database should allow this.

Speeding up processing

The comments above will enable all departments to have access to up-to-date data. Other suggestions for speeding up processing are as follows.

(i) An upgrade to the existing processor may be necessary. If the number of users or volume of transactions processed is higher than was ever envisaged when the existing system was purchased, it may be necessary to install a more powerful, and faster, processor.

(ii) An increase in available RAM (random access memory) would allow more relevant program files and data files to be stored in RAM during processing. This would reduce the number of transfers between RAM and hard disks during processing.

(iii) The system could be redesigned so that more local processing is performed using PCs and perhaps minicomputers at local sites. The mainframe could then be used for the stock database and for bulk storage and printing applications. Local terminals could be replaced by processors and used for small/medium-sized local requirements.

(iv) An analysis could be performed of how time-critical various processing operations are. Batch processing of non-critical operations could be scheduled for overnight/weekend running: this might improve processing speeds for higher priority operations done during working hours.

(v) A new operating system (perhaps an open system) might be appropriate. This would be likely to provide improvements in processing speed. Of course, this might require the mainframe to be replaced too.

(vi) A separate processor designed specifically to deal with communications and related issues could be installed 'between' the mainframe and the terminals. This 'front-end processor' would deal with protocols, sending and receiving messages, terminal allocation, security and related technical matters, leaving the mainframe free to continue with processing.

16   SWM LTD: SYSTEM CONTROLS

Controls

Information is a vital resource of any organisation, and steps have to be taken to insure its security and integrity as if it were any other valuable asset. Just as there are systems to ensure against theft or destruction of tangible assets, so too are measures taken to protect data and information.

Physical access

It is possible to enumerate any number of threats to the integrity and privacy of data held in any system. There are basic physical dangers such as fire, which need guarding against. Controls to minimise risk include fireproof cabinets where important files are kept. Also, there are basic measures relating to physical access by unauthorised people to an organisation's premises. These physical controls relate both to the equipment and the storage media. In a database system like the one described, this is likely to be a random access storage medium. Both backup copies and backup systems can be maintained in case of disasters.

Particular risks at SWM Ltd relate to the use of couriers and floppy disks to transfer data between sites. Even assuming back-ups are available, it is still possible that loss or corruption of disks could retard processing by 24 hours.

In a new multi-user database system, the database file will be held centrally, and the problem of physical access to the medium on which the data is stored will not be multiplied over several sites. Also, it will be easier to keep backup copies of one set of files than of several.

Logical access

The database contains data relating to a number of different applications, some of which might be for restricted viewing only. Access to the entire database should be restricted also, for the same reasons. The type of control that will serve both functions is a password system, in which each user is given a unique code. The password can determine entry to the database, and also restrict users to specific views of it.

A further measure would be to restrict an individual user to one terminal, so that the password keyed in from that terminal could be checked to see that it corresponds in some way to the terminal itself.

For this system to work, passwords must be kept strictly confidential between users, and also as far as outsiders are concerned. Passwords should be changed regularly.

Communications

If data is transferred over a telecommunications link (as proposed earlier in this solution), controls should be made as far as possible to minimise the risks of hacking. Data sent over the link can be subjected to encryption and authentication procedures. Dial-back procedures can be used: they request callers to hang up and they then telephone the caller ensuring that the number is taken from a pre-set database.

Errors

The integrity of data can also be threatened by error. Human error can occur both in systems design and programming. Controls in the design stage, to avoid bugs, include adherence to programming standards, testing and so forth, before the database system is implemented. The same can be said for controls over system maintenance and updating. Proper documentation, testing and authorisation should minimise the risk of further design error.

Other forms of error can occur in the operational stage. There can be programmed controls over data input. These include check digits, range checks, format checks and so forth. The user interface can be so designed to make input of data strictly guided.

Personnel

Controls over personnel relate to a separation of functions as far as possible between programming staff and operational staff, so that operational staff do not have the opportunity to amend programs fraudulently, and so that programming staff do not get the opportunity to interfere with live data for fraudulent ends. For sensitive positions strict recruitment procedures should be followed.

With end-user computing, some of these controls are hard to maintain. In the situation outlined in this case, however, control over the database is maintained centrally so this is not so much of a problem.

17   SWM LTD: SOFTWARE MAINTENANCE

REPORT

To: Chief Executive
From: Systems Accountant
Date: 10 May 200X
Subject: **Report on software maintenance**

This report will explain the types of software maintenance necessary to ensure software remains efficient.

Software maintenance is carried out for three possible reasons.

- To correct errors or 'bugs' (Corrective maintenance)
- To meet changes in internal operating procedures or external regulations (Adaptive maintenance)
- To keep up with new technical developments (Perfective maintenance)

We will look at each type of maintenance in turn.

Corrective maintenance

Testing procedures should identify most potential faults prior to installation. However, faults may not become apparent until certain combinations of conditions occur. Correction of these more obscure faults may be time-consuming and expensive.

Faults may also become apparent when consistently higher than expected volumes of data are processed. Volume limits are a key part of any transaction processing software and it is important that these are reviewed regularly to maintain efficiency. Increases in volume may require software and hardware upgrades (such as additional RAM).

Hardware failures can require changes to the operating system software. Additional warnings or error messages may be introduced. Procedures to back up files automatically when a system fails may be written into the software.

Some 'bugs' may only become apparent under certain hardware environments.

Adaptive maintenance

Software houses may regularly upgrade standard applications or general-purpose packages to provide additional features or make them user-friendlier. Customers need to decide whether to accept the upgrade, which is rarely supplied free of charge and will involve staff commitment to the new software. Non-acceptance of upgrades may lead to less effective support from the software supplier whose expertise is focused on the latest version of the package.

The operating procedures and needs of the user may change. This is very common with outputs such as reports and screen layouts, which are often changed to suit user requirements. Data processing operations are less often changed because they are more likely to reflect standard procedures whereas computer outputs evolve to meet the needs of the business. Many applications packages now allow users to customise the software (to a certain extent) themselves. For example, one person's 'standard' Excel spreadsheet screen may look different to another's - toolbars, the number of sheets, gridlines, the formula bar are all subject to user settings. Customised user generated reports are a common feature of accounting packages.

Hardware upgrades are common in larger systems and this often results in operating software being changed or entirely rewritten. Hardware changes range from a simple memory upgrade to changing from multi-user to networked systems.

External regulation often leads to mandatory changes in software, which can be quite extensive. A typical example is the change to various tax rates after the annual budget statement in the UK. These are normally straightforward and are often planned for in financial applications packages. However, the consequences of, for example, introducing multiple VAT rates would generally be complex and expensive for most businesses.

Perfective maintenance

Users may request enhancements to software which is not producing errors, but which could be made more user-friendly or improved in some other way. This may involve, for example, redesigning menu screens or switching to graphical user interfaces.

It may be possible to rewrite sections of programs to improve efficiency and response times. As noted above, output may be redesigned to provide better quality information.

Index

BPP
PUBLISHING

REVIEW FORM & FREE PRIZE DRAW

All original review forms from the entire BPP range, completed with genuine comments, will be entered into a draw on 31 January 2002 and 31 July 2002. The names on the first four forms picked out will be sent a cheque for £50.

Name: _____   **Address**: _____

_____

How have you used this Text? *(Tick one box only)*	**During the past six months do you recall seeing/receiving any of the following?** *(Tick as many boxes as are relevant)*

☐ Home study (book only)

☐ On a course: college _____

☐ With 'correspondence' package

☐ Other _____

☐ Our advertisement in *ACCA Students' Newsletter*

☐ Our advertisement in *Pass*

☐ Our brochure with a letter through the post

Why did you decide to purchase this Text?
(Tick one box only)

☐ Have used complementary Study Text

☐ Have used BPP Texts in the past

☐ Recommendation by friend/colleague

☐ Recommendation by a lecturer at college

☐ Saw advertising

☐ Other _____

Which (if any) aspects of our advertising do you find useful?
(Tick as many boxes as are relevant)

☐ Prices and publication dates of new editions

☐ Information on Text content

☐ Facility to order books off-the-page

☐ None of the above

Have you used the companion Kit/Passcard/Video/Tape * for this subject? ☐ Yes ☐ No
(* Please circle)

Your ratings, comments and suggestions would be appreciated on the following areas

	Very useful	Useful	Not useful
Introductory section (Key study steps, personal study)	☐	☐	☐
Chapter introductions	☐	☐	☐
Key terms	☐	☐	☐
Quality of explanations	☐	☐	☐
Case examples and other examples	☐	☐	☐
Questions and answers in each chapter	☐	☐	☐
Chapter roundups	☐	☐	☐
Quick quizzes	☐	☐	☐
Exam focus points	☐	☐	☐
Question bank	☐	☐	☐
Answer bank	☐	☐	☐
List of key terms and index	☐	☐	☐
Icons	☐	☐	☐
Mind maps	☐	☐	☐

	Excellent	Good	Adequate	Poor
Overall opinion of this Text	☐	☐	☐	☐

Do you intend to continue using BPP Products? ☐ Yes ☐ No

Please note any further comments and suggestions/errors on the reverse of this page. The BPP author of this edition can be e-mailed at: barrywalsh@bpp.com

Please return to: Katy Hibbert, ACCA Range Manager, BPP Publishing Ltd, FREEPOST, London, W12 8BR

REVIEW FORM & FREE PRIZE DRAW (continued)

Please note any further comments and suggestions/errors below

FREE PRIZE DRAW RULES

1   Closing date for 31 July 2002 draw is 30 June 2002. Closing date for 31 January 2002 draw is 31 December 2001.

2   No purchase necessary. Entry forms are available upon request from BPP Publishing. No more than one entry per title, per person. Draw restricted to persons aged 16 and over.

3   Winners will be notified by post and receive their cheques not later than 6 weeks after the draw date.

4   The decision of the promoter in all matters is final and binding. No correspondence will be entered into.

See overleaf for information on other
BPP products and how to order

ACCA Order – New Syllabus

To BPP Publishing Ltd, Aldine Place, London W12 8AA
Tel: 020 8740 2211. Fax: 020 8740 1184

Mr/Mrs/Ms (Full name)

Daytime delivery address

Postcode

Daytime Tel

Date of exam (month/year)

	2/01 Texts	9/01 Kits	9/01 Passcards	MCQ cards	Tapes	Videos
PART 1						
1.1 Preparing Financial Statements	£19.95	£10.95	£5.95	£5.95	£12.95	£25.00
1.2 Financial Information for Management	£19.95	£10.95	£5.95	£5.95	£12.95	£25.00
1.3 Managing People	£19.95	£10.95	£5.95		£12.95	£25.00
PART 2						
2.1 Information Systems	£19.95	£10.95	£5.95		£12.95	£25.00
2.2 Corporate and Business Law (6/01)	£19.95	£10.95	£5.95		£12.95	£25.00
2.3 Business Taxation FA 2000 (for 12/01 exam)	£19.95	£10.95 (4/01)	£5.95 (4/01)		£12.95	£25.00
2.4 Financial Management and Control	£19.95	£10.95	£5.95		£12.95	£25.00
2.5 Financial Reporting (6/01)	£19.95	£10.95	£5.95		£12.95	£25.00
2.6 Audit and Internal Review (6/01)	£19.95	£10.95	£5.95		£12.95	£25.00
PART 3						
3.1 Audit and Assurance Services (6/01)	£20.95	£10.95	£5.95		£12.95	£25.00
3.2 Advanced Taxation FA 2000 (for 12/01 exam)	£20.95	£10.95 (4/01)	£5.95 (4/01)		£12.95	£25.00
3.3 Performance Management	£20.95	£10.95	£5.95		£12.95	£25.00
3.4 Business Information Management	£20.95	£10.95	£5.95		£12.95	£25.00
3.5 Strategic Business Planning and Development	£20.95	£10.95	£5.95		£12.95	£25.00
3.6 Advanced Corporate Reporting (6/01)	£20.95	£10.95	£5.95		£12.95	£25.00
3.7 Strategic Financial Management	£20.95	£10.95	£5.95		£12.95	£25.00
INTERNATIONAL STREAM						
1.1 Preparing Financial Statements	£19.95	£10.95	£5.95	£5.95	£12.95	£25.00
2.5 Financial Reporting (6/01)	£19.95	£10.95	£5.95		£12.95	£25.00
2.6 Audit and Internal Review (6/01)	£19.95	£10.95	£5.95		£12.95	£25.00
3.1 Audit and Assurance services (6/01)	£20.95	£10.95	£5.95		£12.95	£25.00
3.6 Advanced Corporate Reporting (6/01)	£20.95	£10.95	£5.95		£12.95	£25.00
SUCCESS IN YOUR RESEARCH AND ANALYSIS PROJECT						
Tutorial Text (9/00)	£19.95					

SUBTOTAL £

POSTAGE & PACKING

Study Texts

	First	Each extra
UK	£3.00	£2.00	£
Europe*	£5.00	£4.00	£
Rest of world	£20.00	£10.00	£

Kits/Passcards/Success Tapes/MCQ cards

	First	Each extra
UK	£2.00	£1.00	£
Europe*	£2.50	£1.00	£
Rest of world	£15.00	£8.00	£

Breakthrough Videos

	First	Each extra
UK	£2.00	£2.00	£
Europe*	£2.00	£2.00	£
Rest of world	£20.00	£10.00	£

Grand Total (Cheques to *BPP Publishing*) I enclose
a cheque for (incl. Postage) £

Or charge to Access/Visa/Switch

Card Number

Expiry date   Start Date

Issue Number (Switch Only)

Signature

We aim to deliver to all UK addresses inside 5 working days; a signature will be required. Orders to all EU addresses should be delivered within 6 working days. All other orders to overseas addresses should be delivered within 8 working days. * Europe includes the Republic of Ireland and the Channel Islands.